15 Dec 2020

Aviation in the Raw
When Flying Was Dangerous and Sex Was Safe

Aviation in the Raw

When Flying Was Dangerous
and Sex Was Safe

by

Captain Mike Bennison

Typeset in Palatino
Printed and bound by CPI Group (UK) Ltd, Croydon, CR0 4YYfd

Dedicated to my wife and son

CONTENTS

A PILOT'S PRAYER

'High Flight'
A poem by Canadian John Gillespie Magee Jr.

Oh, I have slipped the surly bonds of Earth
And danced the skies on laughter-silvered wings.
Sunward I've climbed and joined the tumbling mirth
Of sun-split clouds, and done a hundred things
You have not dreamed of – wheeled and soared and swung
High in the sunlit silence. Hovering there,
I've chased the shouting wind along, and flung
My eager craft through footless halls of air,
Up, up the long delirious burning blue.
I've topped the wind-swept heights with easy grace
Where never lark or even eagle flew;
And while with silent uplifting mind I've trod
The high untrespassed sanctity of space,
Put out my hand and touched the face of God!

INTRODUCTION

The sky was dark on the westerly horizon. Only the last vestige of the sun's glow remained, and thousands of thronging stars ahead of us seemed to be mirrored by similar pinpricks of light shining up from the earth below – lights from the villages and towns as though the sky were reflected on the earth. Huge cumulonimbus thunder clouds hung from the heavens, looking like 40,000-foot high Chinese white paper lanterns. Descending within the lanterns were what appeared to be flickering fluorescent light tubes – lightning, which flashed erratically from within, sometimes piercing the side of the lantern and crashing down into the countryside below.

In aviation, one never ceased to be overawed by the power of nature. Sometimes these clouds stretched up into the stratosphere, the layer of the earth's atmosphere extending to 15 km above the earth's surface. Huge anvil-like shapes came off the top and were slowly spread downwind. They are beautiful to watch, but not somewhere voluntarily to venture within.

Our weather radar showed bloody scars in deep red wherever these storms were situated so we could steer well clear of them. One of us often wore sunglasses at night in case lightning flashed near us. In one well-known case, a two-man crew were flying their aircraft manually when they were hit by lightning which temporarily blinded them both. Thankfully, one got his vision back at the last minute and managed to save the aircraft from plummeting into the ground. If they had crashed, it would have been recorded as another case of 'pilot error' as there would have been no way of telling what had caused the crash – rather like killing someone with an ice bullet. Never believe the saying 'pilot error' until you personally know all the facts – often it is easier or more convenient for other interested parties to blame us.

This book is based on my experiences over 35 years. They included private flying, chartered flying, flying for a major airline and my own travel experiences. Some of the identities have been concealed in order to preserve the reputation and blushes of many of my companions along the way.

As you will see, the notes used as a background to this book were written over a period of 35 years, well before 'PC' or 'political correctness' came into fashion. If written today and acknowledging the PC agenda, it would have been an extremely short and boring book.

I have many thousands of flying hours and have flown many types of aircraft. I have lost many friends in flying accidents, and had many laughs and scares. I am convinced that many a pilot's life has been saved through the seemingly inconsequential chatter in conversations in the bar (known as opening the hangar doors), or on overnight stops. Some of our wives got annoyed with their pilot husbands endlessly swapping yarns, but so often when an incident happens, in the back of your mind you suddenly remember someone having mentioned something similar. That tiny bit of an edge can save you, and your passengers, from disaster and death.

I was staggered whilst researching this book to discover how many people were killed in aircraft crashes in the early days of aviation. They sacrificed their lives in the name and advancement of flight. Many of the aeroplanes that I researched crashed, usually with fatalities. It is impossible to put a definite figure on the total that have now become, as we say, 'Icarus', and sprouted their own wings – but this book will, I hope, pay tribute to some of those whose sacrifice is unknown – as is indeed the sacrifice made by their families. I am sure that most, if not all, would be smiling to themselves if they could read what follows – almost all pilots seem to have worked hard and played even harder, and black humour seems to be the norm to try to deal with any doubts and fears. I am also certain they would never have given up that experience of flying, however short it may have been. Nevertheless, we always remember a well-known saying: 'There are old pilots, and bold pilots, but no old, bold, pilots.'

I offer this book therefore to all the aircrew and passengers who gave their lives to further the safety of aviation – a figure perhaps somewhere in the region of 40,000. I am also so grateful to my wife, who has for many years put up with the time that I've had to be away on trips, and also to my son for his support. He flew microlights, has a helicopter pilot's licence and also has been an aircraft dispatcher for many years.

To any of you reading this book that have not actually piloted an aircraft: I recommend you undertake a short flying course with your local flying club. You could then continue on to study for a private pilot's licence, although it would perhaps suffice if you merely manage a solo flight (which will take you about eight hours of flying time). You will see what I mean if you do – it will be one of the two greatest experiences of your life. The first is losing your virginity and the second is your first solo flight – or maybe it is the other way round!

I am often asked whether I miss flying, and the only reply is as follows: there are two distinct sections of a pilot's flying career. Using jargon, the first half of it is on lighter aeroplanes until you eventually start flying aeroplanes which are designated as having the nose wheel behind the pilot – this means that you are now passed to fly on larger aircraft (when you look at any aircraft you will see what this means). Senior pilots are asked to name where they would like to travel. Once they have decided, they are then given a stunning aeroplane with £400 million's worth of hull insurance to fly there, a dozen beautiful girls as companions and whilst at their destinations they are put up in some of the best hotels in the world and given a pocketful of spending money with which to entertain themselves. When they arrive back home, the company takes the aeroplane away, washes it, refuels it, and then asks the pilot where they would like to go next. Not only this but they are paid a huge salary and given a vast pension. Quite simply, what more could one want! I will always remember one pilot who went down to the dole office after his company had recently collapsed – and when he told the person behind the glass partition what his pension was, they nearly dropped dead: some are worth up to £130,000.

However, it's worth remembering that many charter pilots regularly lose their jobs. Aviation seems to go in six-year cycles. When you obtain your pilot's licence, depending where you are in that cycle affects how long it will be before you get your first job. Added to which, many small outfits fold after a couple of years, and they often eke out the summer to get as much income as they can before closing the airline just before the winter season. This more or less guarantees pilots being out of a job for four to six months awaiting the new season and a new airline.

But not only this: always remember when you see an aeroplane flying overhead, that whereas you, in your office, are slaving away with your feet very much on the ground, the pilot up in the sky has the best office in the world, superior to that of Bill Gates or anyone else you might care to mention.

Chapter One
A Brief History of Flying

I can remember as a youngster being with my parents at the house of Lord Sholto Douglas, 1st Baron Douglas of Kirtleside, a World War I fighter ace who eventually became chairman of BOAC. He regularly showed us jerky black-and-white films of early aviation from his extensive collection; these often featured disasters of experimental aeroplanes 'clapping hands', where the wings of the aircraft fold upwards when it crashes, almost inevitably resulting in the occupants being killed. He would be furious at any hint of laughter; he saw them as serious material which ought to be viewed by all. Young as I was, I was deeply impressed by the determination of these men to fly. I knew Henry Kremer, a business partner of my father. Henry put up a reward of £5,000 for the first man-powered flight, and eventually this prize was to rise to £100,000.[1] Not just fame but also fortune was guaranteed to whoever could first securely lift an aircraft away from the ground and fly a figure-of-eight pattern.

So where did it all start? Children at school are taught that it began with Orville and Wilbur Wright on the beach at Kitty Hawk on 17th December 1903 with that well-known flight, the length of which was shorter than the wingspan of modern jets. I shall return to the Wright brothers, and their excellent self-publicity, shortly. But first I would like to make a detour to the small market town of Chard, Somerset, where there is a museum which, although rather small, has a lot of information concerning Frederick John Stringfellow, the Victorian aeronautical pioneer.

John Stringfellow teamed up with William Henson in about 1840, and the two men worked together for some years to

1

produce an aerial steam carriage, for which they patented the design. The museum has models of one of their aircraft, a twin-propeller tri-plane of sorts, which weighed a hefty 3,000 pounds. Stringfellow and Henson exhibited their design at the Crystal Palace Aeronautical Exhibition in 1868, and also had an airline company called 'Aerial Transit' which unfortunately failed. (The Aeronautical Society of Great Britain was founded in 1866.)

There are two notable claims for Stringfellow. The first is that in 1848 he designed and made the first engine-driven monoplane model aeroplane to make free flight, and also that in 1868 he designed and made a steam-driven model aircraft that was capable of free flight – though it never achieved it. His patented specification described a pro-injected steam-driven monoplane with a wingspan of no less than 150 feet. He was an innovative inventor: his other patents were in areas as diverse as photography, medical apparatus and even an armoured gun carriage.

The first steps towards powered flight were no doubt taken even further back than Stringfellow, but of course – as any schoolchild knows – it is the Wright brothers who claimed the title in 1903. However, perhaps the only reason that their claim for the first powered flight is generally accepted is their remarkable talent for publicity. It is now often argued that the Wright brothers' claim is, in fact, false for a variety of reasons, including their use of tracks and skids. But even today it is not widely known who the various other people were in the running for the title of 'first to fly'. One especially strong claim came from a German, Karl Jatho, whose attempt was made during August 1903 – four months before Orville and Wilbur – but the unsung hero with perhaps the best claim of all is one Richard Pearse from New Zealand, whose endeavours are well documented.

Four dates are given for Pearse's flights, all in 1903: 31st March, 11th May, 2nd June, and 10th July. They are recorded as having taken place in New Zealand, on the South Island. He built his own engine, complete with pistons made from cast-iron drainpipes; modern reconstructions suggest this must have had a capacity of 15 horsepower which certainly would have ~ enough to get his aircraft airborne. Today, this remarkable piece of home engineering resides in the Transportation Museum in Auckland, having been discovered in a rubbish tip near his house.

Exhibited alongside is a fascinating book, *Richard Pearse: Early New Zealand Pioneer Aviator* by C. Geoffrey Rodlife, marshalling much proof for the flights. It contains signed statements by schoolchildren who saw him take to the air; they record that they saw him take off, turn right and fly a considerable length of a valley. Their testimony is entirely convincing – and to a reasonable, objective mind provides proof that the flight took place. It is claimed in these records that on one occasion his aircraft landed on the top of a box hedge in the snow; this detail also correlates with what we know of the weather during those dates and confirms that it must have been several feet off the ground. To my mind, it seems indisputable that Pearse flew before the Wright brothers.

Unfortunately, Richard Pearse was not as good as the Wright brothers when it came to publicity. He lacked either the skills or the determination to spread the word about his ascent into the air, an event which back then of course seemed to most people almost miraculous. But during the early 1900s, in the remote outpost of Waitohi on the South Island of New Zealand, it would have been extremely difficult to get the information out to the wondering world. Now, of course, a brief search of the internet is all that is needed to locate for oneself the extensive documents which attest to his flights. In New Zealand, his account is widely accepted; the country's mint issued a commemorative coin in 1982, claiming the '80th Anniversary of the World First Powered Flight', though the date given on the museum's own website is 1903.

There are drawings and many other artefacts in the Auckland museum which is well worth a visit. The site of the flight itself is in the South Island and you can see with your own eyes the valley along which Pearse flew. He was a true aviation pioneer in his inventing as well as his piloting; not only did he build his aircraft's engine, he also created a very strange-looking (to modern eyes) flying machine, the engine of which could rotate to some extent, in a way very similar to that of a gyrocopter or even a helicopter. This actual machine is also displayed in the museum in Auckland. Interestingly, many years ago it was lent to some Americans for an exhibition and never returned – they claimed that it had completely disappeared. Years subsequently, a knowledgeable American visitor to the Auckland museum, when looking at pictures of the lost aircraft, idly mentioned to someone that it was very strange that there were two of the same aeroplane in the world. When members of the staff questioned him further, he stated that there was an identical aeroplane in the cellars of a large bank, possibly in Texas. After investigating, they discovered that it was indeed the original aircraft and it was retrieved.

Perhaps this aircraft had been innocently mislaid, but a documentary broadcast about the Smithsonian Museum, which houses the Wright brothers' original aircraft, made an intriguing allegation. The claim was that the Wright family had given the Museum their aeroplane on one condition: that the Smithsonian never admitted at any point in the future the possibility of someone having flown before Orville and Wilbur. If such an admission were made, then the aeroplane would immediately be forfeit and would have had to be returned to the family. An early blueprint of this agreement is shown on the documentary (of which I have a copy) – and the notion that the Smithsonian might actually be capable of withholding such information has, in the eyes of many, damaged its credibility around the world.

However, there is another very strong contender for the title of being the first to fly: Gustave Whitehead. Born in Germany, he settled in Bridgeport, Connecticut. Officials claim that on 14th August 1901 Gustave flew for half a mile at a height of approximately fifty feet after taking off from Fairfield. Campaigners claim that Gustave beat the Wright brothers by two years and, by this yardstick, he would have beaten the ingenious Richard Pearse too.[2]

Officials in North Carolina reject the claim by supporters of Whitehead, insisting that the Wright brothers were responsible for the first powered flight in Kitty Hawk in 1903, pointing to the photographs taken whilst their aeroplane was airborne. It must be said that, despite all their careful records of events, even they struggled to gain acceptance for their claims – and a so-called 'fliers or liars?' discussion heatedly continued for years, with them being confirmed in their achievement only after a series of public demonstrations. But Whitehead has his supporters, even today; in 2013, Connecticut Governor Dannell Malloy signed a bill into law acknowledging Whitehead as a father of flight – and so not the Wright brothers.

Why did he make this bold step? His decision to do so was based on contemporary newspaper reports which describe Whitehead's flight. These began with an exclusive in the local paper, the *Bridgeport Sunday Herald*, which included details of two flights, one on the afternoon of 14th August 1901 and one the morning after. Their story was carried as international news shortly afterwards, but despite this, the Wright brothers' meticulous evidence without doubt works in their favour, even after all these years.

A Connecticut museum article describes Whitehead as 'a man with little money, who took jobs to support his family while he invented on a part-time basis'. But, it claims, 'Whitehead accomplished what no one else before him had – true sustained flight, with power and control, for a distance of half a mile, landing without damage, in 1901.' It further notes that he never obtained adequate funding to continue developing his own designs, and generously shared his ideas with other inventors, thus having 'a considerable impact on the development of the airplane'.

However, experts continue to disagree. The National Air and Space Museum note the 'controversial' nature of the claims made for Whitehead and describe the news articles as 'questionable' and 'contradictory'. Further, they note that a photograph apparently showing Whitehead's machine in the air has not been seen since 1906. They also note that the journal *The Scientific American* recorded Whitehead as experimenting with a glider in

1903; surely, they argue, he would not have abandoned a successful aircraft in favour of an unsuccessful glider? But perhaps the nail in Whitehead's coffin is their note that not one aircraft that he subsequently built for other enthusiasts ever left the ground. 'Had he,' they ask sarcastically, 'forgotten the secrets of flight?'

Aviation progressed as aircraft became more reliable and innovation focused on the required steering and direction. The original concept of turning an aeroplane left or right was based on 'wing warping', achieved quite physically by twisting the ends of the wing by means of the joystick. This was then overtaken by controls connected by wires to ailerons, or large sections on the trailing edge of the wings. To turn left, the control stick, or the 'spectacle' or 'yoke', is pushed to the left, which brings the left aileron section up, thus pushing that wing down, whereas on the opposite wing the section goes down, pushing that wing up. This commences a turn to the left (or 'port' as is said in the air, borrowing the term used in shipping). It must be remembered that, in doing this, the wings appear shorter to the horizon so, as the aircraft starts to lose height, you need to pull the nose up. Doing this, however, those early pioneers found, produces a skidding motion in the air; this is where the rudder, the section on the vertical tail fin, comes in. If controlled correctly by the foot pedals, it gives a pleasant, smooth turn.

All of this of course had to be learned by the designers, mostly through the risky process of trial and error. Many if not most of the first painstaking steps forward were forgotten as time went on. It was only when the new fashion of microlight aircraft started recently, that engineers repeated the same learning curve as their predecessors a century earlier, replicating some of their mistakes. One such error, that of failing to put a strengthening sleeve through a hole in the material of the wing before threading the cables, nearly killed my son – he happened to spot the resulting fracture in the wing in the nick of time, just managing an emergency landing before the wing split apart. Others, sadly, were less lucky.

Aviation developed through increased ingenuity and improving technical understanding of the principles of flight. It was discovered that if the wings were fixed so that the tips were higher than the base of the wing, the aircraft became more stable, creating more lift by having a slightly longer section below. These became known as 'dihedral wings'. Manœuvrability, however, is lessened by the stability that these wings create; when this is the principal requirement, such as in fighter aircraft, the opposite effect is built into the design of the wings and they droop down at the tips, in much the same way as one would see in birds coming in to land. These are known as 'anhedral wings' or the downward inclination of an aircraft's wing, compared with 'dihedral'.

As is well known, aircraft were used during World War I, principally for reconnaissance. When they came close to each other, pilots would attack each other by firing at the enemy aircraft with shotguns and pistols; now, of course, this seems almost quaint. Eventually, fully armed fighters and bombers were developed.

I had the privilege at one time of owning a World War I leather flying uniform. The accompanying helmet was rather like a leather balaclava with loops of leather (about half an inch in diameter by three inches high) and a sausage-shaped wind-break in front of where the Gosport tubing went (these were the equivalent of earphones and enabled the observer to talk to the pilot).

I also possessed a seat from that iconic aircraft of the Great War, the Sopwith Camel. This was no more than a simple wooden base upon which one perched, with wickerwork forming the back and sides. A canvas rim round the top gave it some rudimentary comfort and a little more support, but it was not a seat upon which one could relax. There was no lap strap to hold the pilot in (a lap strap being similar to the one given to passengers on airliners today). If violent manœuvres were being performed, the pilot simply had to clutch with his knees and hold on tight so as not to fall out!

A notable aspect in the performance of the Sopwith Camel was that, due to the gyroscopic effect of the engine, it could turn in one direction through 270° as quickly as it could through 90° in the other direction. A pilot had to be careful when being attacked because the Germans were more than aware of this; a relatively slow turn in one direction under pressure in a dog-fight could be fatal. This feature of the engine also created significant pull during take-off so the pilot would have to use a lot of rudder through the feet to keep the aircraft straight. It is salutary to remember that there were more fatal crashes on take-off and landings and in training accidents than there were in actual combat. Not only this but 25% of pilots did not survive the training – around 8,000 died before ever managing to climb into the skies to do battle. One in twenty would gain the coveted title of being an 'ace', this being given when one had shot down five enemy aircraft. The average age of survival once beyond training was three weeks.

After World War I, interest in aviation returned to more peaceable development. John Alcock, a wartime pilot who had been captured and kept in a prisoner-of-war camp in Turkey, was chosen to pilot a British Vickers Vimy bomber across the Atlantic, starting in Lester's Field in St John's, Newfoundland, America. He and Arthur Brown, his navigator, flew all the way to Ireland where they crashed but survived in a field near Clifden, Connemara, on 15th June 1919. Alcock was killed six months later at the age of 37 when piloting a Vickers Viking amphibian to the Paris air show. Many years later, when I ran an antique shop, I was unable to purchase, much to my chagrin, a plant pot stand in black ebony-type wood that had a plaque in the drawer stating that it had been made from the wood from the crashed Alcock and Brown aircraft. I had a strong personal interest in this, apart from my interest in aviation, as I went to school with John Alcock's grandson.

A statue of Alcock and Brown in all their leather flying gear stood for many years outside the old Air Traffic Control tower at Central Area, London Heathrow Airport. Each year on 1st April, we would call the police and inform them that there were two suspicious-looking characters in leather jackets hanging around the control tower base. The police were caught out year after year! The statue now stands in a small museum at the entrance to Heathrow Airport, near the police station.[3]

I went to Heathrow Airport many times as a child. My father used to fly as a passenger on the Lancastrian (a Lancaster Bomber converted into a civilian passenger aeroplane) to Australia on business. The main Heathrow buildings back then were simply very large tents. This in fact remained the state of the terminals for several years before aviation 'took off' in the area. After World War II, most civilian aircraft were in fact refitted combat aeroplanes. The Vikings, of which I flew many, were military derivatives. One had been retrofitted with Nene jet engines and flew to Paris faster than modern scheduled services. Indeed, to this day, it still takes longer to fly from London to Paris than it did back in 1947 which seems remarkable but nonetheless is true.

As time went on, aircraft safety greatly improved; crashes became exceptions rather than the accepted rule. Gone were the days of unreliable engines, poor navigation aids and sketchy maintenance procedures. Instead, human factors became the main and often needless cause of aircraft fatalities, not least due to what was termed the 'Atlantic Baron' syndrome. Here, Captains of what were considered large aircraft at the time ruled the cockpit by fear and did not engage constructively with their co-pilots. This situation was fostered not least because the co-pilot knew that his chances for promotion were based on the Captain's reports which were submitted after each flight; upsetting the Captain or (worst of all) suggesting he was doing something wrong was a sure and certain way to stay, career-wise, exactly where you were. With relative frequency, this led to aircraft getting into desperate situations and at times there were crashes which resulted in the deaths of all on board – all because of a nervous co-pilot's fear of upsetting a tyrannical Captain.

This aggressive hierarchy perhaps developed out of wartime flying, and is certainly well-illustrated by an example of exactly this kind of behaviour from World War II. A friend of mine who was responsible for training new-entry pilots would tell them what happened to his father who had been a Squadron Leader (no less) on a Lancaster bomber during the war. They were returning from a mission over Germany with the Squadron Leader flying the aircraft. He was a bristling and acerbic man whom the crew feared greatly. They could all see that the fuel was starting to run out – all, it seemed, apart from the Squadron Leader. But they were in such fear of him that they did not dare speak up.

They sat nervously and in silence. Eventually and inevitably, the Lancaster ran out of fuel, the engines stopped, and they crashed. Many on board died, including the Squadron Leader, who thus became a victim of his own tyranny. Some of the crew bailed out and survived to tell the story. My friend recounted this to every new entry, hurtful though it was for him to relate; he well knew from the needless death of his father. The Captain must create an environment where the co-pilot and crew feel free to speak up, for the sake of the safety of everyone on board.

Cockpit hierarchy has been a pernicious issue. Speaking personally, I can attest that I have lost many dear friends in my 35 years in aviation because they would not speak up and risk a Captain's wrath. However, airlines now use a most welcome innovation known as Cockpit Resource Management (CRM); type this into Google and you will discover many reports and examples as to how it should be used to create an appropriate atmosphere on an aircraft. This innovation needed no technological trial and error; it required no innovatory brilliance. Nonetheless, its effects have been far-reaching and it has helped to counter one well-known stereotype of aviation, that of the manager who has no idea how to get the best out of their staff because of the culture of fear they (perhaps unwittingly) perpetuate and because of the power they have over the careers of their subordinates.

Perhaps a final way in which on-board safety has been increased over the years is that of creating systems to ensure that information that might save an aircraft from a crash is passed on formally, not anecdotally. These include the Notice to Airmen

(NOTAM).[4] If an incident occurs on, around, or near an aeroplane, it is now mandatory that the crew submit a full report which is forwarded to the appropriate government departments. I have never been able to establish whether this could be used in evidence against someone if taken to court for negligence or manslaughter – in other words, whether you could condemn yourself by your own words.

One of the best-known British air disasters of recent times was the result of such procedures not being followed. One 4th June 1967, the Argonaut G-ALHG crashed about fifteen miles short of the runway at Stockport, near Manchester. Eighty-four people were killed; only twelve survived. Crucially, a problem with the fuel cross-feed valve which was known to other Argonaut pilots caused the fatal crash.[5]

On the final approach before landing, the Captain had opened one of these valves to enable the use of fuel from a secondary tank, but unfortunately nobody had told him a key bit of information that other pilots of this aircraft had discovered for themselves – namely, that there was a flaw within the selector valves in the cross-feed system. This permitted fuel to be drawn from any of the eight fuel tanks to feed the engine that required it, but unless you hit the valve heavily with your hand it would often fail to open fully.

On short final approach, with no warning, engines three and four suddenly cut out. The aircraft became uncontrollable and crashed at 1009 hours. One consolation was that, despite being in an overwhelmingly urban area and very close to the town centre, it hit the ground in a small open area between buildings. Members of the public and police, at considerable danger to themselves, managed to pull twelve people from the wreckage, but minutes after hitting the ground it was engulfed in flames, killing those survivors who remained on board. It was believed that this, tragically, accounted for the majority of the passengers; the investigation found that most of the passengers' legs had been crushed on impact by the rows of seats moving forwards, imprisoning them in the aircraft. This should not have happened, but the bracing bars, which were supposed to stop the seats from moving in a crash, were too weak to do their job. Had they been stronger, the investigation concluded, the majority of the passengers would have survived.

Investigators studied the issue with the selector valves and found that, although their control was designed to 'click' when it was set correctly, it was actually impossible for the pilot to lean forward far enough to hear this, given the requirement for Argonaut pilots to wear snug shoulder-harnesses during flight. They also found that, although other pilots of this aircraft were aware of this issue, none of the airlines using the Argonaut had reported it to the manufacturer. Without this information, the investigators concluded, pilots of G-ALHG would have found it impossible to determine the exact nature of this emergency.

The aircraft was being piloted by Captain Harry Marlow who survived but remembered nothing of the crash. He was cleared of all blame – but since the investigation concluded that the aircraft would have immediately become uncontrollable once engines three and four had ceased, he was not given the credit for what a number of witnesses stated that they saw – namely, that in the final seconds of its flight the aircraft made a very pronounced turn to port before levelling out and descending into the crash site. Their accounts strongly suggest that Captain Marlow did exert a degree of control and manage to put the aircraft down in an extremely small open space.

It is sobering to reflect on the history of aviation. Many of the men whose innovations have given us the regular access to the world that we enjoy today paid for doing so with their lives. Like the Greek myth, they have 'gone Icarus' (died); the least that we can do, we who take to the skies so regularly and with such little thought, is to remember them and, in doing so, honour the sacrifice they made. As a side note, engines are identified by the crew by giving them a number – the engine outboard of the wing on the left-hand side is number one, the one between that and the fuselage number two, while on the other side the near one is three and the outside one is four.

Gustave Whitehead

Richard Pearse

Amphibious Vickers Viking

Chapter Two
GLIDING SCHOLARSHIP

When I was very young, I joined the Boys' Brigade, and after a number of years there, I went on to the Air Training Corps at 18F Wimbledon Squadron. There was strict discipline in the squadron – if you didn't conform, you were given a toothbrush and told to scrub the staircase from top to bottom. It was run by Squadron Leader Nicholas, who was referred to by us boys as 'Copper Bum' for reasons that now are lost in the mists of time. My career in aviation nearly met a premature end one evening: I was in one of the upstairs rooms listening to a flight lecture, when someone opened a tin cupboard door and a steel splinter shot out into my eye. This caused quite agonising pain as well as the possibility of lost sight. Thankfully, the hospital managed to remove the splinter and save my eye.

I became somewhat of an expert rifle shot, owning my own Martini Mark 111 rifle. I started at the Wimbledon Park Rifle Club and moved on to shoot for the ATC squadron, for Surrey and finally for the whole Cadet Corps. One year I was occupying the top of the leader-board in a competition at Bisley and needed five more bull's-eyes at 300 yards in order to win. It started pouring with rain and I hurriedly grabbed a gas cape to cover myself and my rifle, which for this range was my .303 Lee Enfield. I squeezed the trigger for my next shot, which to my horror completely missed the target – I could not understand this at all. I looked over the rifle carefully, checked the sights and found that, when I had pulled my rifle under the gas cape, I had accidentally wound the rear site down with the cape. I reset them and scored another four bulls to finish, but unfortunately lost by four points.

I spent a lot of time at Bisley with a Group Captain Macken, firing all sorts of weapons, and I became the mascot for the RAF submachine gun team. We did most of our training on the army ranges at Aldershot; here I was put in a small quarry about 25 yards long by 15 yards wide and given various pistols, rifles and automatic weapons, which I fired all day long. On one occasion, instead of using the target, I drew a 45 colt and fired at a rock. I did not expect to hit it, but I did and the bullet ricocheted off and planted itself in the ground just alongside me which was an alarming experience. The next day I spent firing on a shorter range with a Sten gun and won half a crown (12½p) for my efforts. I still have the targets to this day. I have continued shooting for the rest of my life, ending up as chairman of my rifle and pistol club. I raised a huge amount of money for the club which paid to renovate the indoor and outdoor ranges, the outdoor one being 100 yards long; unfortunately, this has now been sold off.

Having been in 18F Squadron for some time, my first experience of actually getting into the air was at the RAF airfield in Little Rissington, an RAF aerodrome and RAF station in Gloucestershire. At summer camp, I got a ride in an Oxford aircraft. The weather was pretty awful and we ended up lost in thick cloud, not being able to find the airport after some thirty minutes of going round and round in circles. There was suddenly a break in the cloud where the crew managed to identify where they were and flew below the cloud, back to Little Rissington. It was once home to the Central Flying School, the Vintage Pair and the Red Arrows. Built during the 1930s, the station was opened in 1938 and closed in 1994. (Note that the ICAO code for this airfield is EGLV – each airfield has its own designated four-letter code and individual beacons flash their code at night – for instance, EGLL stands for London Heathrow, EGJJ for Jersey.)

Later I was awarded a Gliding Scholarship at RAF Kenley Airport, with the Air Training Corps, qualifying on 15th November 1959. On arrival at the airfield, we were shepherded into an old World War II Crew Room which was decorated with many pictures of (mostly fatal) aviation accidents. In our first briefing, we were told that the previous day one of the cadets had taken off in a Kirby Cadet glider, released the tow rope and simply froze – he continued in a straight line until he eventually crashed, killing himself.

After this somewhat sobering introduction, we were taken out onto the field and watched a Slingsby T.21 and a Sedbergh TX1 Glider being launched with an antiquated winch which was positioned at the opposite end of the runway to the aircraft. We spent the first half of the day retrieving the gliders whenever they landed, rushing out and holding onto the wing tips to keep the wings themselves parallel to the ground, and helping to get them pulled back into position at the end of the runway, ready to connect back to the winch.

Finally, it was my turn! I boarded with an instructor next to me (the seats in the Sedbergh were side-by-side) and watched in trepidation as the long cable was stretched the length of the runway and attached to my glider. After the appropriate signals, the controls were operated in the winch and the glider accelerated at a considerable and alarming pace down the runway. Seconds later, I was airborne and the ground was stretching out beneath me, the people, roads and houses suddenly impossibly small.

After releasing the winch, we completed a left-hand circuit until the glider was lined up to land. Everything was silent apart from the rushing wind. The only real concern was that the cable might snap during launch and put us in the awkward position of having to find somewhere quickly to land.

Gliding gave me a good feel for aviation. I carried out several circuits over several days until eventually it became time for a major milestone – my turn for my first solo in the Kirby cadet glider. I sat in the cockpit by myself. The command came to take up the slack, which I did. When I was ready, I took a deep breath and gave the command to the winch operator. It leapt into life and I was pulled down the runway. I allowed the speed to build up steadily, pulled back on the stick and there I was – airborne, all on my own, with nobody to help me. This was my first solo flight!

It was the most wonderful experience. I turned to the left, climbing up to about 1,000 feet, before finally making the parallel downwind traverse. I could see all the minute figures standing on the runway and looking expectantly up at me – some of them probably hoping that I would crash so that they could have something exciting to talk about in the bar that night! As they say, 'any landing is a good landing', the analogy being that, as long your logbook shows that the same number of take-offs is reflected by the same number of landings, you should be okay.

Eventually, and yet also far too soon, there I was on finals with everything set up nicely. I was singing to myself as I came in to carry out my first solo landing. My relieved-looking instructor congratulated me. I then had to carry out a few more retrievals for other people before I performed the two more solo take-offs and landings which would gain me my A & B Gliding Licence. The 'A' Badge required: 'One solo circuit in a glider or motor glider in unpowered flight after the launch, followed by a satisfactory landing. An appropriate level of knowledge of rules of the air and local airspace restrictions must be demonstrated to the supervising instructor at the time of the first solo flight.' The 'B' Badge required: 'A soaring flight of at least five minutes, at or above the previous lowest point after launch, followed by a satisfactory landing.'

It was a terrible shame to have to leave such a wonderful bunch of people who had given me my first real taste of aviation. But the future lay before me: I was ready to tackle flying powered aircraft.

Air Speed Oxford (at Duxford Museum)

Sedbergh

Slingsby

Sten Gun

Chapter Three
FAIROAKS AERODROME

After I had finished my Gliding Scholarship, I started training for my Private Pilot's Licence (PPL) at Fairoaks Aerodrome, Chobham, Surrey, on 4th March 1962. My first dual flight was for 55 minutes on a Tiger Moth G-AODS.[6] As we had open cockpits, I had to buy a WW2 flying helmet and goggles. She was written off in 1970 after an accident at an air show, but at the time she was believed to have been flown in the past by Squadron Leader B A 'Jimmy' James (1915-2008), a survivor of 'The Great Escape'.

My first powered solo was on Tiger G-AOBX on 16th March 1962. I have recently found on the internet pictures of this aircraft, now painted yellow; it is kept at Shoreham airfield.[7] One of the Tigers was an interesting aircraft – it did not have an air speed indicator as such, only a calibrated metal plate with a spring-loaded piece of metal on it. This contraption was mounted on the wing; the spring-loaded piece would be pushed back as the aircraft got faster and faster, and you could then read off your speed from the calibrated markings on the plate!

The de Havilland DH.82 Tiger Moth was one of the main training aircraft used during World War II. It had a wartime role, occasionally being used as a bomber. Of the 8,866 originally built, many are still around, even after all these years. It is considered gentle in stalls and spins as it can go as slowly as 25 knots, is fully aerobatic and also has a tail wheel. It is hand-started by swinging the prop – you must be careful not to be hit by it.

On one of my first visits to Fairoaks, I bumped into the comedian Dick Emery. He owned a Miles Magister, a low-wing aeroplane, almost like a Tiger Moth, but with no upper wing, which was used to train World War II pilots who were converting onto Spitfires. At his invitation, I joined him for a flight. We both got into the aircraft, someone spun the propeller and off we went at an exhilarating speed. We performed some aerobatics which left me dizzy with delight, after which we arrived over Blackbushe Airport, which at that time was more or less completely deserted (at one time it had been quite a busy airport with Vikings and Dakotas flying out of it). We flew gently over the runway just for a look-see, but when we got to the halfway position, we saw that there were a number of workmen digging a trench across it, presumably putting in an electricity cable. They were about waist-deep and hacking away. Dick looked at me mischievously and set the aircraft towards them; we dive-bombed them, scattering them into the ditch as we flew over at about ten feet – we must have frightened the life out of them! Thankfully, we never heard any more about it.

Twelve years later, I was flying in command on a Viscount 800 from the Channel Islands to London when I was told that Emery was on board the aircraft. I hadn't seen him since that one flight. I put my uniform jacket on with my four rings and cap and went back towards the window seat where he was sitting on his own. I introduced myself to him, saying that I was now Captain of the aircraft which was in part thanks to him and that flight with him that had kept my interest in aviation kindled. I thought he would be tickled pink with this; however, all he did was shrug his shoulders and look back out the window, completely ignoring me. Later I heard that he had died and the newspapers reported that he had had his coffin stored away in a garage for a considerable length of time previously. He may have been depressed as so many comedians are said to be in their private lives.

It was at Fairoaks that I met a dear friend Paul, who was a fantastic driver and a particular fan of Aston Martins. He was later to become an Aston Martin saloon car champion, due in part (or so he said modestly after the race) to the two favourites driving too fast in wet conditions and sliding off the track, leaving him to win. His father had been a Beach Master at Dunkirk. Every now and then you would get the impression that Paul's father was an agent with MI5 or MI6 due to his mysterious air and carefree confidence. Sadly, he has long since passed away.

On one occasion, Paul took me for a spin in his British Racing Green Triumph TR3 and particularly impressed me with his reactions and driving skills. It had been raining heavily, and just in front of us, when we went over a virtually flat railway bridge at about 35 mph, a cyclist slipped and fell over. I thought we would certainly hit him and kill him; had anyone other than Paul been behind the wheel, the cyclist would no doubt have been dead. But Paul flipped the wheel to one side, jabbed the brakes and slid to a sideways halt, stopping about an inch from the cyclist's head. I have never seen driving like it. We had a pint of ale to celebrate!

Driving with Paul was invariably an adventure. On another occasion, he and I popped down the road for lunch at a pub near Fairoaks Aerodrome. Driving at an exhilarating 60 mph, we shot over a hump in the road – only to discover that the road turned 90° to the right immediately after it! This was a little awkward as we were airborne at the moment of realisation. We flew off the road into a thick wood – tree trunks and imminent death were ahead. Somehow, and I still do not know how, Paul managed to navigate the car between all the trees that lay in front of us until we bumped to a halt.

We had adventures on his motorcycle too. On one occasion, I mounted the back of it, and before I could make myself secure, he accelerated, at his customary high velocity, off down the road. I lost my balance and tipped over backwards; the only thing that saved me was my feet getting caught under his arms. I came upright when he changed gear. I did not have a crash helmet in those days.

A lot of pilots seem to be interested in fast cars and driving at great speed. Another pilot at Fairoaks was a multimillionaire who had six beautiful cars, one of which was a Brooklands Bentley in British Racing Green that he had spent a fortune having renovated. He then decided that he wanted to buy an Auster or Taylorcraft aircraft, but to raise cash to buy it, he decided to sell the Bentley. He offered it to me, but unfortunately he wanted £600 for it, which was way above what I could afford at the time. He was well known for hurtling down the road to Chertsey in one of his other cars, an AC Cobra, which had eight Webber carburettors. On one occasion, he went through a police speed trap and was stopped; he offered to take the officers one at a time in the Cobra to demonstrate its performance if they would let him off. They accepted his offer and he was never charged!

Paul and I enjoyed our time at Fairoaks and were shown the ropes with great thoroughness by the instructors there. The first and most important thing before flying is the pre-flight check. For this, you walk round the aircraft checking everything and trusting nothing to luck. You always start at the same place, just where you are going to board the aircraft. The tyre check is perhaps the most important; you look for any cuts or creep on the tyres, making sure that they have not 'turned' when striking the ground during a previous landing which could bend the valve.

You also have to be sure that you check every orifice of the aircraft for insects and dirt. It is surprising how bees and wasps take a liking to an aircraft's pitot heads. Part of the air speed indicator, the pitot head measures the air coming towards the aircraft whilst a static plate (a plate with a hole in it) on the side of the aircraft measures static pressure – the difference between the two is calibrated to give you your speed, which is usually in knots. A simple and approximate way of converting knots to mph is to subtract the equivalent of VAT (when it was 15%!). Pilots like these systems and analogies, as they make life easier.

A pilot normally needs someone to start the aircraft for them by checking that the chocks are in place and by turning the propeller – this is usually turned in the opposite direction to its normal rotation, which is to suck in fuel and avoid what is called hydraulicing. This is with the Magneto switches off ('mags off'), whilst turning a few propeller blades before starting. After several turns, the operator will call out 'Switches on'; the pilot then puts the two Magneto switches on and calls out, 'Contact', meaning mags on for starting. The ground crew member will then spin the propeller which will turn and give the pilot full control of the engine – provided it starts first time.

We didn't have a radio in those days, but today you would call up the control tower and get permission to taxi. Taxiing is done by zigzagging left and right in order to see clearly past the engine – if you go in a straight line, it's far too easy to taxi into something or someone. Years later, during the making of a Battle of Britain film at Jersey Airport, the Spanish pilot of a ME 109 failed to zigzag when taxiing and went propeller-first into a Heinkel HE 111 aircraft – he was immediately sent home in disgrace.

Whilst heading towards the end of the runway, a pilot must carry out certain taxi checks to ensure that all the instruments work. At the end of the runway, it is vital to run the engine up to the correct rpm and check the magnetos by switching off one at a time. This is to see what sort of drop happens on the gauges and to make sure that it is within the limits of the aircraft. Once confident that the aircraft is ready, there are then the pre-take-off checks which are very similar in all types of light aircraft but become slightly more complicated as one progresses to larger aircraft.

Having been cleared by the ATC (Air Traffic Control) with a green flash from an Aldis Lamp (there was an old aviation joke – if you saw a black flash from an Aldis Lamp at night, what did that mean?) and checked that the runway is now clear and no one is on final approaches, the pilot turns onto the runway, takes a last look all round, opens the throttle and the aircraft gathers speed. He then pushes the stick forward slightly during the roll, holding the aircraft level with the tail wheel off the ground, pulls gently back on the stick when the correct speed is reached, and then suddenly the aircraft is airborne.

If you learn to fly, your instructor will gradually introduce you to the different control movements. Before you're allowed to go solo, he will put you through a stalling and spinning exercise, which is quite daunting the first time it happens. Basically, for stalling you will check all around you (in particular, below you), and that you have enough height. Then you will gently close the throttle, allowing the speed to slowly creep back. Eventually, at about 25-40 knots, or even less, the aircraft will suddenly lurch forward with the nose dropping away: you are in a stall.

In most aircraft, it is quite easy to get out of a stall. You just push the column straight forward, hold the wings level, open the throttle slowly and bring the nose back above the horizon until you regain full control.

The spin, however, is much more fun. In this case, just as the stall begins, you kick a full boot of rudder and the aircraft will now spin round and round, going nose-down towards the ground. In order to stop the spin, you simply apply opposite rudder, level the wings and apply throttle – but you must stop the spin first, and **then** level the wings – in that order – or you can get into trouble, especially in cloud. You then gently raise the nose up until you are flying in the normal manner and climb back up. It is quite exhilarating, and after practising that several times (and probably carrying out a loop-the-loop), you will be well on your way to becoming a solo pilot.

The exercises at Fairoaks Aerodrome are usually held over the Hog's Back – a long, straight ridge with a main road along the spine of the North Downs. Running down the centre of the Hog's Back at a few thousand feet means that, when you come out of a spin, you can get a clear visual check on the direction of required travel; it is a good landmark.

Fairoaks itself is at the end of a narrow air corridor cut into the side of the London Control Zone. When returning, the start of the corridor can easily be identified by a water tower. You join the circuit by flying over the airfield, checking the signals square (a large square cut out of the grass next to the control tower about 40' x 40' containing cutouts which give information to the pilots both on the ground and airborne) and carrying out, in most cases, a left-hand circuit of 90° turns until you are on finals. Then the throttle is reduced and the pilot concentrates on the runway itself, aiming to land some way into it. It is never advisable to land on the end of the runway; if there is a last-minute downdraught or a problem with the engine, you're certain to fall short and crash.

Attaining the correct glide path is done by watching the end of the runway as you descend and seeing how the 'picture' of the runway changes. If it goes away from you, then you are going to fall short and need to apply a little more power; if it goes down, you are going to land too far down it and so need a little less. The aim is for the picture to stay about the same and simply grow larger – then you know you are on the right glide path. As you come over the end of the runway, you close the throttle and start to flare by pulling the stick back in towards your tummy. After practising this many times, you will eventually be able to land on all three points of the aeroplane – tail wheel or skid and main wheels. However, in the early stages, as I found, you will either stall the plane with a huge thump, or 'wheel' it on, and if this is not done properly, you will bounce more and more and will then have to go round again by opening the throttle.

One final test before you go solo is a practice engine failure after take-off. For this, you get to 300 to 400 feet and the instructor will pull the throttle back, simulating engine failure. You immediately have to look for somewhere to land. You **must not** try to return to the airfield; any pilot trying to do so would invariably kill himself and his passengers as he would more than likely crash before getting back. One of the main reasons for this is that, in making the turn needed to return, you would lose too much height – an aircraft's wings create less lift on a turn because they are shorter at this moment. This will probably result in a stall and a crash.

Before getting a Private Pilot's Licence, we had to take some written exams which basically consisted of very useful meteorological (or weather) papers. There were also tests on how to join a circuit and how to read the airfield signals square – these contain some large, toy-like symbols which you view when you initially fly over the airfield before joining the circuit. The signal square is usually positioned next to the control tower and there are various different symbols which one must know: for example, a dumb-bell symbol in white suggests that the airfield is unserviceable or unreliable except for the runways, so you must use the runways only. Two white crosses on a vertical arm indicate that there is glider flying in progress. An arrow indicates which circuit you will use, the right or left-hand circuit. A white cross indicates that there is parachuting in progress. This is very important as, obviously, you can easily kill a parachutist, and it is particularly important for helicopters as down-wash will collapse the parachute if you fly over the top of them.

There was an accident fairly recently where a helicopter landed with its rotors spinning and a parachutist came straight in from above him and went right through the rotor blades, which was not a pretty sight. (While on the subject, with a helicopter around, always make sure that you duck down below the blades. A number of years ago, a helicopter pilot landed at his house and stepped out of the helicopter; his young child ran towards him shouting, "Hello, Daddy!" The pilot picked him up and lifted him above his head, right into the path of the rotor blades.) We were taught always to remember, when approaching an airfield, to fly over the top of the checkout signals square and keep a really good look out.

The Landing-T clearly indicates wind direction and therefore which way you should land – you land along the base of the 'T' towards the cross arm. It is vitally important that you land into wind, because landing with the wind behind you will cause a lot of difficulties and probably an accident as it considerably increases your landing ground speed and you may then run out of runway.

Always submit a flight plan before a flight, otherwise if you crash somewhere and the trees close up above you, rescuers will have no way of knowing where you might be – it might make the difference between life and death for you. After every flight, you have to fill in your logbook (this is a must if you want to obtain a higher licence), stating whether you were the pilot under training or the pilot in command; if you are under training, then you name the Captain of the aircraft and get him to sign your logbook. You can also make any notes that you may wish. Many of my Captains in the earlier days were the World War II bomber and fighter pilots who had various entries in their logbooks showing bombing missions, whom they had shot down, and whether there had been death or injury to their crew.

My friend Paul and I both qualified for our Private Pilot's Licence (PPL) on the same day. The test consisted of a flying exam followed by a short cross-country flight, and went very smoothly indeed. The PPL entitles you to fly solo; one danger is the rush of confidence it engenders, many people behaving as though they were now expert pilots and then rushing out to ask their friends to accompany them in an aircraft. This can be a very dangerous period of your flying career as you think you have the knowledge and experience that you still lack. If a new pilot flies into difficult conditions with which he is unfamiliar, it can be fatal. At this point in time, you have not been taught to fly in cloud – and woe betide anyone who thinks they can just do it! Because you cannot; you **have** to be trained.

One extremely fortunate pilot I know suffered from exactly this over-confidence. Not long after gaining his PPL, he took off from an airport in England to fly back to Ireland, where he was from. He flew at about 1,000 feet from the Oxford area straight to Ireland. Most of the journey was clear, but he encountered some cloud. Whilst in some clouds, quite unable to see where he was going, he suddenly saw what we call 'cumulus granite' – i.e. a mountain! He pulled the stick back in order to gain height as quickly as possible but crashed straight onto the mountain. But instead of hitting it nose on, because of the angle the aircraft was at, he managed to land flat-belly onto it. Somehow, he survived. We joked afterwards that, if you looked closely at his forehead, you could see where the altimeter imprinted its shape with the needles showing 1,000 feet!

WWII Flying Helmet

Bentley

Tiger Moth

Miles Magister

Taylorcraft

Chapter Four
OXFORD, KIDLINGTON AERODROME

A fter various adventures and with the required thirty hours of flying under our belts (in addition to several technical exams), Paul and I finally had the hard-covered Private Pilot's Licence in our hands. We both made applications to the Oxford Air Training School at Kidlington Aerodrome to undertake a commercial pilot's course. The aerodrome dates from 1935 and has the rather sad claim to fame that in 1941 Amy Johnson died on a flight to Kidlington from Blackpool when she diverted from Oxford and crashed her airspeed Oxford into the Thames estuary. If you don't know her story, it is worth reading.[8]

We arrived at Kidlington Aerodrome, Oxford, on 7th August 1962 and were duly in awe of our surroundings and our instructors. We discovered however that one of them, a man with a slightly withered hand, had – shortly before we arrived – decided to show off to some young ladies visiting the aerodrome. He took an aircraft up and carried out a series of aerobatic manoeuvres over the top of the airfield; he got lower and lower, and nearer and nearer the ground. Coming out of his last loop, he misjudged his height and went straight into the hangar roof – thankfully surviving.

Paul and I became well acquainted with him, mainly because he was a good chap, but also because he was a Bell's Whisky representative. Naturally, we felt it our duty to accompany him to each of the many local pubs that were customers of his. It was the norm for us to have free whisky at each and every one of the pubs, and my affinity for Bell's Whisky dates from those times.

Oxford, it turned out, had seen plenty of accidents and my first experience of losing a friend came soon after arriving there.[9] A pilot

I had known for only a few days, whom I'd met shortly after my arrival, took his secretary for a flight and they crashed in a nearby field. The investigation discovered that there was an amorous element in what had occurred; it turned out that his trousers, which were lowered, had got caught around the controls of the aircraft, resulting in it plummeting straight to the ground. That was the end of him and his secretary – though as we talked about it in the bar, we agreed that it must have been one hell of a climax!

Our accommodation at the airport consisted of World War II-style long wooden huts that had been divided into individual rooms. They were dark and cold, even when the sun was out. The only way you could heat or lighten them was by means of a coin meter in the room, which you had to fill with coins on a regular basis. The main fuse box was at the end of the corridor and the fuses continually blew, leaving us in the dark and freezing cold until some bright spark hit upon the idea (perhaps none too safely) of putting a large nail in place of the fuse. It was so cold that you could actually wake up in the morning with a glass of water by your bed that was solid ice.

My first flight on arrival at Oxford Kidlington Airport is recorded in my logbook. It was in a Piper Colt G-ARKN on 7th August 1962 at 1730, lasting 1hr 05mins, with my instructor Dave Ryles. I believe he was an RAF pilot on leave, and he was a very good instructor. Ironically, he later ended up as my First Officer when I had become a Captain, having eventually left the Air Force to join the company. At 2000hrs we were airborne again for thirty minutes and practised spins, stalls and forced landings. The purpose of the forced landing is not only training in the event of a general engine failure, but also to keep in mind the worst-case scenario of an engine failure shortly after take-off. It is always vital to have a clear idea of where you are going to land if the engine fails, particularly on a single-engine airplane.

Paul and I had to do about 200 flying hours and numerous exams over approximately a six-month period. Much of our time was spent in the classroom on theoretical work, in preparation for taking written exams. Relaxation took place mostly in the airport bar, swapping stories – or, as we did not have any money – we had a system of playing liar dice at which we rapidly became expert. If we didn't win at it, we wouldn't eat or drink.

I made some very good friends at Kidlington, with whom over the years I've unfortunately lost contact. Two of them were Sikh pilots from the Indian Air Force, who were the most fantastic, polite gentlemen that I have ever met. Indeed, such was our friendship that something happened that I will always treasure: I was allowed to see one of the Sikh officers prepare his hair and put on his turban, which I understand is a great honour – I certainly considered it as such.

There were also two outstanding Arab gentlemen. One, Ali, was the son of the chief of the palace guard in his home country, and there were many occasions where he was protective towards me, safeguarding me during difficult situations. He was extremely tough and knew how to defend himself, and he was also a real ladies' man – he often went AWOL to meet ladies in London! On one occasion, some parachutists came onto the airfield and ended up getting exceedingly drunk; they became aggressive and picked a fight with Ali round the back of the bar area. They had picked the wrong person – he took two bottles, broke them and with one in each hand was so fearsome that they thought better of it and departed swiftly!

One of the instructors was a pilot from the Royal Air Force bombing crew that bombed (or, to be more accurate, missed) the Torrey Canyon oil tanker. This was carrying 120,000 tons of crude oil when it became grounded on Seven Stones Reef near Land's End on 18th March 1967. It was leaking oil and it was decided that the Fleet Air Arm would bomb it in order to break it open; despite the target being stationary, they could not hit it. Needless to say, the press printed embarrassing stories about the incident and it was not the Fleet Air Arm's finest hour. This instructor went on to teach Churchill's grandson (who passed away in 2010) and also The Rt Hon the Lord Trefgarne, who later became a supporter of Brooklands Museum.

Another friend was Paddy, a six-foot-two Irishman with a background as a racing driver. One day he decided that he would put a blower on the engine of his yellow Triumph Vitesse. I was with him when he managed to get it up to 115 mph on a back road, not a speed for which that car was ever designed, and it was at this very moment that the pipe from the blower came adrift – you couldn't see back down the road for smoke pouring out of the car. It was not on fire, but the oil had gone all over the engine. Stopping was a hairy business as the brakes were certainly not designed for that sort of speed, particularly not when covered in oil!

Breakfast flights were all the rage at that time. As a squadron, we would take off very early in the morning and fly to an aerodrome for breakfast, often Le Touquet. It is amazing how refreshing it is to take breakfast in a foreign country just as the sun is coming up. One of these flights took place from Biggin Hill, the famous World War II fighter station. There were five aircraft going and I was to captain one of them. During my pre-flight, I noticed that we were one life-jacket short. I had already demonstrated to my passengers how to put their life-jackets on, pointing out that, as we were flying at 1,000 feet, if the engine failed, I would have no time to give them instructions on how to put them on before we hit the sea. I refused to go without one; one of the other Captains, I thought rather stupidly, gave me his. I don't know what would have happened if he had had an engine failure.

At Oxford I also met Howard Greenaway. He was a well-built man with blonde hair who had a maroon-coloured MG Y-Type 1¼-litre saloon and tourer, a model that I have rarely seen either before or since. His parents owned a farm on one of the well-known battlefields from the English Civil War; I believe it was Edgehill. I often hired the car from him, but there was one difficulty – the back of the driver's seat was broken, meaning you had to sit bolt upright with no support whilst driving the car. However, I found that a large suitcase wedged between the front and rear seats served the purpose well.

Paul and I inevitably ended up goading and challenging each other. On one occasion, I was flying a Tipsy Nipper T 66 Series 2 (G-ARDY), and he a Piper Colt – and we were finishing at the same time. I was established on final approach when, all of a sudden, he cut in below me. I could see him through what was basically a piece of Perspex cut into the side of each wing on the Tipsy Nipper – made so that you could actually see directly below you. I wasn't surrendering my approach; I continued my path, getting lower and lower and getting nearer and nearer to him when finally, at the last minute, he chickened out! I went ahead and landed.

We heatedly discussed what had happened on landing, I with the triumph of the victor, he with the chagrin of the defeated. He claimed he had the right of way, which I completely denied. We eventually decided to continue the discussion at the local hostelry. Driving into Woodstock village, we met up with several more of the trainee pilots, one of whom drove a MGA sports car in red. At the end of a wet evening and very many pints of beer later, we all set off back to the airfield in the dark. I was passenger in Paul's British Racing Green TR-3 and the MG pursued us at top speed. It was freezing cold and wet, and there were no seat belts in those days so it was not the safest of conditions. The two cars were side-by-side on the dual carriageway running from Woodstock to the airfield doing 70-80 mph, both drivers going as fast as they could, when we realised we were approaching a roundabout which had a three-inch kerb round it.

Paul and I just about got into the roundabout first, but as we were going too fast, we slid sideways all the way to the middle, bumping over the kerbs with a terrible bang. We came to a crunching and inglorious halt with the roof of the car having flown off with the force of the impact, leaving us sitting in the rain! We got the engine restarted and gingerly inched the car forward onto the road, where we found that it wobbled alarmingly left and right, left and right, pitching first one way and then the other. We managed to wedge the top back on which just about kept us dry and coaxed it back to the airfield where we parked it in an old hangar.

We inspected the car in the light of day, discovering that all four stub-axles had been badly bent. Purchasing new ones, we made the car more or less serviceable again. The roof no longer fitted due to the damage it had sustained but in other regards it was a going concern. To celebrate, we drove it back to London late at night. It had already been snowing for several hours and, with no top, we were soon frozen stiff. We were driving along the outside lane of another dual carriageway, hurrying past a large Ford Zephyr Zodiac on the inside lane, but the snow, which was drifting and piling in the middle of the road, was slowly invading our lane. It became progressively narrower and narrower. Eventually, the inevitable happened and we sideswiped the Ford.

Both cars drove along, stuck firmly together, for some 200 yards. We both managed finally to stop in a convenient pub car park and prised the two vehicles apart. The other driver got out and inspected the damage to his car, which was considerable. We assumed that he would try to take Paul to court. As was our custom, we retreated into the pub and warmed ourselves up, feeling gloomy at the prospect. To our surprise, we never heard any more about it!

This was by no means the end of incidents in cars; Paul did eventually end up in court. On the occasion in question, we were driving down a hill on a two-lane road in a glorious Nash Metropolitan, finished in turquoise and white. There was a flat-backed three-ton lorry in front of us on the inside lane and we came alongside, slowly overtaking him in the empty lane on the other side of the road. However, there was a bend coming up, about 200 yards ahead.

There was plenty of time for us to overtake him before the bend but the truck driver deliberately put his foot down to stop us from getting in. Naturally, it would have been more sensible and conciliatory to have slowed down, but that was never on Paul's mind! We therefore ended up going round the bend on the wrong side of the road with the truck blocking us from pulling in.

Immediately on doing so, we saw a coach speeding towards us. At the last second, Paul managed to get in front of the truck but just as we pulled in we heard the sound of shattering glass coming from the back of the coach. It appeared that the coach driver had slammed his brakes on and the car behind him had crashed into the back.

There were now cars flying all over the place, skidding chaotically. Paul calmly weaved between them, missing everything and we sped on round the corner where we stopped. Feeling rather guilty, we parked the car and walked back under the cover of some trees to see what had happened. It seemed that no one was hurt, but there was a lot of damage to a lot of vehicles.

The law at the time stated that, in order to prosecute someone for a driving offence, the police had to inform the driver within 56 days. We waited with bated breath and the days passed. It was actually on the 55th day that Paul received in the post a summons for dangerous driving – a serious charge. One can only assume that they got his number plate either from a photograph, by luck from a passenger, or by someone noticing us when we were parked up round the corner.

We appeared uneasily at court on the due date. I was Paul's only witness, whereas there were about forty people on the other side! Paul had a very good barrister so I did not actually have to testify for him, although I would have said that the driver of the truck was driving provocatively and was determined to make sure that we did not get in. After a long plea by his counsel about his future career as a pilot, Paul was found guilty of a lesser charge of careless driving (instead of dangerous driving) and fined £50. We walked out with a due sense of relief and celebrated at a pub.

Paul later married into a fairly wealthy family and ran a small chain of tool shops, from which he, as a member of the family, made a reasonable living, allowing him to indulge his passion for cars and drive Aston Martins and eventually start his own flying club at Biggin Hill. I will never forget the driving escapades we shared or the first-hand experience I had of his brilliance behind the wheel. I was not surprised that he became the Aston Martin champion that year; his modesty should not be allowed to conceal his ability.

We worked towards the 200 hours of flying required for our commercial licence. Available for our use were Tipsy Nippers (the cheapest to hire at £1 10s per hour), Piper Colts, Tripacers, Airdales and twin-engine Apaches and Aztecs. My particular favourite bird was the small, single-engine single-seat Tipsy Nipper (G-ARDY). It had a Volkswagen engine, short stubby wings and very small wheels, complete with the smallest set of disc brakes I had ever seen. It was very aerobatic but was not without quirks; it had a troubling tendency for the engine to stop, which sometimes occurred mid-flight, but more often at the end of the runway when you were lining up to accelerate for take-off. Whenever this happened, which was frequently, I would have to jump out of the aircraft, spin the propeller until it started, then hold onto the wing tips while the aircraft went round and round in circles until I could make a lunge at the side of the aircraft. When I managed to secure a handhold, I would then jump into the seat, strap myself in and finally take off.

This particular aircraft outlived me for time in the skies – it was still going long after I had retired. Not only that, I was amused to read an accident report for her in November 2000, where this same quirk was still in evidence. The pilot, exactly as I had done so many years before, started her up himself at the end of the runway by spinning the propeller, but he did so with the throttle on a relatively high setting. He then slipped and fell over and could not catch her, leaving her to speed merrily into a fabric hangar! Less amusing was her final accident report, in 2011, where her propeller bolts mysteriously snapped off when flying at 2,000 feet. Her pilot somehow managed to land her and survived, but his horror at suddenly seeing his aircraft had no propeller must have been truly traumatic! Both reports are in the appendices.

As Paul and I neared the end of our 200 hours, we had to take various exams and pilot cross-country flights, a vital part of the flying course. The flying exam consisted of a three-leg (or triangular) cross-country flight with an examiner; at his chosen moment on the second leg, the examiner would tell you to divert back to base. You were closely watched as you set a course back to the field laying off a few degrees on your heading to allow for wind and then called up the airfield for a magnetic bearing (QDM) that would take you back home.

MG TR-3

MG Y Type

Nash Metropolitan

Nipper

Piper Colt

Chapter Five
COMMERCIAL PILOT'S QUALIFICATIONS

I took my CPL (Commercial Pilot's Licence) when I was 19 years old, in 1962, which was eventually followed by the senior Air Transport Pilot's Licence (ATPL) which I passed at the age of 22.

One of the first means of progression for Paul and me was the radio licence exam. This saw us going up to London for a fairly intense test where we more or less re-enacted a full flight with headsets on in the classroom. I know this may not seem quite right, but we were given a glimpse of the script for the entire exam. As we drove to London in Paul's Triumph TR3, we practised over and over again until we were word-for-word perfect on what we had been told would be in the exam. Goodness knows what would have happened if it had been a different exercise!

On arrival, we were solemnly taken to our cubicles where a headset and microphone awaited us. The examiner explained the scenario; to our absolute delight, it was indeed the one we had expected. We were taken through an entire imaginary flight for which we were both word-perfect all the way through. We both emerged with the necessary stamp on our licences.

A full Professional Flying Licence comes in stages: the first part is the CPL, or Commercial Pilot's Licence, which allows you to fly aircraft up to about the size of a Dakota, known as a DC3 (although colloquially known as a 'Goony bird' in the trade – due to the way it appears to waddle down the runway). You require about 200 hours' flying experience before you can take the exam which consists of about six parts, including a written exam and a cross-country flying test.

Although we had been taught the technical exams at Kidlington Aerodrome, they always seemed somewhat cursory and, indeed, were not enough for a detailed written exam. I felt deficient in this regard, so I went to crammer courses at Cass College in London, which were based on past exam papers, but Paul didn't. These brought me up to a very high standard which enabled me to pass the exam, although I'm not sure that they gave me the complete knowledge that I was expected to have later in my career.

The first exam was to be astral navigation, but this was in fact done away with about two weeks before I was due to sit it. Navigation technology had advanced to such a degree in the previous years that an exam in it would have been an irrelevance. Indeed, by then most aircraft did not even have any vantage from where an astral shot could be taken.

Morse Code took the greatest amount of concentration, both to learn, and also in which to demonstrate proficiency under exam conditions. You were expected to be proficient in it up to a pretty high standard and it was widely used in aircraft; in practice, Morse Code was the only way that you could actually identify most of the navigation aids. It is used still today on every single flight to ascertain that the radio aid to which you are tuned is the correct beacon or landing aid. I can still remember most of it, even to this day. I have included a Morse Code chart in the appendices.

We also needed to complete at least five hours of night-flight instruction. This included three hours of dual instruction, which would include at least one hour of cross-country navigation as well as five solo take-offs and five solo full-stop landings.

Paul and I undertook our five exams at the same time. These were:

1. Air Law: the rules of the air. [Pass mark 70%]
2. Navigation Part 1: Interpretation of weather forecasts to ensure a safe flight. [Pass mark 70%]
3. Navigation Part 2 and radio aids: Navigation aids available to the pilot. [Pass mark 70%]
4. Met. [Pass mark 70%]
5. Signals [Pass / Fail]

Our study on meteorology took us to a very high standard in our reading of the weather, which I have always found useful in life. Within this was the climatology section, which we all dreaded. Here, the world is split into five parts, and in the examination you could be asked to describe what the weather would be like at any time of year in any part of the world. This was an extremely difficult exam, and I was lucky on the day when Europe was the examined topic.

You may have heard of 'Buys Ballot's Law'. This describes how the wind blows and your bathwater spirals one way in the northern hemisphere and the other in the southern. In the northern hemisphere, if you stand with your back to the wind, the low pressure is on the left-hand side (low-pressure normally meaning bad weather), so that once you know which way the wind is blowing, you then know whether you're flying into bad weather or away from it.

The speed of the wind is taken by measuring the distance between the isobars (these are the sweeping, long lines on a weather-chart which look rather like a greatly distorted dartboard). The closer together they are, the stronger the wind and the worse the weather will be.

Altimeters work on air pressure – you can see the pressures on the television met forecasts which are indicated by a series of lines that look rather like a dartboard. Some of the meteorological maps will show you a low pressure area, probably in the form of a circle, and the nearer the isobars (as they are called) are together, the stronger the wind will be. If they are very, very close, there may be a hurricane or other such system. Whichever, flying into low pressure is dangerous, while going into high pressure is not usually such a problem.

So with different pressures as you travel on your trip round the world, you might think your altimeter is showing one particular height but, in actual fact, you are going up and down depending on whether you are entering high or low pressure. The danger is when you're flying into an area of low pressure, which means that you think you're at a certain height, when in fact you might actually be lower. Therefore if you are setting your safety height to take this into account for a mountain, if the pressure is extremely low, you may actually strike the mountain. Obviously this causes problems round the world, with not only the changes in pressure due to the weather system and pressure systems as you progress, but also from the fact that your airfield is at a different height from all the others – you might have no idea really how high your airfield is, except by testing your altimeter on the ground with what is called the 'QFE'. When you set this on your altimeter, it will read zero. If you wind it to what the tower gives you as the QNH, it should then match up with the height of the airfield. If it does not, then your altimeter is unserviceable (get it checked by the Ground Engineer).

So the only way to manage all the aircraft flying around is to have the average pressure in the world set on your altimeter the same as everyone else – this has been designated as 1013.2. This is also needed to calculate technical aspects of an aeroplane in the form of its performance etc. All of the aircraft that are flying on designated airways – this is the way pilots navigate, almost like a normal road map showing motorways – and pilots all know exactly how high they are compared with the other aircraft on that airway. This should prevent the possibility of hitting other aircraft.

So once more, when you come in to land, there are two altimeter settings. The same applies for take-off, but in the landing particularly, you can have QNH or QFE – if you select QNH, which you will get from the Met Office before you leave and/or the Air Traffic Controller at the airfield that you are arriving at, this will give you your height above the runway – although not necessarily above any mountains or other things. QFE will read zero on landing on your altimeter. You usually land with QFE so the altimeter reads zero when you touch down. (By the way, QFE and QNH are named after the Q code, a code used in aviation where the Q code FE would stand for field elevation and NH should stand for nautical height.)

Another quite fascinating point, and a necessary piece of knowledge, is that in low pressure, the altimeter will make you think you are higher than you are by 27 feet per millibar. Every change in pressure of one millibar is equivalent to 27 feet in the height shown on your altimeter, so flying into a low pressure system is dangerous. For instance, if you are flying towards a low pressure area and at, say, 1,000 feet, if the pressure drops by ten millibars, your altimeter will be over-reading by 270 feet – your height is actually 730 feet above ground, which could mean the difference of flying over a mountain or into it. Most mainstream aircraft fly on airways (a sort of road map system, starting at about 5,000 feet) with the altimeter set to 1013.2. This is the average pressure throughout the world and is used by aircraft so that they are all flying on the same altimeter setting. It is also used for many engineering measurements. You might presume that once you zero an altimeter on the ground at point A, it will be accurately calibrated. However, as you will see, once you go to another airfield at point B at a different height above sea level, it will not register zero feet at the other end of the flight. You can therefore make it read zero on your altimeter by asking for and setting the QFE of that field. QFE is a Q code used by pilots and Air Traffic Controllers that refers to atmospheric pressure and altimeter settings – Quick Fix Engineering, also known as 'hotfix'.

To standardise all this, once you are on the airway, you use 1013.2 until prior to landing when you ask the airfield for its QFE so that your altimeter will show zero altitude when you land. You also might ask for the QNH, which will show the height of the airfield at that particular time when you land. You have to be particularly cautious of your altimeter's reading when you are flying towards a low-pressure area.

Normally the weather between the fronts is made up of low cloud and rain. When this has passed, you end up with cumulus cloud, or rain showers on hot sunny days with cumulonimbus (large anvil-shaped clouds), often stretching up to the troposphere. This is the lowest layer, right below the stratosphere; the next layer above the stratosphere is the mesosphere; the bottom of the stratosphere is about 10 km (6.2 miles or about

33,000 feet) above the ground at middle latitudes; the top of the stratosphere occurs at an altitude of 50 km (31 miles).

You might also get thunderstorms, which are shown on the weather radar as a big red splodge. If you don't have radar and it is extremely cloudy, you may accidentally run into one – you will soon know that you have done so as you will be violently shaken around and possibly struck by lightning.

Being struck by lightning is actually no big deal. I have carried out four flights in one day where I have gone over the same beacon, near Midhurst, and been struck each time. I have also seen St Elmo's Fire – this is an effect caused by pulses of electricity running down the cabin and seemingly along the heads of all the passengers, pulling their hair in sprightly straight vertical lines. It also often plays on the windshield too and you see a beautiful blue sparkly spider-like web in front of you.

The best case I had of being hit by lightning was when I came out of Tel Aviv just after take-off on a Trident. I had just selected the undercarriage up and was starting to climb when we were hit by the most terrific bolt of lightning which made the aircraft shudder and shake. However, all seemed well in the cockpit, all instruments reading as normal, so we carried on flying towards the Alps. Here, I had to make a decision as to whether we flew over them (4,808m, or nearly 16,000 feet) and landed in Geneva, Switzerland, or instead landed in Italy, to see if there was any structural damage. However, the lunch allowance was much higher in Geneva than Italy; that decided it for me! On landing and inspecting the outside of the aircraft, I counted 164 holes with burn marks that looked rather as though someone had taken a machine-gun and fired down the entire length of the Trident. As usual, this sort of damage is patched up with duct tape (we call it speed tape); the public may not realise it, but it is a regular temporary fix for items that come loose or hang off the aircraft, so that one can get them back home for repairs. (You notice I used the term 'selected the undercarriage up' and not the old American phrase of 'gear up'. This is because a Captain once said on a take off roll to the First Officer, "Cheer up," at which point the First Officer selected 'Gear Up' whilst they were still on the ground!)

Weather forecasting today is not a patch on how it was in the old days – it seems to be a broad-brush concept applied to a quarter of the country. When I was new to flying, every airport had its own weather forecaster. In Jersey, for instance, there was a forecaster known to us as 'Windless' who could forecast to within five minutes or so when the weather in Jersey might worsen or improve. After some time of observing and discussing his forecasting with him, I was actually able to emulate his ideas. I can remember sitting in London Heathrow Airport with other crews, all waiting for the weather to clear so we could head to Jersey. When I studied the weather map, I detected a 10° change in the wind. I told them to get my aircraft ready, to the consternation of the other pilots, and I took off and flew down just in time for clearance in Jersey.

The weather window in which I arrived was very small; a couple of hours later the weather had closed in again. I needed to go to Guernsey next, and as Windless told me that there would be a very short clearance or window of opportunity, I asked for the aircraft to be made ready for take-off. On board, the Duty Manager advised me that we had the correct passengers but the wrong baggage; our bags were on another aircraft that was also going to Guernsey. I told them that there was insufficient time for both of us to fly over, and that we should take off immediately. However, the officer refused to do so, and spent nearly 1½ hours changing the bags over. I am afraid I was a little forceful with him when I got back to my base, which was then in Birmingham.

There, the Flight Manager was not particularly pleased with me and told me in no uncertain terms that the Duty Manager had spoken to him in order to get me reprimanded. I merely said that if he had checked the weather forecast for that period, he would have seen that I could have got over there and that I was absolutely correct in what I had aimed to do. He glared at me and told me to leave his office. At no time did he apologise to me for making the correct command decision. But more of him later.

Snow and ice on the runway can drastically affect an aircraft, not least because landing on a runway with more than half an inch of snow can physically damage it. However, snow leads to other incidents. On one occasion, a Trident aircraft landed at Heathrow and taxied, in the snow, towards its stand. However, the Captain misjudged its route as the tarmac and grass were both covered in a crisp blanket of white, and he strayed onto the grass, the Trident sinking down right to its axles. Eventually, it was towed away onto the stand by a large tug where, much delayed, it unloaded and the passengers disembarked.

That aircraft later departed on another route and took off, but the next aircraft replacing it on the stand after coming into land simply (and naturally) followed its tracks. Nobody had bothered putting any warnings out. The result: it also went axle-deep in grass and mud, leaving its Captain fuming whilst the tug was fetched. Lack of foresight involving tugs was not a one-off occurrence; on one occasion at Heathrow a very expensive brand-new batch of tugs arrived from Canada. They were used all day until they seized up – they had been delivered without gearbox oil!

Much of the commercial training was spent familiarising us with radio aids. It is difficult to believe how much is involved in these, which use both long-wave radio and VHF (the latter stretching just over the horizon). One key aspect was the radio range beacons, one of which used to be at Dunsfold and was used to guide us into Gatwick Airport. The pilot navigated in by listening to a stream of automated 'As' and 'Ns' in Morse Code. If you heard an 'N-stream' ('dah-dit, dah-dit, …'), you turned the aircraft to the right; if you head an 'A' stream ('dit-dah, dit-dah, …'), you navigated to the left. When hearing a steady tone, you flew straight ahead.

More complex was another radio aid, 'Consul' (designed by the Germans during the war and used by us), which we used when flying to Stavanger in Norway. You had to listen very carefully to a series of dashes or dots and take the number that you heard away from 60; if you heard 30 dashes and 20 dots, you had to take 50 away from 60, leaving 10, and then divide by two and add five back onto each figure. You would then know whether you were left or right of a certain track. It sounds complicated, but it was really an exercise of concentration.

It was probably whilst using this radio aid that a Vickers Viking flying from London to Stavanger flew straight into the top of a mountain northeast of Stavanger on 9th August 1961. The accident killed 39 people, three crew and 36 passengers who were a class of schoolboys aged 13 to 16 with their two teachers, all from Lanfranc Secondary Modern School for Boys.

Perhaps most feared of all was the Load and Balance Exam. This was a calculation headache consisting of weights data and baggage data, and was based on the number of passengers expected on your flight. We had to transcribe this onto a load sheet and use the information to calculate the correct fuel, the reserve fuel and the diversion fuel. It was also the basis of where passengers should be seated; even on an aircraft as stable as a Viscount, if all the passengers sat at the front, or at the back, the aircraft would be unmanageable. The cabin crew had the onerous and unpopular job of moving passengers around, and theirs was the task of convincing them that the inconvenience was necessary for safety purposes.

I was lucky enough to pass all my exams in one sitting. I must admit that, at the back of my mind, I've always wondered whether I was fortunate to be sitting them at a moment when there was a great shortage of pilots. Paul did not pass his, despite re-sitting the parts he had failed, and consequently never managed to gain his CPL – he was a superb pilot and a great loss to commercial aviation. He went on to obtain an instructor's rating and ran a flying club from Biggin Hill.

To fly in IMC weather (meaning Instrument Flight Rules), thick cloud and reduced visibility, an Instrument Rating is required. This is an expensive exam to pass and requires thirty hours in a twin-engine aircraft as well as the exam itself, where you must fly to a very high standard in simulated snow-and-ice conditions and be monitored from the flight planning stage through all the checks, and of course throughout the flight itself. The focus is the references to snow and ice. You are expected to fly extremely accurately, within tight horizontal and vertical tolerances similar to the following.

IFR flight limits;

Height ± 100 feet

Starting a go-around at decision height + 50 feet/-0 feet

Minimum descent height/altitude decision height/altitude + 50 feet/-0 feet

Tracking On radio aids ± 5°

Precision approach

DME Arcing ± 1nm

Speed Generally ± 10 knots

You have to work out by means of a circular slide-rule your holding pattern upon arrival as you wait for clearance to land, and you need to get it as near as possible to exactly four minutes. Having followed various complex procedures from charts and having followed a single beacon, you then fly an Instrument System approach which guides you in holding your line on the flight path; you keep two needles crossed on a gauge, one which indicates whether you are above or below the flight path and one which shows whether you are moving to the left or right of it. If you keep these crossed and adjust speed by using power setting and flap settings, you should arrive at exactly 1,000 feet into the runway itself – as long as all the calculations for your landing weight are correct.

Pilots with their IR are often 'boldly' confident in their abilities after passing such a rigorous exam. Many famous people have, however, been killed on charter aircraft in bad weather – one thinks of Audie Murphy, Patsey Cline, Jim Reeves and Rocky Marciano. There is not the slightest margin for error; any mistake at any point can prove fatal. It is thought that the difference between a European and an American artificial horizon caused one crash – on one, the turn is shown at the bottom, and on the other, at the top. There is no room for complacency.

Instruments are highly complicated, and it is expected that the pilot will have a detailed knowledge of how all his instruments work. In this day and age, most aeroplanes have display screens;

there's not so much to learn because the screens are just pulled out and replaced when you land. When they first came out, some pilots went to Boeing in Seattle for a course on them. One asked how the artificial horizon worked; the instructor replied, "It's SFM."

Puzzled, he asked what that meant.

In reply, he was told that it stood for "Sheer F...ing Magic".

This became an expression I adopted frequently throughout my life!

We had to learn many aspects of aviation so we knew what to do in almost any conceivable situation. Knowing how to fly on one engine if one of your engines failed is one example. Here, you have to 'lean' slightly on the live engine by turning towards it. If you try to turn leaning towards the dead engine, you may well crash and kill everyone on board (which happened to an aircraft over Jersey). Also, we had to do an individual exam on every aircraft type we elected to fly, though we were able to buy most of the answers to these in the form of 'Pop Speller's Notes' (he was a retired examiner who had copied all the answers before retiring and sold them). We also had to be able to calculate the direction of travel from an aircraft's lights at night; the ones on the wing 110°: port red, starboard green. Tail white covering 140°, making a total of 360°, so you can then tell whether the aeroplane is going away from you or crossing your path safely.

Aircraft navigation lights are placed in a way similar to that of marine vessels, with a red navigation light located on the left wing tip leading edge and a green light on the right wing tip leading edge. Anti-collision lights are flashing lights on the top and bottom of the fuselage, wing tips and tail tip. Since the colour is in relation to the direction from which an aircraft can be seen, we can immediately determine the trajectory of any aeroplanes. Therefore, the following conclusions can be drawn:

1. If a green and a red light are seen, this aircraft is facing us, flying towards us: collision is probable!
2. If a red light is seen, this aircraft will fly from right to left: collision is possible.

3. If a green light is seen, this aircraft will fly from left to right: collision is possible.
4. If a white and a red light are seen, this aircraft will fly away from right to left: collision is possible.
5. If a white and a green light are seen, this aircraft will fly away from left to right: collision is possible.
6. If a white light is seen, this aircraft is seen from the rear, flying away: collision is remote.

Gaining my CPL was a moment of great triumph. As well as opening up my career, it allowed me to aim for a final goal: my Air Transport Pilot's Licence (ATPL). This requires 3,000 hours of flying time and allows you to fly larger aircraft such as Jumbos or Concordes. It was an extremely difficult exam for which you have to study hard in your spare time. I worked very diligently for mine; any delay getting it costs you seniority as you cannot go on your command course without it, and thus have no route to becoming a Captain on most of the larger airlines.

A considerable number of pilots managed to get distracted by their love life. I remember one in particular for whom this was the case. He had been married four times and was an ex-professional golfer, and he seemed to spend all his spare time not studying for his ATPL but instead either getting divorced or playing golf; he never took his senior exam. Another had a very attractive girlfriend; as far as I could gather, he felt he had better things to do than study when at home! She took him to task in the end, banning him from the bedroom until he passed the exam. This, finally, was the motivation he needed and he secured his APTL!

Then, having passed, one was not allowed to sit on one's laurels. I had as routine every year two medicals, a route check by a Training Captain on an actual route, and two simulator checks, one of which included my instrument rating. But this rigour was of course entirely correct. If one hoped to be an 'old' pilot, one could not afford to become a 'bold' pilot. I always remembered that there was never a flight where I was not one mistake away from disaster. For all the fun and delight of the job, the sense of responsibility was always there – and rightly so.

ICA Computer

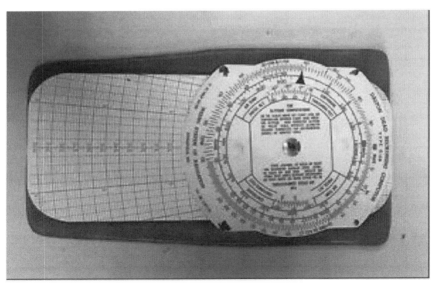

Dalton Computer

Chapter Six
CHARTER OUTFIT

There is an old saying, 'You know you have made it, when the nose wheel is behind you.' I wrote to as many airlines as I could find and got a reply from Autair, a charter outfit in Luton. This was by following the suggestions that I make to youngsters or their parents – that they consider their future for their children, although it seems too early for most of them, but here is my idea: they should buy a copy of the Financial Times, go to the Top 100 Index and pick out at random ten companies, all slightly different in their products. Send a letter to each of the ten companies saying that you're (in the child's name) interested in a career with them, and although you're still very young, when you have taken your exams, you would like to apply to the company for consideration of a job. You know very well that you will not get a reply, but keep a copy on file for each of the ten companies. Then, when you've done your first set of school exams, write back saying that you are still interested – again, you will not get a reply, but keep the copy. When you do your higher exams, write again, and then do the same if you happen to go to university. This should give you four copies per company. Finally, you apply for an interview, and if accepted, when you turn up with 20 or 30 other applicants, the interviewer will ask you why you want to join that company. You can then produce the four copies, showing that over a period of years you have consistently shown an interest in that company – and this should give you an advantage over the other applicants.

At last I had the chance of a professional career in aviation as, since passing my Commercial Pilot's Licence, I had failed to get any form of aviation job. It seems that throughout history the aviation jobs market has gone up and down on a six-year cycle. I had spent the previous eighteen months working for the pink trading stamp company, Sperry and Hutchinson, as an accounts clerk and then as an internal auditor. I had written to every single aviation company in Europe without any opportunity of a job interview – virtually none of them exist any more. Then at last it paid off. I now had my first real interview.

I drove to Luton Airport – there was no security on airfields at that time and I was able to drive straight in and across the tarmac, where a number of really old Lockheed Constellation aircraft were lined up – one, I believe, was G-NURL Constellation.[10] On the right-hand side between two hangars was an Avro York freighter, possibly G-AGJE, built between 1943 and 1949 and belonging to Skyways of London.[11] She had long seen her best days. I stopped and climbed into its huge cargo hold. As I turned towards the front of the aircraft, the floor sloped upwards and I climbed steps until I was in this magnificent old cockpit. Most of the glass up in the top half of the cockpit and over the roof was dark amber in colour and gave an eerie yet tantalising glow to the whole cockpit. It reeked of history and oil, and creaked and groaned as if she were talking to me. There were banks of instruments – the throttles were fascinating because, instead of being on a central pedestal, they hung from the roof where you took hold of them and pushed them forward, feeling just like a character in a John Wayne movie. A museum wanted her, but only if they could repaint her as they pleased, and her owners refused as they wanted to keep the Skyways colours. I believe Cosford Museum in Shropshire now has one.

The interview at Luton Airport, which seemed quite straightforward, was held in an office at the top, back end of a really dark hangar. I passed there and then, and was offered the job on the spot at £1,200 per year, with half-a-crown (or 2s 6d – 12½p in today's money) per hour allowances for every hour from chocks away to chocks back, and also thirty shillings (£1.50) for each night stop.

However, it was pointed out that I did not have a thing called a 'twin-engine aircraft rating', which seemed slightly ridiculous because I had already been flying twin aircraft for some thirty hours. So I had to rush round to a local flying club on the airport base and ask them if they could issue one for me. Within thirty minutes we were airborne, flying an Apache aircraft, registration G-ASHC. It was a twin and I had to fly it around on one engine to finally get the signature in my logbook – and so I was all ready to start in a charter company. There followed a quick trip to London to pick up my uniform – black with one gold ring on each arm, and of course the all-important pair of wings.

I went back to my benefactor in the trading stamp company where I had been working as an auditor. He had originally given me the job and I showed him my acceptance letter for the charter company. Surprisingly, he was very pleased for me and called William Schafer, the American Head Auditor, into the office where they both congratulated me and supported me in deciding to take the job. William had been in the American forces that had landed on Omaha Beach and had somehow survived the decimation of his fellow soldiers. He was an absolutely charming gentleman.

By this time I'd been made an internal auditor and some of the female staff (who seemed to like me) came up to me and said that they'd had a lot of problems with the oldest auditor, propositioning and touching them. The last thing I did before I left the company was to do a favour for these women and tell William about the whole issue – I assume that he acted on it, as it certainly was unfair to the staff.[12]

My aviation contract was initially for six months during the summer period, flying Vickers Viking aircraft – these had been converted or at least developed from Wellington bombers (there were 11,500 Wellingtons built during the war). The first Viking flew from Wisley Airfield, Surrey, in June 1945; nearly a year later, one crashed when both engines failed. It used the original Wellington wing-and-undercarriage design, and basically the whole of the cockpit, but the fuselage was a brand-new design.

About 160 civilian Vikings were built, of which at least fifty seem to have been destroyed in some crash or another. Before I flew the Viking, at least one of them had been used as a test-bed and fitted with Rolls-Royce Nene turbojets, flown in about 1948 as the world's first pure jet, civil aircraft. It actually flew from London to Paris in 1948, taking about 35 minutes – which, considering it now takes well over an hour to do the same flight, was quite an achievement. We flew it in a configuration of 36 passengers with two cabin crew or stewardesses (although we called them hostesses), plus a pilot and co-pilot.

However, Catch 22, before I could start my training on the actual aircraft, I had to get an ARB (Air Registraion Board) technical test for the aircraft. This was a multiple choice exam paper with three choices for each question all about the Viking. Problem number one (remember there was no Google in those days): I had never even seen a Viking, let alone been in one. There were no manuals available, as they were all on the aircraft, and they were all away on flights also known as 'down route'. We were advised to buy a set of 'Pop Speller's Notes' – as previously mentioned, Pop Speller was a retired examiner who used to mark the papers, but appeared to have accidently got a full set for most, if not all aircraft. I seem to remember paying about thirty shillings for his Notes, but there was no other way to pass the exam. Such a small airline did not have any form of training school policy for the technical side, only for the flying side.

I went up to London, sat the exam, and passed – although I remember that I did not even know where the undercarriage lever was, and this had been the first question! Was the lever (a) on the top left of the throttle quadrant; (b) on the top right; or (c) on the right-hand side below the throttles?

But with the notes, I got through.

I returned to Luton to find some accommodation and located a large boarding house, although I didn't realise that, at the time, it had a very dubious reputation in the town. The unmarried landlady was a fairly pretty, middle-aged blonde who had lived in Rhodesia (modern Zimbabwe) most of her life, and had just decided to move back to England. The next day, having found this accommodation, eight of us (all Second Officers – S/Os), all proudly displaying one gold ring on each sleeve plus the all-important pair of wings (or brevet) proudly displayed on our chest – plus the ARB stamp on our licences – reported for duty at the airport.

I had bought a very nice second-hand black Riley 1.5 for £400. I arrived proudly in uniform at the main gate, informing them that I was reporting for duty. It was a great moment driving once again across the tarmac. There were several different aircraft types belonging to different airlines – two of our Vikings and one of our Ambassadors (also known as AS 57 or Elizabethans), plus DC3s, a DC4, an Argonaut, and a Euravia Constellation. This particular Constellation was full of passengers and fully loaded with fuel, but it had jacks under one wing with the wheels removed! This aircraft had an unserviceable brake pack on one of the wheels, and they were awaiting the next Constellation to land so that they could jack that one up and steal the brake pad from it – not a very professional way to run an airline!

It is amazing how much 'shrapnel' there is on the tarmac – vans, catering trucks, tractors, ground power units and starter packs, fuel tankers, baggage trucks, engineering vans and fuelling trucks. I arrived at the hangar, which to me was more like a cathedral, a huge corrugated iron building that would eat up even an Elizabethan aircraft. Huge girders held up the roof, stores were stacked all along and down each side, including bits of tail plane and even an engine or two, and at the end stood the steps leading up to the office where I had taken my original interview. Several of my new colleagues were wandering around, awestruck at the immense size of everything – it seems laughable in this day and age.

At last we were all put together in the Ops Room, at the back left-hand side of the hangar, with boards not dissimilar to World War II – except they were Perspex with lots of black chinagraph writing on them, giving the names of the pilots and how much flying time they had available. We were all allowed 115 hours flying or actually being airborne in any consecutive period. If your first flight was of five hours, and you then continued flying up to 115 hours, the total would drop to 110 and you could do a flight of less than five hours. Or if you were really lucky, you might get a day off flying but had to serve in the Ops Room all night, usually on your own.

Various teleprinters were clattering away, and people seem to be busy at their desks. The Chief Pilot gave us a general lecture. He was about 55, of medium height, with grey eyes, and had a slight stoop. He was known by his nickname 'Around Again', due to some incidents in his life when it seems he bounced the aircraft so many times that it had to 'go round again'. He lectured to us about the new company contract that we had just gained, which was to fly every night to Perpignan in the south of France, close to the Mediterranean coast. He said that there was so little profit in the contract that if anyone diverted, delayed a flight due to technical reasons, refused to carry out a flight due to being ill, or exceeded their flight time limitations, we would lose money on the whole contract and some of us would have to be fired. He left us in no doubt whatsoever that if we did not get into the airfield every time, and we did not make the return flight every time without diverting (bearing in mind that there was a strong headwind component on the way back, and technically it was outside the range of our aircraft), we would either be fired immediately or certainly would not have a job at the end of the six-month season. This was certainly not what I was led to believe happened in aviation. However, it was the first of many shocks to my system.

We were then taken outside to actually touch one of our Viking aircraft – this one was G-AHPB. It was basically a Wellington Bomber – it may have been old, it may have been decrepit, but it was our old decrepit aircraft. We immediately fell in love with it. We passed a very embarrassed senior member of management who was filling his car up from the aircraft's fuel tanks. I think the car was a grey Armstrong Siddeley Sapphire. He was not only nicking company fuel, but avoiding tax!

Six of us, plus two new Captains, were taken round the aircraft and shown how to do a pre-flight – it was very similar to the one that I wrote about previously, checking each part of the aeroplane to make absolutely sure there was nothing wrong with it, including the tyres, which take a tremendous battering as the aircraft lands.

After checking the rear right, or starboard, side rear hold for bags of ballast, you enter the Viking by a door on the back left, or port, side of the aircraft and walk past 36 seats and then into the cockpit. Going through the aircraft uphill, climbing over the main spar with two steps up and two down, you continue to the cockpit. This main spar was huge because Vickers had experienced problems on a Varsity (the militay version) test showing up. These problems were compensated for by this substantial spar. The aircraft could easily tip on its nose, and in order to stop this, you had to make absolutely sure that there were large sacks of stones in the rear right-hand hold. Once the aeroplane was fully loaded with passengers and freight, these bags of stones would be lifted from the rear hold and put into the front freight right-hand hold, just before the engines were started. On landing, before the passengers left the aircraft, you had to get the load of stones from the front starboard hold to the rear hold. Otherwise, if the passengers disembarked and the crew were still in the cockpit, the aircraft would go on its nose, damaging the propellers.

The eight of us, plus the Training Captain, then boarded the aircraft to see the toilet/galley to the right. The Training Captain took his correct seat on the left-hand (or port) seat, the same as in any aircraft (as opposed to a helicopter where the Captain sits on the right-hand side). Always remember, and this is very important: an aircraft is like a ship and has a port and starboard side. The port side has four letters, as in the word 'port', which is equivalent to the left side of the aeroplane as you face the front. The engine on this side is called Number One. The starboard side has more letters and represents the right-hand side of the aircraft as you look towards the nose. There're no ifs or buts on this, and it's vital that, if you should happen to lose an engine, you know which side of the aeroplane you're talking about. It is no good looking backwards and saying it is on the left, when it is in actual fact the right-hand side of the aircraft. You will notice my comments much later on about the Kegworth 737 crash on the M1 motorway (G-OBME 8th January 1989 on Flight 92 from Heathrow to Belfast) and my theory on how that happened.

One of the new pilots took the right-hand seat. Signals were made out of the window to move the ballast bags from the rear to the front hold. The engines were started and the roar of power just seemed amazing to us in our innocence, as the two Bristol engines roared into life, shaking the aircraft. The Captain gave a cross-hand signal to the engineers for the chocks to be removed, the Captain received ATC clearance to taxi, applied the power, and then we taxied off down the taxiway towards the runway. Taxiing on a Viking aircraft is quite interesting, as there is no steering wheel as such, and the only way to really taxi the aircraft is to apply pressure to the foot pedals or rudders left or right, and then squeeze the brakes, which are situated on the back of the spectacle (the yoke or control column).

Training had now begun in earnest. At the end of the runway, we came to a halt and applied the brakes. The engines were run up and checks were carried out, including feathering the engine – or at least, partly feathering the engine. This basically meant that, if you lost an engine in-flight and the propeller 'windmilled', it would cause tremendous drag. In the case of an underpowered Viking on full load, you would barely be able to climb away or even hold height – so you turn the blades of the propeller sideways so that they are end-on to the slipstream, thus avoiding any drag.

When the run-up checks were complete, the guy in the right-hand seat carried out the pre-take-off checks and called for take-off clearance. One of the most important parts of these checks is to adjust your seat so that you can reach the rudder pedals. You then look down at the runners that your seat slides backwards and forwards on, and check that you can visually see the pin locking your seat in place. If you do not do this and the seat is not locked, you will find that, as you taxi out, you will slide back and you will not be able to reach the brake peddles and you could hit something on the tarmac. Really serious issues can occur if your seat runs back during take-off, when it is easy to grab hold of the control, pull the nose violently up and stall the aeroplane, with the resulting probable crash from height, killing all on board.

Also, make sure that you can get full rudder with the pedals. On most aircraft, when you get an engine failure, you will find it extremely difficult to get enough pressure on a rudder in order to keep the aircraft straight. Indeed, it is often termed 'knee jerk', when you find that your knee is literary juddering under the pressure – at least, until you can wind on trim to take up the strain. You will need to lock your leg in a straight position before you can finally get the trims to work – that means turning a small wheel to take the pressure and weight off your leg. We term it 'dead foot, dead engine' – that is, in order to keep the aircraft straight, you have to apply full rudder, the leg doing nothing is on the side of the failed engine.

We were finally given clearance to take off and turned onto the runway, applying power and feeling a punch in the back as we accelerated towards take-off speed. As speed increases, you actually pass a speed called V1, which is a speed after which you cannot stop on the runway – whatever happens. At this speed, you will just go off the end of the runway. The next part is hitting the speed of V2, which means you now have sufficient speed to control the aircraft if you lose an engine, and finally rotate speed. If you had lost an engine after V2, you would have to compensate with the controls – you may naturally look out of the windscreen and see that the aircraft is veering off the centreline. In order to keep it straight, you would apply rudder with one of your feet. As you apply the rudder to keep the aircraft straight, the live engine would need to be compensated for, so you end up either seeing the engine instruments run down on a duff engine, or you can feel which foot has gone forward with the compensation of your holding that wing down. Again, we use the phrase 'dead foot, dead engine'. Now you would call for the appropriate engine failure drill and name the engine – Number One if it is the left, or port, one, or Number Two for the right, or starboard, one. If you get this wrong, you have the strong possibility of dying along with your passengers – it is something to practise and make sure you have it clearly in your mind what would happen if that engine failed as you take off.

We flew off to the west, clear of airways, and each of us in turn got into the right-hand seat. The Captain would talk us through a simulated procedure for an engine failure by throttling back the engine, and pretending to carry out the full feather drill which stopped the propeller and turned it end-on to the airflow, so that there was little or no drag from the failed engine. The aircraft would try to go in one direction or another. In order to keep it straight, either by looking straight ahead at the horizon or in cloud by looking at the instruments, you would find that you needed full power and more rudder pedal in order to hold it straight. So you need a great big boot full of rudder to keep it straight – as I indicated, so much so that you could easily suffer knee jerk where your knee is actually trembling under the weight of trying to compensate for the dead engine. If possible, lock your knee in a straight line so that your leg is dead straight and rigid – this makes it much easier to hold it on course. You then use a trim wheel to take the weight off the rudder until eventually you can relax your leg. Now apply the aileron to keep the wings level, and the aircraft should now fly roughly straight and level. It is only affected when you move the live engine throttle backwards or forwards – if you pull it back so that there is less power coming from the live engine, you would need less rudder; if you increase the power on the live engine, you would need more rudder. Remember, if you have to turn, always turn after an engine failure so that you rest on the live engine, and never (if possible) lean on the dead engine.

When we had all tried this, we then changed round and carried out six take-offs and landings. This is thrilling while you're doing it yourself, but not quite so exciting when you're sitting in the passenger seat with brand-new pilots attempting to land the aircraft either in a three-point landing (on all three wheels at once) or wheeling it on the front two wheels and then getting it wrong. The Viking was well known as the 'pig' due mainly to its shape, but also to the fact that it was one of the hardest aircraft ever to actually land. If you messed it up first time, it could easily bounce and then bounce higher and higher until the aeroplane would eventually crash, unless you threw the whole thing away. You would have to apply the power and climb away and do it all over again. We had to endure 48 landings until we were all cleared.

When it was my turn, I called for the pre-take-off check. I then had control and applied the throttles, remembering that the aircraft was a tail-wheel aircraft. As we gathered speed along the runway, I slowly applied forward pressure on the joystick (this is sometimes called the yoke or the spectacle). As speed increased, and with a slight forward pressure, the tail slowly came away from the runway. All the time you are controlling the aircraft with your rudder pedals, linked to the vertical fin on the tail of the aircraft. At about 90 knots, I pulled back on the stick slowly and she slowly came away from the ground.

I then called for the undercarriage to be retracted and the non-handling pilot then reduced the throttle to the appropriate setting, followed by a change in the pitch – the angle that the propeller cuts into the air. Once I had a reasonable height, I then started playing with the oil coolers and gills, as these control the engine temperatures. We were then cleared by Air Traffic Control for a left-hand circuit which consists of 90° turns. Once you are on finals, it is similar to what I described in a light aircraft – you apply the power or reduce the power in order to change the picture presented by the runway, and on whether it was going up or going down as to whether you applied more or less power. When established on finals, and you get clearance to land, you then do the pre-landing checks, and at about 1,500 feet drop the undercarriage slowly, increasing the amount of flap that you have until you have full flap before landing. All the time you're on final approach you will need to nail the speed as near as possible by increasing and decreasing the throttle. Every time you increase the throttle to increase speed, the aircrafts nose will rise, taking you above the glide path or the correct approach path to the runway. Alternatively, every time you reduce the throttle setting to bring the speed back, the aircraft will naturally go below the glide path or back onto it if you were high in the first place.

We normally tried to land the plane on the front two wheels, but woe betide you if you did not get it exactly right, as the aircraft would ricochet off the runway, bounce and then 34,000 pounds (15,420 kg) would come back heavily on the main wheels again – and unless you can regain control, it would continue to bounce, getting higher and higher. If you do not do anything, it will come down and break into thousands of pieces, so it would not be a good day for you or the 36 passengers. The only way round this is to apply full power, start to climb away, retract the undercarriage and some of the landing flap, climb away and start all over again. Remember – the Viking was christened the pig for this very reason!

I have in my possession a newsletter sent from the Chief Pilot later in the year, warning that the aircraft G-AHPB should not complete any three-point landings (that is, aiming to touch the ground with both wheels and tail at exactly the same time). The missive stated that, if this aircraft had carried out one more take-off and landing, the tail would have failed on the aircraft and it would have crashed. We were to stop doing three points with immediate effect. The aircraft's registration ended in PB and it was quite daunting to consider that you might have been the one to do the next flight on that aircraft... you suddenly become aware of your fallibility.

If you think that having touched down was the end of the subject, you would be wrong. You controlled the aircraft with the rudder and the aircraft would slowly lose speed due to its nose-up attitude on all three wheels, and also to the fact that the landing flaps were down. However, as the aircraft slowed, you would need to control it by means of the rudder and brakes. We continued by making this a touch-and-go – that is, the Captain applied full power, selecting the land flap to take-off position, and down the runway we lifted off for the next circuit and landing.

By the way, we had a very 'stiff-shirt' Training Captain who insisted that you waited until you cleared the runway, and only when he had called for the after-landing checks could you then start them, commencing with selecting the landing flap to the up position. The stupid thing is he used to forget, and when you got onto the stand and shut the engines down, you would find that the flaps were in the fully down position, getting in the way of the loaders and everyone else. Through no fault of your own, you would then be expected to go into the cupboard at the back of the cockpit and hand-pump 160 times in order to select the flaps to the up position. Just to assert his authority, he continued to make the mistake over and over again, and most First Officers would be quite belligerent and would not operate them until requested.

This is a typical case of a Captain trying to prove that he is very important. A similar case happened later on in my story when the Captain was taxiing out with a Trident aircraft towards the runway at London Heathrow and the FO started to do the taxi checks. He went ballistic, saying that he had not asked for them and that they were to put everything back – the First Officer was only to start to do the checks when he (the Captain) asked for it. The FO did as he requested and the aircraft approached the end of the runway and was given an immediate take-off. It turned onto the runway and the pompous Captain applied full power and started the take-off. They were at about 80 knots when all hell let loose – bells and lights started flashing, giving a warning that the aircraft was in a dangerous state and could not take off, because there had been no flap or droop selected. In bringing the aircraft to a halt with maximum brake and full reverse thrust, the brakes were virtually burnt out, so they had to have an aircraft change. Again, this type of Captain typically refused point blank to apologise, merely saying, "Why didn't you put the flaps and droop down?" Being a senior Captain on the training side and in management, one assumes that he managed to lose the appropriate paperwork so that he did not get into trouble.

The brake control on the Viking aircraft was mounted on the control column, just behind the yoke. If you held the two rudder peddles in a central position and squeezed the brake controls (which were in the shape of small levers on the front of the flying controls), the aircraft would continue straight ahead and slow down. If you wished to turn left, you would apply left rudder and squeeze the brake control; similarly, to turn to the right, apply right rudder and squeeze the brake control. This was great if you were continuing on a level surface, but at Luton the end of the runway was an S-bend going downhill, so somehow you had to slow the aircraft down – which meant that the rudders should be in the centre – and touch the brakes. Unfortunately, as you would have to turn left and right round the turns, you would find yourself going downhill, trying to slow the aircraft down, and trying to turn it to the left or right, all of which formed a great party trick. If you did not do it right, the aircraft would just become faster and faster, and you would be more than likely to come off the taxi track.

Anyway, we had six take-off and landings to do each, so we either did a touch-and-go or had to make a 180° turn at the end of the runway after the landing and return back to the take-off point. Then we had to await the clearance and take off and repeat the whole thing five more times.

At last it was all over, and after getting the ballast moved, we then climbed from the aircraft. We then went into the briefing room where we expected to be told about a whole lot more training... but that was it. I completed nine supernumerary flights (that is, observing). We were now fully converted onto Viking aircraft, and indeed I was now allocated a flight that very night.

We carried out the flight planning for a flight to Luxembourg (on G-AHPJ), which the Captain did in this case, working out the shortest route on airways to our destination. Thank goodness I was not responsible for this, because as we ploughed into the late evening, it became darker and darker, and we continued talking to Air Traffic Control until all of a sudden their traffic control in France went ballistic, complaining that the Captain had flown the wrong way along a one-way airway. Remember that aircraft have their own system of roads in the air. Whilst on these roads, you have to keep to certain height restrictions given to you by Air Traffic Control.

Working as a charter pilot for a small outfit is certainly not the best-paid position in life. The starting salary was £1,200 a year. Many charter pilots earned less than United Dairy milkmen. I soon found out that we as pilots were not supplied with any food, so Lesson Number One, taught to me very early on in my charter career, was if you want to eat on the flight, then after take-off go straight into cloud and make the flight as bumpy as you possibly can so that everyone is sick and you can eat their food!

Unbeknown to me, the Captain I flew with to Luxembourg had a very torrid second marriage, culminating in him strangling his wife. There were a lot of stories about this in the press where she was referred to as a cow. Coincidently, very many years later, I met the man who said that he was the one who had helped the Captain in a small way in the disposal of his wife's body. He described what happened roughly in the following words: he said that the Captain had had children by a previous marriage and was unable to get access to them. He had two more children with his second wife, who had taken a lover, continuously rubbed his nose with this fact, boasting about it to all and sundry at parties and other occasions.

He did not want to divorce this wife as he might have lost access to these two children as well, but finally one night she returned to the house, boasting again about being with her lover. Evidently, she regularly brought back washing from the liaison and even made the Captain wash it for her on a threat of barring access to the children. It was said that he had told her, "I loved you so much that I had a vasectomy for you, but it went wrong and I have lost part of my tackle because of you." To which she had replied, "No, you didn't; you had the vasectomy because I wanted to know for sure that if I had another child, it would be with my lover and not with you." She continued laughing and throwing things, at which point he just broke and strangled her.

The person relaying this story to me lived opposite the man and said that he had supplied him with a dinghy in order to dispose of the body. The Captain took the body and wrapped it in a carpet, drove past Gatwick Airport and picked up a piece of large concrete which he attached to the body. Finally, arriving at a lake in northern England, he rowed onto the lake and pushed the package over the side. Unfortunately, it wasn't quite in the deepest part of the lake, and many years later, when a German woman went missing on a hiking trip in the area, people started to look for her body. Some divers discovered the carpet and brought it to the surface. The body was supposedly virtually intact with only a few minor nibbles by fish. However, the Captain had forgotten to remove her wedding ring, which had both her and his initials engraved inside. It appeared in the paper a couple of days later. A female neighbour who was a friend of the dead woman recognised the two sets of initials and reported them to the police. The neighbour who had supplied the dinghy saw the police cars waiting at his house and tried to intercept him on his normal route back from the airport, but for some reason he used a different route and was arrested.

He was released on £20,000 bail, which was very unusual for a murder case. He was found not guilty of murder, but of manslaughter, and received a minimal custodial sentence of some three years plus one year for obstructing the coroner.[13] He had previously been a hero when his company went bust and he was stranded in Canada with a full load of passengers. He had gone round in the middle of the night, waking up the passengers and getting them on board the plane and flying them back to England before the aircraft could be impounded.

Eventually, we arrived back at Luton and I was given another Luxembourg flight the next day on the same aircraft, but with a different Captain.

We never really knew where we were going to fly the next day until the evening before, but we had a scheduled service from Luton to Blackpool, and even one from Blackpool to London Heathrow. Many other pilots whom I flew with during my nine months' attachment were WW2 fighter or bomber pilots. One in particular was Pancho Villa, the first person to shoot a 109 down with a cannon-equipped Spitfire. He had had fifteen kills and is mentioned in the Battle of Britain roll of honour.

The Blackpool service was quite pleasant and usually resulted in some form of night stop. The next day you might either return to Luton or fly to London Heathrow, back to Blackpool and down to Luton. On one flight was a little old lady who decided she wanted to go to the toilet. Somehow she got lost walking towards the back of the aircraft and missed the only toilet door. She pushed a door open, right at the very back of the aircraft, but unfortunately this was an entrance to the baggage hold just in front of the tail fin. There were no lights that she could find, and being too embarrassed to ask, she squatted down and obviously had a tinkle. She then left the freight hold and went back to her seat. Luckily, the hostess had noticed her and investigated to discover that the cucumber sandwiches, which she had just laid out in the freight hold, were soaking wet. Partly out of panic and partly using her initiative, she dabbed them with a paper towel and then served them all to the passengers. No one made any comment other than that they thought they were the best cucumber sandwiches they had ever had – quite unlike the dried-up British Railways sandwiches!

On another occasion, with a different Captain, we were flying back towards Luton from Blackpool when a vicious storm passed over Luton Airport. Each aircraft type had been tested to certain crosswind limits. In the case of the Viking, it was 30 knots across the runway, 20 in the wet, but any more than this and the aircraft would be in danger of getting out of control and crashing. It is quite an exciting art to land an aeroplane in maximum crosswind conditions. The crosswind limits are less in wet weather.

On this occasion, it was wet and the weather was awful, with a crosswind of over 35 knots. The Captain used the radio to talk to company operations and said that he was going to have to divert because it was well over 30 knots across the runway. Indeed, it was more than the 20 knots across the runway that was allowed on a wet runway. On hearing this, the ops officer contacted the Duty Manager who came on the radio fuming because we were not going to land at Luton. The aircraft would have been out of place and passengers severely disrupted. He therefore stated, tongue-in-cheek, "I have just been rewriting the manual and we have got a Ministry of Aviation clearance to increase the crosswind limit to 35 – therefore you have no reason whatsoever not to land and I expect you to do so." It was blatantly obvious to me that this was an outright porky pie – however, my Captain, who was always worried about losing his job, continued and proceeded to land well outside limits. He had been employed in something like fifteen jobs in the previous eight years. These companies had either folded and gone bankrupt, or he had just been fired for one reason or another. He said categorically that he had no intention of losing this job as he thought that there was a future in this one.

Personally, I could see no future in this, other than a wooden box. However, I was in no position to wrest the aircraft from the large senior Captain. We therefore turned onto final approach where the buffeting from the wind was positively awful. We were looking out of the side windows, and with a high crosswind, the aircraft crabbed in to land. At the last minute, the Captain had to kick the rudders to force the aeroplane straight and parallel to the centre of the runway and make sure it hit the runway almost immediately, or she would have been pushed off to the side of it. The aeroplane could also have aquaplaned. The wheels, which were not rotating in the air, would be expected to spin as you hit the runway. However, if you did a really smooth landing, this might not happen, and you find that the wheels or tyres remain static and just get burned by the friction with the wet runway, probably bursting them. There is a formula to work this out – you can use it on your own car when you find that if you go over bumps when travelling fast on a wet road, the car momentarily gets airborne – when you come down, the tyres are not going at the same speed as you would expect and they behave just like the aircraft. The formula is nine times the square root of the tyre pressure. It sounds complicated, but the simplest thing in the aircraft is to make sure that you thump the aircraft onto the runway in the wet. This breaks through the film of water and spins the wheels up so you can now get a grip when you put the brakes on.

Our aircraft touched down and the Captain managed to bring it to a halt. We could barely get the aircraft off the runway as the wind was so strong. Partly through skill and partly due to luck, we made it. I can assure you that there had been no alterations to the manuals and there had been no Ministry of Aviation clearance of 35 knots – it was merely a threat from the Duty Manager that if we had not got in, we would have been fired!

One night, our Ambassador (also called Elizabethan or AS57) aircraft was at the holding point at the end of runway just in front of us. We saw it revving up its engines in the usual manner, but while doing the run-up and checking its magnetos to see if the engines were okay, the tail plane was shaking about a frightening amount. Although this was perfectly normal, these aircraft had three tail fins. The plane lined up, the brakes were released and the aircraft went down the runway – although I would describe it more as hurtling down, as it carried on and on and on. The runway had a big drop at the end of it over Luton and the aircraft barely became airborne, sinking in just the way you see fighter aircraft taking off from aircraft carriers, and at the last minute it manages to climb away. I assume the crew would have needed a change of trousers. Evidently what happened was that someone (possibly, but unlikely, an engineer) had been playing around in the aircraft before the flight and turned the trimmers to full nose down. In other words, the trimmers or large wheel which you can move in order to take the strain or effort out of the flying controls, were in the wrong position, and the crew had not noticed this during their pre-flight checks. Anyway, when they reached the end of the runway and pulled back, nothing happened. Both the pilots had to put their feet on the control panel and pull back with all their might just to keep the aircraft airborne. The incident was kept quiet because it's more than likely they would have lost their jobs straightaway. The aircraft continued and eventually returned from its trip and nothing more was said.

This was the same type of aircraft that crashed on its third attempted take-off at Munich on 6th February 1958, Flight Number 609, killing a large proportion of the Manchester United football team. The total casualties were 23 dead and nineteen injured. Its biggest problem in snow conditions was the fact that you could not get up onto the extremely high wing to check for ice. An example of how vitally important it is that you carry out pre-flight checks correctly.

During its pre-flight check on a Hermes aircraft, the engineer mistakenly put a correction on the compass for a variation of 30° instead of 3°. The aircraft took off and the crew realised there was a difference between the two compasses. After taking Astra navigation fixes, they decided incorrectly that the CL2 compass was the good one. On top of this, the navigator changed the 3° west setting to a 6° west setting, which was in actual fact 60° out. They flew for some six hours before the navigator realised the error and reset the variation to zero, at which point the two compasses agreed with each other, having flown for six hours miles and miles off their proper course. Several other things went wrong on the flight – as is normal in aviation, things happen in threes. Finally, the aircraft crash-landed in the desert – thankfully, only three people were slightly hurt, but the aircraft was a write-off. Many years later I met the Captain's wife.

There have been two types of Vickers aircraft called Vikings. First was a single-engine sea-going biplane, which achieved infamy in being the plane which was flown by Sir John Alcock, who died on 18th December 1919, ferrying one to Paris. He was flying solo and attempted to land in bad weather while taking the aircraft to an aeronautical exhibition in Paris. The second Vickers Viking was a twin-engine monoplane airliner that was designed in the dying stages of WW2, using the wings and engines of the RAF's Vickers Wellington bomber fastened to a new fuselage. It had a maximum speed of about 180 knots, with a range of about 1,500 miles. In the mid-1950s on a Paris flight, one of the Viking aircraft suffered a bomb blast on board, damaging the back of the aircraft and badly injuring a stewardess. However, the aircraft was strong enough to survive and landed in London.

We regularly flew to Perpignan, close to the French Mediterranean coast and surrounded by hills – rather like an airfield being built in the middle of what appeared to be an old volcano. It seemed as though every other night an aircraft was lost – I'm sure it's an exaggeration, but one of the examples was I believe an Argonaut which had problems with its air system in the cabin and the crew suffered from carbon monoxide fumes. The pilots, if not the passengers, all passed out and the aircraft crashed into the mountain, killing everyone on board. The enquiry blamed the pilots.

Anyway, back to the Viking. The Perpignan flights consisted of a maximum range flight of nearly four hours down to the French airfield. When we passed Paris, there was a tremendous gap in navigation aids – we were looking for a beacon called Carcassonne, which was extremely low-powered and virtually impossible to pick up unless you were almost overhead.

This was a constant problem on every flight. We went there one evening, the 21st anniversary of another charter outfit to celebrate their birthday, when two of their aircraft slid off the Portsmouth runway.

When flying near mountains that are covered in cloud, we use a terminology 'cumulus granite' – that is, clouds full of mountain. Most pilots have a very black sense of humour and you will constantly find that the deaths of colleagues in air accidents usually end up with some wry joke.

One of the skippers was a schoolteacher, a large guy about 6' 3" tall and roughly sixty years old. The flight used to take off late in the evening, somewhere about eight o'clock when the sun was beginning to set. It was usual when I was flying with him that I would have to load all the passengers, do all the flight planning and all the pre-flight checks, and have started the engines with everything ready, including moving the ballast to the front hold. He would appear in his car at the last second – jumping out of the car, he would throw his car keys to the engineer, take the left-hand seat, sign the load sheet, call for chocks away and, with the engines already going, would open the throttles and taxi out for take-off.

He would then fly all night, four hours each way, eight hours actual flying time, plus the turnaround time – certainly a ten-hour night. Remember that he had been teaching at school all day long – and he did this regularly, but never seemed to get tired. He also had another annoying habit of bringing his children's pet projects onto the flight, which usually consisted of looking for a castle, a river, town or anything of interest which the children were plotting on a big school map back at school. Believe it or not, on one occasion we were travelling along at 10,000 feet and, all of a sudden, he turned the aircraft on its wing and dived down low so that he could check out the appropriate site of interest. We would then spend half-an-hour climbing back up through all the different levels without telling Air Traffic Control. How on earth we didn't get killed, I will never know, but eventually we would get back to 10,000 feet and finally land in Perpignan.

As I have mentioned, going down to Perpignan was virtually at the maximum range of the aircraft. With the full amount of fuel on board, the aircraft was up to maximum weight when it left Luton (with half-an-hour's extra flying time as reserve plus a nearby diversion airfield). However, the return flight was totally different from most nights due to headwinds. There was no way that the aircraft could get off with sufficient fuel to fly back to Luton due to prevailing headwinds.

We often needed approximately sixty more gallons of fuel. The way this was done was that the 'flying spanner', whom I've mentioned elsewhere, was sent down on a tour of duty. Quite simply, he had to make sure that when the load balance sheets were produced for the return flight, there was little or no cabin baggage – but this doesn't make sense. People went down on holiday, as you can imagine, with cabin baggage, and you would expect them to bring more back, including large donkeys and hats and goodness knows what else, that they had bought as souvenirs.

However, none of this extra weight appeared on the load sheet. We were still too heavy to get the extra fuel on board, so the passengers were made to eat the food on the ground! By making them eat the food on the ground, we did not have to show it on the load sheet. I have mentioned this to other airlines that I've flown with, and the ground instructors would just not believe me. It was then that sixty gallons of extra fuel was put into the fuel tanks, although not shown on the technical log. The aircraft sat on the end of the runway, the engines were run up as much as we dared, and then the brakes were released and the aircraft went hurtling down the runway towards the mountains in front of us. At the last minute, we just managed to get clear of the ground and airborne. The undercarriage was brought up as quickly as possible, then a steep turn within the mountains, climbing up and away and setting course as soon as we were above them. When you're watching aircraft at air shows, you often see them sitting at the end of the runway with the brakes on, running the engines up to full power, and then releasing the brakes. Many believe that this merely stalls the propeller, and in actual fact the best way of getting maximum effort from the aircraft would be to release the brakes and then apply full power. I can assure you that this really, really, concentrates the mind on the flight.

I don't know whether you have noticed, but engineers and flight engineers have purple in between the normal gold, silver or platinum braid on their arms. This is due to the fact that the King gave them the right to wear the royal colour as a mark of respect for the engineers on board the Titanic who went down with the ship, trying to keep it afloat as long as possible.

On the flight home, when you had got your pulse down and the adrenaline had worn off, or down to a suitable level, one of you would normally decide that they would have a sleep. Remember that we used to fly a pattern of approximately one Perpignan (for a ten-hour duty), rest for ten hours and then fly for, say, five hours, take eight off, then, say, a four-hour flight, eight hours off… by the end of the week you would have flown possibly seven or eight duties in five or six days. It was quite exhausting and natural for pilots to take turns to sleep in flight. However, you must remember that at 10,000 feet in the cockpit with a couple of pieces of Perspex for windows which slid back, it was freezing cold (with no heaters), and in the winter period I would wear long johns and have a couple of blankets over me, just to keep reasonably comfortable. One of us would sleep for an hour and then the other. Many years ago, someone appeared on the television during an interview and said he had done this, thus confirming what I have just said – and it was a fairly normal practice in aviation at the time.

In the meantime, the other pilot would relax in his seat. There was a simple wing-leveller system, instead of the modern autopilot, which consisted of a large box in the centre lower part of the instrument panel, with a large artificial horizon and a small knob which you could turn. This moved a small aeroplane up and down, above or below the horizon. With this selected, the aircraft would keep its wings level. However, you needed to turn this little knob in order to move the little aeroplane to keep its height, as this was not automatic. The trick was to take the metal bar that was used for pumping the hydraulics (if there had been a hydraulic failure), put a piece of paper in the end of that and rest it from your stomach across the two throttles to a small knob that you turned to make aircraft climb or descend – you could then sit back and relax and turn the tube clockwise or anticlockwise, thus making the aeroplane go up or down whilst remaining at the correct altitude!

On one of these all-night trips, I got one of the aircraft which had a rubbish radio. It was barely possible to hear anything. Paris complained like mad for nearly two weeks as the same aeroplane shunted across the Paris airspace, unable to communicate. Paris Air Traffic Control eventually said that the aircraft would no longer be allowed to fly through their airspace unless they had the radio was fixed. Remember that the radio was a World War II unit and it was not easy to get spare parts, so all the company did was to swap the really bad radio with one from another aircraft. It was at least ten days before Paris realised what had happened, and they would keep changing it every so often to a different aircraft. Only one Captain could hear Paris as he had absolutely superb hearing. The radio had a dial marked with 'a', 'b', 'c', etc. for different frequencies – if you did not have it , you would have a box of assorted crystals and go to the back of the cockpit and tune a new one and plug it into the radio.

Another pilot was very reminiscent of Tony Hancock, except
that he was a really handsome version (or so it would appear,
because all the ladies used to throw themselves at him). His
technique was to take off, keep the throttles almost flat out and fly
as fast as he could on the flight and all the way back. He said he
had never had an engine failure, but another Captain said, "No,
but *we* get them, thanks to you."

On one trip, I remember flying to Düsseldorf, and one of the
company's much larger Ambassador aircraft flew there just after
us. (Düsseldorf was the only airport in the world where they
checked your flying licences.) We were preparing both aircraft for
the return trip when the Captain of the Ambassador found that he
couldn't take all the baggage on his aircraft, otherwise he would
have been overweight. My Viking Captain told him to load it on
our old Viking and we would take it for him, which indeed we
did. The Ambassador Captain was very embarrassed at our old
aircraft taking his bags. Still to this day, I don't know how we got
airborne with all the extra weight, but we had a good laugh about
it once we had survived the flight. If we had lost an engine, we
would have crashed.

Another trick of this Captain was to request 6,000 feet as the
cruising altitude, and then in the dark fly all the way up to 10,000
feet – which I can assure you is extremely dangerous as other
aircraft are going backwards and forwards on the different levels.
He would then put the nose of the aircraft slightly forward and
spend nearly an hour getting back down to 6,000 feet, but in the
meantime the airspeed increased by 15 to 20 knots, so with the
extra power and the extra speed from the slow descent, we
always got home a lot quicker than anyone else.

He was an extremely generous pilot who lived with a Euravia
stewardess. He had built the most fantastic bar up in the roof of
his house, apparently cutting joists away, but the house never
seemed to collapse. The bar was certainly fifteen feet long and
had a fantastic free booze selection and masses of cigarettes – it
was a regular meeting-place. You would often see him serving
and having a number of drinks at the bar, being hale and hearty

to everyone, when all of a sudden he would disappear, gone off on a flight – bearing in mind that he drank drink-for-drink with all his guests. Later, he would be back in behind the bar as if nothing had happened.

I can remember he had a white Sunbeam Alpine sports car and we went to Farnborough Air Display where my father had a stand, so we could drink as much as we wanted as guests on various other stands at the end of the Air Show. We got in the car and he drove back along the Hog's Back towards my house. At the Guildford end of the Hog's Back, he literally couldn't drive any further, he was so drunk, so we changed seats – I had had very little to drink so continued to drive the car to my house where he collapsed in one of the armchairs.

You may ask where he got all the alcohol and cigarettes. When we arrived in, say, Perpignan, he would go into the duty-free shop and buy thousands of cigarettes and bottles of brandy and whisky, etc. He would then take up the battery floor panel behind the Captain's seat and hide everything in the battery hold – quite frightening, actually. Goodness knows what would have happened if the bottles had broken. He then replaced the panel, which very few people knew even existed, except for the engineers. We flew the usual four hours back to Luton and, on landing at Luton Airport, he would immediately approach the engineers to get the aircraft towed to the hangar as fast as they could. In the meantime, Customs would come on board and look round, and finding nothing wrong, would leave the aircraft. We were only allowed half-a-bottle a month by Customs who kept a running list. The panel was eventually lifted off in the hangar and all the goods were transferred to his car. The engineers were given their appropriate packs of cigarettes and a bottle, and away he would drive – back to his house where he took everything upstairs to his bar and carried on partying, as if nothing had happened. In the meantime, I can assure you I was petrified that we would be done by Customs and I would lose my job – at the very least – if not end up in prison. The interesting thing is that he gave virtually all of it away, even though it actually cost him a vast amount of money.

The only other use the battery hatch had was when we got a new stewardess and the Captain would hide himself in the battery hold. I would ask the stewardess in flight where the Captain and gone, she would search the cabin and toilets and come back saying he had completely disappeared. When she next returned to the cockpit, he was sitting quite happily in his seat, much to her confusion!

We took off from Blackpool en route for Luton, but the weather was so bad that we diverted to London in thick cloud. On the way, we were told to go into a holding pattern, but before we got there, a hostess came into the cockpit and said, "Did you see that Air France aircraft, it went right past us in the cloud and I could read the registration." Goodness knows how we had missed it.

With the same Captain going to Perpignan again, I had a flight to remember. We flew down towards Carcassonne – the weather was foul and there were many aircraft in the air, and we had very little surplus fuel. We were allowed to make an approach and fly down amongst the mountains, lower and lower, when at the last minute I saw the runway off to the right-hand side of aeroplane. With no hope of landing, the Captain called for full power. I selected the undercarriage and flaps up and we climbed away. He then asked Air Traffic Control to go round again and make another approach – bearing in mind we were in the middle of what looked like a volcano all around us. It was pitch-black in dense cloud and very turbulent. When we turned again onto final approach, with the lousy radio aids that were available at the time, we made another attempt, coming down below limits. At the last minute, again we missed the runway and couldn't land. We applied the power again, went through the same process of undercarriage, up flaps up and climbed away.

At this point, the pilots in the aircraft circling above started to shout, saying, "Get out of the way, it's our turn, you go and divert." Some were running out of fuel and an argument ensued with several aircraft shouting and swearing and cursing, just like a night in a Glasgow bar. My Captain was shouting back, telling them to mind their own business and swearing back at them. We went round again, completely ignoring Air Traffic Controllers' requests. On our final approach, at the last minute we broke cloud and managed to land. I've never been so scared in my life and it wasn't until a month later – when I actually landed there in daylight – that I saw the mountains for the very first time. How we had survived, I have absolutely no idea – we could have been added to the other two or three dozen aeroplanes that had crashed in that area over several years.

At one point, the number of crashes in the area had been so bad that there was a statement made in the House of Commons. A Derby Aviation aeroplane had crashed in 1961 and the 34 on board had all died. There had been a suggestion that the compasses had been affected by the magnetic field associated with the iron mines in the area. In Germany, there is a similar area between Berlin and Munich where compasses went off-course and this was attributed to the lodestones in the area.

I made a great friend who was a fellow co-pilot and an absolute natural in the air. Driving to work one day, he went down a small dip under a bridge when some idiot fired an air rifle at him – it went straight through the windshield and hit him in one eye and he never flew again.

Another pilot, Captain James, had a great head for figures. Wherever he flew, he would get the cabin crew and myself to club together all the money we had, including the bar money or ship's float, and then go and buy different currencies. When we arrived back in Luton, he would swap it around again and somehow every single time he used to make profit and split it between us.

We had several enjoyable morning flights across to Rotterdam to pick up flowers, where we had a fantastic breakfast which was basically eggs and bits and pieces on toast, with gherkins, of all things. During this time, we waited for the flowers to be loaded. Once again, I made a very dear friend from one of the other companies that were there, but I found out some time later that he was killed in a flying accident.

Flights now became slightly more varied. I drew a very good flight, namely the champagne flight to Reims, France. We had 36 passengers on board, all of whom were dressed up to the nines. Initially all went well, until we got to roughly where the airport was supposed to be. We circled until eventually we found a totally deserted airfield, where we tried to contact the tower, but there was nobody there at all. Finally the Captain took it on himself to land, which was not a good idea because we didn't have a fire service available. The Captain landed the aeroplane and taxied to the end of the runway. On the right-hand side was a small, very old wooden building, which looked vaguely like a 1930s terminal. It had been an RAF airfield during the phoney war from September 1939 to April 1940. I have since found this airport is mentioned in some wartime books.

We really couldn't say that it was Reims Airport. We asked passengers to remain seated while I jumped down from the back of the aircraft and walked towards the old building, generally looking around, until eventually I found an old pair of broken aircraft steps. Written on the side in really faded writing was the name 'Reims Airport'. I called up to the Captain in the cockpit to say that this must be the right place, and after moving all the ballast, we disembarked everybody. We stood around for probably half-an-hour, and eventually an old Citroën charabanc came driving up and someone jumped out. We all boarded and drove off to a beautiful chateau where we were entertained for most of the day, including a superb lunch. As the pilots, we couldn't participate in the champagne, but we were given a couple of bottles to take home with us. A very memorable trip.

Some other flights were taking oil rig workers across to Scandinavia or up towards Aberdeen. Hostesses used to make quite a lot of money and tips from workers. There were two steps up and over the main spar in the Vickers, due to the fact that early aircraft had clapped hands – a euphemism for the fact that the wings came off, so they had a really strong spar joining the wings together. The hostesses took advantage of this and deliberately wore long red pantaloons or knickers under their skirts, so that the guys sitting in the seats on either side of the steps got a flash of stockings and red knickers – good for tips!

Another wheeze of the girls was to come up and ask me as the co-pilot to draw up or fill in the passenger information slips which consisted of heights, times, where we were, when to adjust your watches, etc. These they managed to sell for about half a crown or five shillings (12½p or 25p) each, thus topping up their pretty paltry salaries. Added to which, the free orange juice cost 2/- (10p). On one of the international airlines, one of the sections on the passenger information slips read: 'Adjust your watches by — so many hours', written in different languages – including Portuguese. Unfortunately, the Portuguese for 'Please adjust your watch by one hour' is slang in Brazilian for 'Please enjoy your next erection'.

Or a cabin address could include the statement: 'Please put your watches back 100 years'.

Every time we left the aircraft, we had to make sure that the control locks were in place, which were basically wooden blocks to stop all the control surfaces thrashing around during windy nights. You also had to 'dress' the propellers – basically making them look nice and smart by having the four-bladed propeller set top and bottom left and right, like a cross.

I now had a good number of flights under my belt and the routes began to get a little bit more interesting. We got a contract to operate Berlin Tempelhof-Amsterdam-Berlin Tempelhof, flying flowers very early in the morning to Berlin. Berlin had been a virtual island ever since the Second World War.

Berlin Tempelhof had only three major airlines that were allowed to carry out scheduled services – namely, Air France, Pan American and BEA (later British Airways), although charter companies were allowed and there were several oddball aircraft parked on the tarmac, including our Viking.

One day, it was my turn to complete a tour in Berlin. There were two Captains based there permanently, who had been living in Berlin since the end of the war. Alex Imrie (who died on 4th June 2011, aged 80) had a fantastic knowledge of the Nazi era and World War II. He actually had one of the huge books that kept all the records of the Luftwaffe kills during part of the war, identifying the pilot, the aircraft and who was shot down, as well as when and where. He had numerous other artefacts, some to do with the Red Baron and all sorts of priceless items. I suggest you look up his aviation books online.

The Viking being an unpressurised aeroplane was already at 10,000 feet when it approached the central Berlin corridor, 10,000 feet being the upper limit for all three airways into Berlin. On arrival, I was introduced to the Station Manager who was the only employee there and turned out to be an ex-SS officer. I took a liking to Berlin and spent much of my flying career flying out of there. I arrived for the first time with my Captain and another Second Officer on board so that we could operate these early flights for a week.

Initially, we arrived with the Captain, the one whom I referred to earlier as looking like Tony Hancock and who was a real devil for his alcohol and women. The most amazing part of the flight was actually just after passing Hanover when we came into the airway that started from the East-West border in a straight line to Berlin. The feeling of going over this border (the 'Iron Curtain') was quite dramatic – you almost felt as if the engines changed note, and you were more than aware that you were over virtual enemy territory. Our destination airport was Tempelhof, which if you looked at the map of the airport itself, was designed in the shape of an eagle, housing an aircraft factory underneath it – the main parking area for aircraft was under cover. It had been built in the early 1920s and altered by the Nazis when they were in power. It consisted of two fairly short runways, one of which had a block of flats at the end of it, the other a graveyard, which was reputed to house the reinterred grave of Manfred von Richthofen, the infamous 'Red Baron'. It was more than interesting ducking over the flats and making sure you landed as soon as possible – otherwise you could easily run off the end, as many aeroplanes did during the Berlin airlift.

We parked under cover. The Station Manager appeared very rapidly in typical Germanic fashion. He was naturally very efficient, although there wasn't a lot for him to do. We shut the engines down and the ground personnel moved the bags of ballast as required, and we shut the doors and left the aircraft. The Captain himself and the other Second Officer eventually walked to a small hotel just across from the main entrance. In doing so, we walked past the memorial for the 39 crew members killed during the Berlin airlift which had kept the Berlin air corridors open. This represented the flights of aircraft between 1948 and 1949, when the Soviets cut Berlin off completely. Anything that was needed in Berlin to keep it going (mainly coal) had to be ferried in on aircraft. A recent television programme identified a tunnel running under the grass area from the U-Bahn (short for 'Untergrundbahn', meaning 'underground railway') to the airport itself, once a possible escape route for Hitler.

Berlin is served by three airways (routes), all emanating from Berlin itself – one going due west, one going north-west and one going south-west. All of these have an upper limit of 10,000 feet – go any higher than that or off to one side, and you would rapidly find a Russian fighter alongside you, raising and lowering its undercarriage, signalling that you must follow him to a Soviet airfield... which would spoil your day. A TV quiz show host, Hughie Green, experienced this when he strayed off the narrow airway and was forced to land. It took quite a lot of diplomatic discussion before he was allowed to leave. Consider the problems of flying in these corridors with heavy thunderstorms around. You had to keep on the airway, otherwise you would either be shot down or at the very least told to put your wheels down and follow a Russian jet fighter onto an East German or Russian airfield. Indeed, early one morning a Pan-American freighter on the way along a central corridor heading due west just disappeared. The wreckage of it was actually returned to the western powers, minus one of the engines. It was always thought that they had been shot down specifically to obtain one of the engines off the aircraft. The Allied forces in Berlin had a very good radar system to ensure that flights were always on track – if you deviated by just a small amount, they would be onto you immediately, giving advice about which way to turn. However, on a clear day some of the really experienced Berlin skippers knew exactly where the centre line of the airways was by line of sight. Occasionally, it was fun to hear the Americans saying they were off-track – the usual response from the pilot was, "I think your weapon's bent; you should get it checked."

Anyway, the three of us checked into a cheap hotel, changed into civilian clothes, and at the skipper's suggestion, made a beeline for the local fleshpots down in Berlin. We arrived there fairly early on and drank copious amounts of German beer. The skipper spent most of his evening chatting up the hostesses, which was a stupid idea because the hostess invariably poured the drink on the floor. Anyway, much the worse for wear, probably at something like one or two in the morning he called for the bill, which was huge. One must remember back then that the only allowances we received for flying was half-a-crown an hour (12½p),plus £1.50d for the hotel, on top of our flying pay to cover expenses at the hotel, such as tipping, food and other things.

We went through all our pockets, but in no way did we have sufficient money to pay the bill. After many threats by huge bouncers (of cutting our throats and other bits), the skipper negotiated that the other Second Officer would be left as a hostage while we went back to the hotel and got as much money as we could and then returned to pay the bill – there were no credit cards in those days. We left this particular club in a taxi, and the skipper and myself returned to the hotel. Rummaging through our pockets, I found some more money, he had a little more, and we borrowed quite a lot from the hall porter. We called a taxi, got in and shut the door, when the skipper turned round to me and said, "OK, Mike tell him the name of the club." I hadn't a clue, nor did he. We then spent the next 3½ hours driving round Berlin looking at any night club that vaguely fitted the bill, while I suppose our hostage was sitting in fear of his life. Finally, we hit the right club and went in, paid the money and all three of us left, much the wiser.

This is a similar story to one a friend of mine told, whom I will call the Bear. He took the entire crew out one night in Nairobi, some way out of town. They had a whale of a time with copious amounts of alcohol, but were presented again with a massive bill, which had obviously been inflated. After many threats against life, person and family jewels, the Bear had a brainwave and paid the entire bill with his credit card and then somehow got a taxi back to the hotel… whereupon he rang the credit card company and told them that the credit card had been stolen and would they cancel it. He never got the bill!

We would fly out of Berlin extremely early in the morning, hoping to be back by 8.00 am with a full load of flowers from Amsterdam. It is amazing how many flowers the Berliners used to buy in the 1960s. One of the best flower shops was in the lobby of the Kapinski Hotel, just off the Kurfürstendamm, or 'Ku Dam'. At six o'clock every morning, the early crews would muster in the lobby and take up their seats as the flower girl used to come along and bend over, revealing that she never wore any form of underwear as she proceeded to do all the flower arranging. It was a very good start to the day.

We managed to gain a couple of extra charter flights from Tempelhof, one going to Sylt (a German North Sea island) and the other one to Copenhagen. I was due for the latter trip, flying with one of the oldest Captains, known as 'Speedy Williams'. An excellent pilot, his nickname was due to the extremely slow but precise nature of any of his reactions. However, the other Second Officer, who was supposed to go to Sylt, had already flown there and was collecting airports in his logbook. He asked if I would do a swap – it didn't bother me where I was going, so I readily agreed. Sylt is a nudist colony and it was great fun to fly over the sands at almost zero feet on finals to the airport, causing consternation and a lot of sand being blown into places where it shouldn't have been.

We both set off at roughly the same time. I was now crewed with Alex Imery, one of the most respected early aviation experts ever. I later thanked my lucky stars that I had done the swap, because the trip to Copenhagen for the other guy became a nightmare. As they flew at 10,000 feet over Hamburg Airport, one of the engines started going rough and played up to such an extent that Speedy, whilst rolling a cigarette, slowly moved the seat forward and carried out the feather drill on the engine, closing it down very slowly. He was actually an excellent Captain. Just as this engine feathered and spluttered to a halt, the other one gave a huge cough, followed by another, and virtually seized up. It was lucky that Speedy managed to feather this engine as well. Remember, on a twin-engine aeroplane, with both of them shut down, the only way to go is down. Luckily, they were directly over Hamburg Airport and managed to do a series of circles, landing safely on the runway. From what I remember, the undercarriage would free-fall without a problem. Putting the flaps down meant getting out of one's seat, putting a pole into a slot to pump 160 times in order to move the flaps. Anyway, all was well and they survived, and eventually we saw them back in Berlin a day or two later.

One morning, we tried to start the engines and nothing happened. I was shocked to find that the entire toolkit for the company in Berlin consisted of a small screwdriver and a penknife – and not even a Swiss penknife at that! There was no engineer, and the Captain and myself had to open the cowlings and bang around inside to see what we could do… but to no avail. Eventually we managed to bribe a Pan-American engineer to come over to our historic plane. With a couple of wrenches and percussing the engine in several places (i.e. hitting it hard), it finally burst into life, with black smoke pouring out of it for a while until it settled itself down.

During the Berlin airlift, streams and streams of aircraft full of coal used to fly into the city one after the other. In total, 1,534 tons were needed every day to keep in excess of two million people alive. That's not including other necessities. The largest quantity of any single item required was coal. If anyone made any mistake whatsoever and couldn't land on the first go, they had to go all the way back to their take-off point, over 100 miles away, refuel and start the flight again – there were just too many aircraft in the stream. The landing at Tempelhof Airport was between two blocks of flats, which caused fantastic wind effects bouncing around the last third of the approach. The runway itself was extremely short – not as short as the parallel runway, which had a block of flats right at the end of it, so aircraft used to have to fly over the flats, close the throttle and drop onto the runway as quickly as they could.

At last I had a day off. The two Captains lived in Berlin, but I didn't see either of them off-duty and I decided that I would go through the Wall and investigate East Berlin. Remember, this was 1964. I had heard that you could get on at the Friedrichstraße U-Bahn station and travel into East Berlin. However, what people had not explained was that it went to East Berlin, but only for one station. After that it came back into West Berlin again. Obviously I'd been told in no way to wear uniform, as this would be like a red rag to a bull for the 'VoPo' or Volkspolizei – the East German guards. I joined the end of the queue in West Berlin to buy a ticket for the Berlin U-Bahn, entered the train, took a seat and away we went. After a very short period, I suddenly became aware of passing between masses of tangled barbed wire. As I said, no one had warned me that it would go into East Berlin so quickly, so I disembarked along with two American guys of about 19 years of age. There were numerous tunnels, none of which meant anything to me. We joined a queue which had several people in front of us, all elderly and shabbily dressed in black. Suddenly a couple of armed soldiers appeared holding a 'Tommy Gun', or the East German equivalent, and began interrogating the passenger in front of us who was petrified, and all the others were cowering.

I asked one of the Yanks whether they thought one of the tunnels would take us back into West Berlin or whether it would be going deeper into East Germany. They said they thought it was the right-hand one. No way did I believe that they had a clue, so I wandered off down one of the tunnels and they followed me. We managed to find someone who spoke 'Pidgin English' who said that the train that we almost got on would have taken us deep into East Germany and probably had us arrested as spies. No one even knew that we were in East Berlin behind the Wall, and we could simply have disappeared. Eventually we found the correct train and managed to return back to West Berlin, remembering that it was divided into four parts – the Russian, French, American and British sectors. We then decided that we would try and go through the American Checkpoint Charlie. We went down scruffy backstreets and eventually found this large white garden shed, which was in fact Checkpoint Charlie. We entered the hut with our passports and were eventually signed out to cross into East Berlin. At least someone would now know if we went missing! We walked across through the barrier area, which was full of huge blocks of concrete where people had tried to find a way across. The buses were being inspected underneath using mirrors, cars were being torn apart or weighed – they knew the exact weight for every single car make or type. In particular, if you drove from Hanover to Berlin by road, you would be stopped halfway along the road, everything would be taken out, and the car would be weighed to make sure that you were not helping anyone to escape.

It was at this point we were told to change money into East German marks, which in no way would ever be changed back again. We went off and I went my own way. It was like going back 30-40 years and was dreadful. There were dirty prams and bicycles which were extremely old, like something out of the ark. People were frightened to talk to you. I walked around for some time and decided it wasn't really for me and came back to go through the museum at Checkpoint Charlie. The museum itself was quite an eye-opener, showing where people have escaped on a glider or been welded into the fuel tanks of cars, used fireman's breathing apparatus to swim under the water, jumped out of the window or tried to climb up over barbed wire and then been torn apart by dogs. It was quite horrific and well worth a visit. I always wondered why people went to such lengths to escape in the way they did. It struck me that it would be quite simple to wait a couple of streets away from Checkpoint Charlie until somebody went past not dissimilar to yourself. You could then merely tap them on the head, take their passport and you would be into West Berlin before anybody realised, leaving the poor sucker on the pavement to argue his way out of an East Berlin jail. All round a very eerie set-up!

We used to dine or drink with quite a few members of MI6 who used to have cars in sheep's clothing – these vehicles didn't look like much, but boy! – did they have fantastic engines! They used to drive into East Berlin, up to some of the airports, take photographs and listen to radio conversations… and whatever else they got up to, possibly meeting spies, etc. They would often end up racing at high speed through the streets with the German Stasi chasing after them until they could manage to get through to Checkpoint Charlie. We used to visit X-Mess, which had a safe house for MI6 (MI6 are 'our' spies, while MI5 is there to catch 'their' spies) in a block of terraced houses where there was a free snooker table and bar. We could help ourselves to alcohol, just leaving a few pfennigs in a box.

My favourite place (bearing in mind that I was paid so little in the way of wages and allowances) was down by Friedrichstraße Station, just opposite the Bahnhof (the surface railway station). This could best be called a soup kitchen, where we could get a large bowl of green pea soup and a beer for virtually nothing. Remember, we were paid very little, even allowing for the fact there were thirteen Deutschmarks to the pound at the time.

Most of the buildings in the centre of Berlin had now been rebuilt from the shells that were left after the war. However, it was painfully obvious that there were very few mature men, as most had been killed during the war. There were plenty of women. Being what appeared to be well-paid pilots and having a fantastic uniform was definitely an advantage – you could certainly get discount at any store if you wore your uniform.

We were driving in a taxi down the Kurfürstendamm when the driver asked if the Captain had been there before. His reply was, "Yes, but I didn't stop." It took a while before the taxi driver understood what he meant… and that was only after the Captain explained that he'd been 'making all their car parks for them'. On another occasion in a situation similar to this, my Captain said that he had actually been in the Kurfürstendamm in 1944. This completely threw the driver. It was explained that he had been shot down and picked up by the Wehrmacht who had taken him on a sightseeing tour around Berlin before delivering him to a prison camp.

Flying from Berlin to Amsterdam one night, we landed in a thunderstorm. As I have explained, taxiing Viking aircraft is difficult, so we ended up in a strange position whereby we had to keep maximum brake on one side in order to stop the wind blowing us round in circles on the ground. We could not use the rudder to turn into wind and we ended up stuck in the middle of this fantastic storm with thunder and lightning crashing all around us.

Back in Luton, I was seconded to Invicta, flying out of Manston Airport, where they had Viking aircraft which had originally belonged to Basle Air (G-AIVF Captain Gibson and G-AIVD 12/09/64 to Ostend and Luxembourg). They had a fantastic cockpit panel in a beautiful light green – an absolute pleasure to fly. The runway was ginormous, not only in its vast length but also in its vast width, which was specially built to take aircraft that had suffered WWII battle damage. The airport was designed as an emergency airfield, a Spitfire and Hurricane base during the WWII.

Sonne (German for 'sun') was a radio navigation system developed in Germany during World War II. The system was used for long-range navigation under the Consol name, and supported by ICAO as one of the suggested long-range air navigation systems. This was copied by the allies and remained in service for many years after the war one in particular was in Stavanger and served the route from Newcastle to Stavanger.

I flew from Newcastle to Stavanger in Norway using the consul system mentioned previously in the book – even then there were very few of these consul beacons as they had become time expired due to new technology.

A couple of years previously, on 9th August 1961, a Viking G-AHPM similar to ours, flying from London, crashed near

Stavanger. I believe it was full of school children and all 39 on board were killed.

On a trip to Stavager, we experienced heavy icing, and we could hear the ice breaking off the propellers and smashing against the fuselage. We flew at a very low altitude and had great fun throwing our bread out at the fishing boats on the way across. I have no idea whether we hit them. However, I can say that in Jersey, Dakotas (DC3s – the ones known as 'Gooney Birds') did the same thing and one was so low that it struck the main mast of a fishing boat – thankfully, the aircraft managed to continue on to land.

We were considerably delayed on one flight when we went to take over an incoming aircraft. We found that it was literally full of thousands of newly-hatched chicks, and due to the heat of the bodies in such close packaging, they had all died – it was the most dreadful sight to see so many having to be disposed of. This can often happen with dogs or cats that had been put into the hold since, unless the temperature was well controlled, they died in flight – especially if one of the crew members forgot to put the heater switch on or leave the lights on in the hold for them.

From the south coast of England, a small company started up a new airline line with DC7s converted where the nose opened up – basically, in order to take cars to Ostend. To open the front up, the cockpit was raised up almost like a camel's hump on the nose of the aircraft. Strangely enough, due to some technical reason the aircraft actually flew almost twenty knots faster with this horrible bulbous nose. Unfortunately, the company eventually went bust.

One Captain in another airline found that, in flight, one of the fire warning lights for one of the engines was consistently on. He put it in the tech log, a large black book which the engineers read religiously after every single flight – this has to be signed off by both the engineer and the Captain. Nobody bothered fixing it, and finally the chief engineer said that the simplest way was just to take the bulb out, which meant that if the engine caught fire, they would have no idea that it was alight until it was too late.

Back at my Luton digs, which had a dubious reputation in the area – if anything happened, it was bound to have something to do with the building, which I will call St Nicholas. A racy well-built blonde South African lady ran it, and she made a beeline for one of the residents, a Customs officer. I spent a lot of time drinking with this officer and eventually he invited me to the airport to visit the Customs offices at night. He had to pick something up before we went to a party – it turned out to be a couple of bottles of Scotch, which had been confiscated the day before. We sat down in the office and I was introduced to the cupboard which housed all the confiscated booze. I spent two hours drinking all sorts of different concoctions and also reading vast amounts of pornography, all of which had been confiscated.

At this point, I decided that I was going to buy a new house and eventually signed a contract and popped it into the post-box, only to find on returning home that I had been offered a job with a major airline. Too late to retrieve the contract, I had to go along with the purchase all for the sake of half-an-hour.

I had been with the company for a reasonable length of time now and was offered the opportunity of flying Ambassador or Elizabethan aircraft, or what was otherwise known as the Airspeed AS57.

The company flew some of the 23 Airspeed AS57 Ambassadors that were built between 1947 and 1953, also known as Elizabethan aircraft by British European Airways – the same aircraft type that had been involved when the Manchester United football team crashed in the snow in Munich on 6th February 1958, whilst being flown by Captain Jimmy Thain. Many pilots feel very sorry that the Captain seemed to take the blame for the whole accident, when it was recognised only after the accident that an aircraft cannot get airborne when there is more than half-an-inch of slush on the runway. It was a very high-wing aircraft with two engines, and took about 55 passengers. Jimmy Thain ended up as a chicken farmer with no real money for the rest of his life.

The aircraft had a funny characteristic – you had to rotate the aircraft 15° on take-off, but if you did more than 8°, it would hit the tail plane on the ground, so you had to almost manoeuvre it off the runway. Once it was airborne, it would climb away very well. The aircraft was fitted with a white wheel under the triple boom tail plane, and at the end of each flight, you would have to check that it hadn't been touched. It was painted white so the engineers would know if you had over-rotated and you would usually be fined about 30/- (£1.50) for them to paint it and do checks. It was also extremely difficult, as was shown at Munich, for anyone to see if there was snow or frost, etc. on top of the wings, as they were so high up.

The propellers were eighteen feet from top to bottom and had to be 'dressed', with one blade vertical – it took quite a lot of effort. Powered by two Bristol Centaurs 661 engines, 2625 hp each, maximum speed was just over 300 mph. However, as described earlier, the only way to get that was to fly up to the level you were allocated by Air Traffic Control, go through it by some 500 feet (which is not only dangerous but illegal), and then dive down to the correct height, thus getting the aircraft off what is called the 'step'. We flew with 55 passengers, two cabin crew and two pilots. Another strange thing with the aeroplane was that you almost had to change gear as she went through certain levels in flight, while it was also known for the smoke trail it left on take-off.

It was a beautiful aircraft, long and sleek with high wings, huge engines and massive propellers – eighteen feet in diameter – and with three tail planes, much like the Constellation. The windows for the passengers were huge, certainly as big as the Viscount, and similar in shape. It had problems during production when, during one incident, both engines fell off.

Training was similar to the Viking, except this time there was one Captain to be trained plus us two Second Officers. We completed the normal engine failure in flight test and returned to the field and each completed six take-offs and landings. We then had to go to London and complete the ARB technical. Again, there was no chance of studying the books, as the aircraft were airborne nearly the whole time, so we had to get another set of Pop Speller's Notes and study for the exam. The questions were either very difficult or new. However, I came up with the bright idea of saying or writing across the paper, 'None of these answers are correct – please check with the chief engineer.' This seemed to suffice because I passed the exam.

With the technical exam complete, I then visited the Civil Aviation Authority to get my licence stamped. We were summoned to the airport and told that we would be required to operate a flight that night – the crew would consist of a Training Captain, the new Captain, us two Second Officers and the usual ground engineer. The ground engineer was in attendance to do any servicing if something went wrong, to fuel the aircraft and to sign off the tech log (you will read reference to one of these engineers a little later on when I arrived at Jersey Airport). It certainly was a nice aeroplane. Once again, we carried the 'flying spanner' to fiddle any paperwork that was required.

We would be flying a charter for some very important travel agents to Djerba on the North African coast in AS57 registration G-ALZS (which crashed when it went off the runway on 14th September 1967). We were chosen for the privilege of the inaugural flight with a full load of passengers. We flew down and landed late in the evening on a comparatively good runway in the middle of the desert, to be met by masses of people with Arab bands, camels and belly-dancing – a fantastic welcome. We were put in a separate villa away from the passengers and were given as much alcohol as we could drink, and then rejoined the passengers for all sorts of typical Arabian food which we took sitting on carpets. By the second night, I had the worst food poisoning I've ever had in my life, bar one.

It was decided that the Training Captain was going to stay on at the resort, while the junior Captain, the other Second Officer and I would fly the aircraft empty back to Luton. We tried to submit a flight plan but found that it was such a barren place that we had to take a taxi to the official building on the airport (which wasn't much larger than a toilet block) where we were supposed to submit the plan. However, none of us could stop being sick long enough to complete the form and it had to be done on a rota basis, with one person rushing in and filling in one part, returning to the back of the building to be sick again, etc. and the next one going in to fill in another part. We understand the flight plan was delivered somewhere by camel, then by a couple of army vehicles to somewhere else from where it could be transmitted. Eventually, we returned to our digs and were ill for hours – we could not take off until we got a message that the flight plan had got through.

Finally, the three of us climbed into the aircraft – thank goodness there was no one around to see us, as we were in a sorry state. We got airborne and rotated around the aeroplane pilot seats and the rear toilets, one at a time, and there would only be one pilot at the controls at any one time. This was a brand-new aircraft to us! Anyway, we continued flying until we were so unwell that we had to put into Marseille. After about six hours we seemed to be well enough to continue the flight and finally landed at Luton late the next morning – thanks be to God. By the way, that counted as our check flight, and we passed!

My next flight was down to the Basque territory and San Sebastian, a difficult airfield because there is a large hill at one end of the runway and you had to do all your take-off calculations before we landed, otherwise it was quite possible you might not to be able to take off.

This aircraft was rather similar in the cockpit to the York and you had to step up to get into the pilot's seat.

When you are climbing and going through about 10,000 feet, you eventually had to change gear in ordered to continue the climb, but the aircraft was very susceptible to being on the 'step' – an expression where, if you can imagine it, the aeroplane is going along nose-up but in level flight; the restriction will cause drag, slowing you down approximately twenty knots. We therefore always carried on climbing up an extra 500 feet and then dived down, getting the aeroplane in a more flat plane and gaining about twenty knots extra speed.

A friend of mine renovates aircraft, including Spitfires, and on one occasion he had an order for three Chipmunk aircraft which he completely overhauled and was required to send to America –

so he got a large freight container and, with a lot of jiggling one way and another, he got all three into the container. On the Customs form, he wrote 'Chipmunks'. The next thing he knew was that American Customs officials were after him for illegally importing animals into the USA as they had never heard of a Chipmunk aircraft.

I was getting near the end of my contract with Autair, and had handed in my notice to the company. It was Christmas Eve and we were flying G-AGRW (eventually this aircraft sustained substantial damage in an accident at Amsterdam-Schiphol International Airport, although all three crew members survived).

I was leaving on New Year's Day. However, I was given a flight to Blackpool and back to Luton. On the return trip to Luton, the weather became worse and worse, until it was absolutely impossible for us to land at Luton. However, the Polish Captain, who was a WWII fighter pilot, became very agitated. He said that there was no way that he wanted to divert as the relief crew had already left Luton and it would lose him his job. Finally, with no other option, we set course to Southend, but due to some mix-up with operations, they sent the new crew to Stansted to take over the aircraft. We therefore switched course to Stansted Airport. We called up Air Traffic Control for the visibility at Stansted, which was about 1,000 metres, and we started to turn onto very long finals, when they said the visibility had gone down to 600 metres. Further down the approach, they then said visibility was virtually zero – and that they would be closing the airport down anyway, because it was Christmas.

There we were at about 300 feet in zero visibility and no Air Traffic Control – an impossible situation. However, the Captain continued flying the aeroplane down the ILS (Instrument Landing System) and I was looking out through the windshield, when at the last second I saw a couple of white flashing centre lines of the runway. I called, "Pull up," and the Captain pulled back on the stick and the aircraft touched the ground. We slowly rolled to a halt, but we couldn't find anywhere to get off the runway and taxi to the building. Finally, the Captain turned the aircraft off the runway onto the grass somewhere and closed the engines down, just abandoning the aircraft. I got out and moved the ballast and then, with the two passengers who were with us, we walked through the fog and eventually found the building and a taxi. We got into the taxi and drove to Luton.

I asked the Captain why he nearly killed all of us and why we hadn't diverted to Southend. Again he argued that under no circumstances was he prepared to lose the job; he would rather die. It was most reassuring to know that the Captain of your aircraft felt like this about your life! This was virtually my last flight in a charter outfit. The very last was again in G-AGRW, Luton-Blackpool-Luton with Peter Hogg from 'The Lady in the Lake'.

I went to buy myself a Lotus sports car but changed my mind at the last minute when one of the guys told me what Lotus stands for 'L O T U S = Lots Of Trouble Usually Serious'.

The night before I left Luton for good, I went for a drink at the Luton Flying Club where I ran into Howard Greenaway, the pilot that I trained with in Oxford, who had owned an MG saloon car and had been brought up on a farm on one of the famous Civil War battlefields, Edgehill.

We had several beers and I asked him what he was doing at that time. He said that, since leaving Oxford, he had run a crop-spraying company. He had been very keen to get into the airline world but every time he trained a new pilot, they crashed and injured or killed themselves. He therefore had to stay on, but this had been going on for at least a year and he was becoming quite exasperated. I write this because it becomes relevant in the next chapter. This was the last but one time I saw him alive.

BAC 111

BAC 111 Hush Kit

HMS Amethyst

Fall of the Berlin Wall

Heron

Trabant

Airspeed Ambassador Cockpit

Airspeed Ambassador Cockpit

Chapter Seven
Co-Piloting Viscounts in Jersey

While still flying for the Autair charter outfit, I applied for a position in a national airline. Eventually, I was told to report to Northolt Airport for an interview one day at 10 o'clock. The roads were sheet ice as I drove my 1.5 Riley, and finding that the traffic was really bad – so much so that I was running behind schedule – I stepped on the throttle and the car hit some black ice and spun through 180°. I finally managed to arrive on time – only to find there were a group of seven pilots to be interviewed, one of whom had worked previously for my charter company. During the conversation, people were quite amazed that the charter outfit actually had checklists, as only a few minor companies in those days did.

I was asked several questions – nothing too complicated – except one which I remember: 'How would you keep a reserve in a hydraulic tank in case of an emergency?' I went into a description of having a pipe either in the side, lower down in the hydraulics and/or one coming in from the base of the hydraulic tank. This seemed to be an acceptable answer.

Lastly, the seven of us were taken to a room and given a subject to debate. One guy said virtually nothing, two were very argumentative, and four of us basically took the midline. You will notice that there is no mention of female applicants – it turned out later that the company had a policy that women did not have spatial awareness and that they could not pass any of the basic tests which they set up for them.

The debating subject was the troubles in Cyprus, and what would we do with the situation between the Turks and Greeks.

Every time I started to say something, one particularly argumentative man started to abuse me verbally. However, I managed to stand my ground and obviously said the right things because I passed this stage. The interesting thing was that there was one chap called Willy who had said nothing throughout the discussion, and the invigilator asked him to sum up. Everything went quiet for a moment, and I was anxious in case he failed to account for himself. However, he only said one sentence: "I would send a gunboat in." That's all he said. Everybody laughed profusely and eventually I met him at Heathrow, where he'd been given a job, so he had obviously said the right thing!

After a while, I was told that I would be advised by post as to whether I would go on to the second interview. I received my invitation letter and progress was subject to my passing a couple of medical checks and a dental check. I arrived at the dentist's surgery and walked into the waiting room to find two very attractive blonde receptionists, one sitting on the other's lap, and both kissing each other. The dentist himself was being a little voyeur and just watching the pair of them. It seemed as if the dentist couldn't get rid of me quickly enough. I merely had to open my mouth whereupon he said, "That's okay," and bundled me out of the door. The medical was also a formality.

I arrived at the second interview to find that there were only two of us who had bothered to turn up. To my astonishment, the interviewing senior Captain merely said, "Well, if nobody else is going to bother turning up, you two might just as well have the two jobs. In the meantime, would you like to come with me to the local squash club where I'm a member and I will buy you a beer?" The two of us then followed him by car.

I had just signed and posted a contract to buy a house in Luton for £3,175 (eventually selling it at a profit of £135). I then walked back to my digs to find the airline contract on my doorstep. It was too late to get the house contract back out of the post box, so there I was committed to buying a house and starting a new job in a totally different area – talk about Murphy's Law! I signed the airline contract and posted it in the very same post-box. I wouldn't be surprised if the two letters landed on top of each other! The next morning I gave the charter company a month's notice. I joined the new company straight after I had served my notice.

My first day in attendance was 5th January 1965. We were all ushered into a classroom and sat at desks. In front of us was an envelope; eventually we were told we could open it. There were forms in it, but the most interesting thing of all was that it told us which aircraft we were to fly.

The options were between the Vickers Vanguard and the Vickers Viscount 800. The Vanguard (nicknamed the 'Guard's Van'), being the larger aircraft, took a maximum of 135 passengers with a three-pilot crew and a changeable number of cabin crew. Being a three-crew aircraft, it did not appeal to me due to the fact that I would get less right-hand seat flying.

I was given the Vickers Viscount 800. The only reason I can see as to why I got the Viscount would be that I had flown Vikings (23,000 pounds max) and the Ambassador (55,025 pounds) with my previous company. These were both considerably larger and heavier than the DC3s (16,865 pounds) that most of the others had flown.

There was a photograph on the wall that looked like a man painted on it, but it turned out that an engineer had been checking the tyre pressure on a single wheel but did not shut the cage safety door. The nitrogen was pumped into the valve but the tyre exploded, smashing him into the wall, leaving a full imprint of him.

After a general initiation, we were given lunch in the canteen and sent to classes where I started to learn, by way of chalk and talk, about the company and the Viscount 800. The course itself was pretty good. In the same vein as the previous aircraft I had flown, we were given a huge number of sample questions which were extremely helpful on passing yet another ARB (Air Registration Board) type of exam and then having the licence stamped by the Civil Aviation Authority.

The course included many hours on a simulator. It was here that I came up against the most argumentative guy from the interview. We were later teamed up together in the Viscount simulator, and it turned out that this guy had been a Flight Lieutenant in the RAF on Armstrong Whitworth AW.660 Argosy aircraft, nicknamed the 'Noddy'. This was a cargo aircraft with a large lozenge-shaped airframe, twin-boomed tail and the same engines as the Viscount. Indeed, it was very similar, including the cockpit. He could have been extremely helpful to me, seeing that he knew virtually everything about the Viscount. However, he chose to be exactly the opposite and did everything to climb over me in order to get top marks. Eventually I had to go to the ground school officer in charge and say to him that we had 'a clash of personalities'. This seemed to be the right wording, as it was accepted. The pilot concerned passed his course, but approximately a year later he left the company. He was arrogant, and it was typical of what we would call the 'Atlantic Barons' – meaning they would do nothing to encourage their co-pilots to be part of a team. More about this later. As this guy had flown the Argosy in the RAF, he was expecting to fly it for the company. However, that was not the system that they used, and he was deliberately put on a different aircraft, namely the Viscount.

A few more comments on the Argosy. One of the pilots stood about 6' 4" and was on one of the aircraft one dreadful night going into Milano-Linate Airport with thunder and lightning, and the ground radio aids there were not very good. The Captain continued an approach starting well out from the field and obviously lost his bearings. As he descended, he hit the side of a hill slowly, partly due to the headwind and partly due the shallow angle of the hillside, just like a cheese grater taking the bottom off the aircraft. Eventually the aircraft came to a grinding halt. Remember that it had a huge bulbous front hold, but this had almost totally disappeared, leaving just the cockpit, situated on the top of the aircraft and wings, and the tail booms. Neither of the pilots were hurt, so they merely stepped out of the back door of the cockpit onto the grass. Normally this would have entailed climbing down the ladder from the cockpit onto the floor of the main part of the aircraft, but nothing else was left of the plane! The official report read: 'The Argosy struck a hilltop at 2,230 feet some 35 nautical miles from the runway 36 threshold. Probable Cause: Navigational error due to 1) Failure to determine the aircraft's position in bad weather; 2) Failure to make fullest possible use of the co-pilot.'

This co-pilot, who I will refer to as 'Thumper', was again on an Argosy several months later at Stansted Airport, this time during a training exercise. When one of the engines was being throttled back to simulate an engine failure, instead of just idling, it went into what I believe is ground fine pitch and spun the aircraft off the runway so that it crashed and was virtually destroyed. Thumper turned to the Training Captain and the other First Officer, telling them to follow him – "I know the way out when this happens." He walked away totally unhurt from the aircraft. However, the management took a different view on this and decided it was about time to move on to a different aircraft, and so he was put on Comets.

Anyway, we had now passed all the technical exams and turned up at five o'clock in the morning to be on the simulator. It usually started out being freezing cold, although as soon as they started chopping engines and various emergency procedures, sweat would be pouring off you, just as though you were sitting on top of a 3kw electric fire. Simulator time was often rented out to other companies and so they had the more sensible times for their courses.

The visual on the Viscount simulator was something to be seen, especially in this day and age when we have computer technology, and everything is generated in what looks like real life. In this particular case, we had a huge map – something like 20 feet across and 40 feet high – which revolved on runners. The runners stood vertically, and a map – or rather, a model of a map – ran up over the runners down the other side and back up from the bottom. The fake trees were made out of sponge with wooden blocks to represent buildings with runways and roads all painted on.

It was pretty realistic considering, and the only drawback that anyone really found was that, if you got too low, the camera automatically jumped to about five feet above the map in order to protect the lens. On one particular occasion, when they were flying very early in the morning, a giant spider appeared in front of the camera down near the main Staines Road, frightening the life out of the crew! By the way, we have nicely renamed towns like Walton-on-Thames, and someone suggested renaming Staines as 'Staines on Trousers'... but it did not catch on.

The six of us Viscount pilots were now put in an interview room for a free discussion as to where we would like to be posted. There were four postings to Glasgow and two to Jersey. I do not expect you to understand or believe this, but I did not actually know where Jersey was. I had heard the name but had no idea that it was an island down near the French coast.

However, it sounded a lot better than being stuck up in Glasgow in the freezing cold doing Highland and Island flights in all sorts of atrocious weather. Three of us therefore put in for Jersey. Between us, we decided to draw lots out of a hat. Much to the annoyance of the ex-RAF Argosy pilot, I got Jersey and he got Glasgow, which is probably why he eventually ended up leaving the company. He was certainly not a happy bunny. The other pilot who got Jersey was also ex-RAF, a great guy and a good pilot. He told me that he had been at the Commanding Officers' cocktail party. The CO was talking to him and a small group of VIPs when the CO's young son came up, pointing at him and said, "That's the man who was in bed with Mummy," to which the CO said, "Now don't be silly, son," and ignored him. His friend was actually court-martialled when caught in bed with another CO's wife, evidently putting up a black was a good way to get promoted. He got his promotion when the Board of Officers came to his name and they said that they knew his name, but could not remember why – so they gave him the promotion on the pretext that he must have done something good.

Ground training finished, I left the training building and went home. Three days later, I put my Riley 1.5 car up for sale.

Posted to Jersey

On 11th January 1965, I was posted to Jersey and arrived there one sunny morning, having allowed sufficient time off to find myself accommodation. I had been recommended a very nice boarding house in town run by a lovely lady called Mrs Stretch. On collecting my bags from the airport to take them to the boarding house, who should come across the tarmac but Howard Greenaway, the guy who owned the MG with the broken seat back that I mentioned earlier. I last saw him just before leaving the Aero Club on Luton Airport about a month before. He had passed all CPL exams and got his Instrument Rating at the same time as I did, but could not get a job and so became a crop sprayer. We stopped for a short chat – it turned out that he had finally got someone to take over his role in the crop-spraying business and had now been offered a job with a Jersey airline. He had completed his basic training and that very evening was about to go on his very first scheduled airline flight from Jersey to Paris Orly and back. We agreed to meet later and celebrate the fact that we were now both airline pilots based in Jersey.

I left, took my bags and settled into Mrs Stretch's B&B and had a bath and an evening meal. Someone put the television on and after about ten minutes there was a newsflash. The announcer said that a DC3 had crashed at the end of the runway, which was about four miles away from my accommodation. They then went on to say that there had been no survivors except one stewardess who had broken both her legs, and that no one was to travel to the airport because it was now in thick fog. Obviously this was Howard's flight. It was his very first flight – and his last. He was sorely missed. It turned out that on the second approach, the Captain had flown the aircraft down the ILS (Instrument Landing System) on runway 27 (he had an alleged reputation for ducking under and always getting in, whatever the weather). On this occasion, things were stacked against him as he got very low and one of the aircraft wheels hit, first a tree, and then one of the leading lights, which was basically a telegraph pole with a light on top of it. If so, it should have been sawn through so that it would give way if an aircraft struck it, but for some reason this had not been the case and the aircraft veered to one side and crashed. It turned out that Howard had been supernumerary on the way to Paris and I believe he had sat in the right-hand pilot seat on the way back.[14]

It was the end of a really nice guy and a good pilot with a very short career. It also turned out that the Captain's wife was pregnant and he was trying to return home before she gave birth.

The next day I was scheduled for training to fly with a Training Captain called Captain Woolland who had been on Swordfish aircraft during the war. He had attacked a German battleship, although I don't know which one – it could possibly have been the Bismarck – when a very large shell from the ship exploded next to him and threw his aircraft on its back. It was ditching into the sea and there was nothing he could do about it, although just before it hit the sea, another shell exploded next to him and threw the aircraft upright. He managed to fly on through the gunfire, and lived to fight another day.

We were supposed to go to Dinard, but Woolland was really keen on getting back home to London early the next day, so asked me if I minded doing the training that night instead. The weather that night was appalling – it was dark, with really strong gusty winds across the Dinard runway (which ran practically due north-south), and it was raining like mad. We certainly should not have left to carry out my six take-offs and landings on G-AOYL. However, he was still determined that he would, then go home first thing in the morning. So much pressure was put on me that there was no way that I could really refuse. I got the aircraft ready, Viscount 800 G-AOYL, and we flogged across the hop which was a short flight. Then we trundled around the circuit and completed six take-offs and landings in the worst weather that I have ever come across, and to this day, I don't know how I managed to get the aircraft to land well on each occasion.

It was pitch-black except for the runway lights and a glow from the distant building. The cockpit lights were dimmed and the red ones turned up, so that we could see out. There was thunder and lightning streaking across the black sky. We turned onto the runway and I called for the power, the Captain wound up the four engines, I released the brakes and off we went. Faster and faster, he called V1, V2 and rotate. Up to V1 we could stop in the distance left of the runway, but after that we were committed as there was no way we could stop without going off the end of the runway. Nor could we get airborne between V1 and V2, which is when we can get rudder control to keep the aircraft straight if we had lost an engine.

Due to the 20+ knots crosswind, I kept the aileron down into wind and used the tiller or steering wheel for a short while until I could get rudder or foot peddle control, then back with the stick and we were airborne, turning the aircraft slightly into wind to keep it going in the same direction as the runway. Then I called for the undercarriage up, climbing to flap retraction height and after take-off checks. Powering back, we bounced around in the black turbulence to 1,000 feet. Then a 90° turn followed by another found us going downwind at an alarming rate due to the terrific tail wind. I called for more checks, and we being the only idiots airborne, got clearance to finals. The last 90° turn slowly brought the runway lights across the three windshields until it was nearly in the centre of mine. I had to crab towards the runway to keep it central, flaps, undercarriage and more flaps, while the turbulence got worse and worse. The lights came towards us, fairly slowly due to the headwind, and then when the lights almost came up above our heads I pulled back on the stick and flared. As the wheels touched, I kicked the aircraft straight and we were on the runway. I slowly took the pressure off the stick and as we slowed down, the Captain applied full power, moved the flaps to take-off position and we were off down the runway again. Just five more circuits and bumps to go! As we finally set course to Jersey, I felt very pleased with the whole exercise. Woolland landed at base, and we retired to the Aero Club for a well-earned beer or two or three.

I had passed and never flew with Woolland again.

At the end of this, he signed up all the paperwork and I was now a fully-fledged co-pilot on Viscounts.

The next morning, on G-AOJB and with Captain Nicolle, I was on the Jersey-London flight. We had it drummed into us over and over again that we must do everything by the checklist, which could take fifteen minutes if you did it by the book. I was supernumerary on this flight, which meant that I was an extra crew member watching to see how it was all done. The co-pilot came out with me to the aircraft to get it ready, while the Captain was doing something in the main building. I expected an experienced co-pilot to pick up the checklist and work his way through it. However, he did not even look at it – to my horror and amazement, all he did was throw the book on the floor and just go around touching all the different levers from left to right around the cockpit, seeing that they were in the right position. It is certainly not the way you would expect it to be done, but it became the norm and is still the norm with some pilots of lots of airlines.

This co-pilot was a pretty good pilot – he was getting on a bit, a stocky ex-professional golfer who played off a handicap of almost scratch. He had been married four times (in this day and age he would be called an 'Audi pilot' after the four rings on the front of all Audi cars). He had never passed his ATPL in order to become a Captain, as he was more dedicated to golf, saying, "All that would have done was to distribute the extra salary as alimony to the other wives," so all he did was enjoy himself on the golf course. He was used to really upsetting the Flight Managers when he arranged golf tournaments and pushed the Flight Manager around as if he were a brand-new rooky. They were not at all amused by him doing this to Senior Captains from his lowly position, but then he really didn't care what they thought, and it just went over his head because it was never his intention of trying to be a Captain. My first trip in the right-hand seat was with the same Captain – back from London to Jersey in G-AOJB.

Two years later, I applied to Captain Pennington, a Battle of Britain pilot, for one of his new houses that he was building. We sold our house in Bell Royal for about £6,500 (it had gone up form

£4,000), and we soon had a potential buyer who was a fascinating person. He was English, but during the war he remained in Jersey during the German occupation. The first thing he'd seen of the Germans invading was when he was walking down to the harbour. Coming the other way were a load of Germans on pushbikes which was the first he knew that they had actually been invaded. A little further down was what looked like hundreds of sheep walking across or down the main drag by the sea wall. When he got closer, he discovered that they were Russian prisoners-of-war in a dreadful state, with sackcloth wrapped round their feet, whilst they were being beaten and whipped. They were taken off and used for building the underground tunnels for the hospital and many other fortifications that to this day survive on Jersey. I had always thought the Germans had built the sea walls as protection against storms, but I am told they are anti-tank fortifications.

The gentleman who bought our house was lucky enough to get a job looking after the Commandant's horse – this seemed to work for many years, but the standard of the Prussian German soldiers became worse and worse as the attrition rate on the main fronts took its toll. (At the main council building, the Jersey workmen laid out a beautiful square of granite, but the Germans never noticed that there was actually a 'V' for victory in the design. Underneath it was eventually found a container holding some documentation and other items which those very brave people had placed there.)

In the end, our buyer was sent to a work camp over in Germany but managed to survive. Anyway, he was interested in buying our house. The system for buying a house in Jersey is this: say there are ten houses and they all cost £5,000; you could only sell those houses for £5,000 plus a small amount of increment for improvements. It didn't really matter whether you spent a fortune on your house or whether you allowed it to go to rack and ruin.

However, residents in Jersey had many ways round this. One would be to sell a picture with the house for maybe £10,000, or sell your car with the house. One of the real favourites for much more wealthy people would be that you would start a joint bank account with the purchaser – the extra money would be put in a new joint account where both had to sign in order to take the money out. You would then go to the main court where you would not have signed anything in order to sell your house – you merely stood up in the court and swore on pain of perjury that you understood what was in the document and that you sold the house to the other person – both of you swore, and that was it, the house is sold – a very simple procedure. However, what normally happened is that there would be an envelope on the seat and the person who was buying the house put their signature on the required form to draw the money, and the person selling then took it to the bank having added their signature, and so withdrew the money from the joint bank account – so many ways around the system!

So we moved towards La Corbière lighthouse in Jersey and into a pleasant detached house which we bought for £10,000. It was more expensive than the others. I was very tempted with one house which was built on a huge German ammunition bunker – you could come out of the front door, go down some steps and be in a huge bunker. However, it was not in the best position.

Being the first person on this estate, I named the road 'Rue de la Pointe'. It was duly accepted. Finally, the house was sold to Lloyds Bank with everything in it – lock, stock and barrel – for £16,500; we just left the keys there and returned to London in January 1972.

I met a solicitor later in my life, who regularly had very large sums of money in his UK bank account on behalf of his clients awaiting the sale of a house. He decided to go to Jersey to see whether he could invest it. The general tax rate was 20% and he said to the tax people that he wished to invest several million pounds in the bank account, but didn't want to pay anything like that in tax on the interest – what could they offer? He said they offered him 5% tax, and after a lot of toing-and-froing they managed to get just 1%. Just shows you what you could do!

One of the tax inspectors lived opposite me, and to the delight of many people, one day he suffered severely from elephantiasis, which I believe meant that he couldn't get out of bed because his testicles were so big. He did not get a lot of sympathy from anyone! Jersey income tax was paid eighteen months to two years late, so everybody put their money in fixed bank accounts and accumulated quite a lot of interest before the money was actually paid to the tax office.

Flights were usually to London Heathrow, Gatwick and Southampton, and occasionally Birmingham, Manchester and Glasgow. It was pretty limited, but one of the tremendous advantages was that we were often sent to Berlin for six-day postings so we had Jersey income tax of 20% (when or if you even paid any), plus the very generous German allowances.

There was a very nice company club down by the bus station in St Helier with a snooker table on the first floor, which everybody enjoyed. One night everybody gathered there to rib and take the micky out of one of the stewardesses. It turned out that she'd just got married to one of the stewards who was exceedingly well endowed. She on the other hand was extremely tight and she had to carry out exercises with different forms of apparatus in order to accommodate her new husband. The crews never stopped taking the micky out of them. Several nights later, the club burned down and the snooker table came crashing through the floor, spelling the end of our club.

It was at this point that Captain P was singing the praises of Williams & Glyn's Bank. As I had just left the Midland Bank who had upset me – I had gone to them with a large bag of coins, which I had collected over a period of time, in order to pay them in when one of the tellers told the female teller in front of everyone to throw me some bags and to 'get him to count it himself'. I called for the manager in order to close my account immediately and went round the corner to Williams & Glyn's (who eventually became the Royal Bank of Scotland) – it was a fantastic bank, with no glass partition between you and the tellers.

I thanked Captain P for his recommendation and we flew together many times. One trip in particular was when we went to Southampton. We landed but it was sheet ice all the way down the runway, and we only just stopped before the end. Thankfully, we didn't run off one side or the other end. We slowly turned round, and he said we would fly back to Jersey, but I refused to, saying that I could see no way that this aircraft would stop if we had an engine problem. We would just have run off the end. After a while, being a good Captain, he listened to what I'd said and the flight was delayed a considerable time until the ice had melted. We flew back to Jersey to find that we were about to undertake some new flights from Heathrow to Milan and Turin. This meant that Captain P was required to fly to London and go as a passenger on a Vanguard for route experience from London to Milan. This was a normal situation, as a Captain would normally go to a difficult new airfield as a passenger in the flight deck before he could operate in command.

Well into the flight on G-APEC from London to Turin, things went wrong over Brussels at 19,000 feet. The aircraft suffered a major rupture of the rear pressure bulkhead – in this case, the metal panels in front of the elevator sprang up, stopping the elevator from being effective and blocking the airflow over them (the elevator is the part that sticks out left and right of the tail and which hold the aeroplane level). Evidently, it was caused by fluid leakage from the toilets at the rear of the aircraft seeping into the tail section and finally corroding away the aluminium panels on the tail plane. There was now no control over the elevators and the aircraft started to lose height and then dive, heading straight into the ground from nearly four miles up. Everybody was killed.

Yet it was well known in the RAF that toilet fluid could rot an aircraft. There was no way that the aircraft could stay straight and level at 19,000 feet, so it eventually dived vertically into the ground with little or nothing being left. We don't believe much was found of Captain P, but what was left was cremated and scattered over Biggin Hill, which is where he had served in the RAF reserves. Unfortunately, when the ashes were put out of the window, they all flew into the back of the aircraft amongst the seats!

It is quite moving when someone is killed like this, because we had to open his locker to see whether there was anything in it. He was married with two children, and as we went through the bits and pieces, it became apparent that there was a stewardess involved in his private life. Some time later, a memorial service was held in Jersey. The church was packed and several of the cabin crew tried to make sure that the stewardess would not appear. However, a disaster occurred – the wife and two children were right in front of the church, when the stewardess came in at the back, screaming and wailing and very distraught. The children realised what was happening and they started crying.

Ironically, just before the accident, Captain P had been mowing his lawn before a flight when a stone had come out from the Flymo, hit a wall and struck him just below the eye – he could have had severe eye damage and so may never have been on board, and so would have been alive to this day. Captain P is sorely missed and was a great pilot and a great friend. Just before the accident, Captain P's father had died of a heart attack – Captain P said his father was going to the toilet standing up in the dark when he probably fell asleep and fell over, suffering a heart attack.

Just before this, an Ambassador AS.57 aircraft, G-AMAD (similar to the ones I had flown), also known as an Elizabethan, flew into Heathrow Airport and onto runway 27 right. It was full of horses and at about 300 feet they applied land flap. Unfortunately, a chunk of the mechanism of the flaps broke and the left flap came down but the right one didn't. The aircraft veered to the left and in the most horrific situation, they flew down between the Charlie and Bravo stands, a cul-de-sac leading towards Terminal One. The only way they could have saved the aircraft was to get out of their seat and reset a circuit breaker, impossible in the circumstances. There was no way that they could get over the building and the aircraft hit the ground, taking the tail plane off a Trident aircraft called G-ARPI or Papa India, soon to become infamous. The horses were all killed or put down. It must have been terrifying in the cockpit and to know that there was no hope whatsoever of surviving the next twenty to thirty seconds.

The Trident G-ARPI was repaired and some time afterwards was involved in a famous accident known as the Staines disaster.

Staines Disaster G-ARPI

On the night before the Staines crash, there had been a trade union meeting of BALPA at the Skyways Hotel because the pilots wanted to strike. The only person who did not want to go on strike was the Captain of G-ARPI, Stan Keys, who was at the meeting which I also attended. He was short in stature and well overweight, puffing and panting and fuming at being the only person to argue against the strike. Eventually the meeting dispersed and the next day I was in the Crew Room when he came in with two First Officers.

Again, he was red and fuming, arguing with everyone in sight that we should not go on strike. The tannoy went and he was called to operate Flight Number BE 548 to Brussels so he left the Crew Room. From what I understand, there was a large number of doctors on the full flight, and there was also another Captain on the fourth seat who was positioning to Brussels.

Stan Keys was the Captain and the First Officers were Ticehurst and Keighley. Stan had a reputation amongst co-pilots of being a domineering Captain who often moved levers himself when they should have been operated by the First Officers. The scenario was roughly as follows (and, in fact, we trained for this on the simulator after the accident, so it's pretty accurate as to what happened). The Trident aircraft has two lift devices – one what you would call the flaps on the back of the wing which is set to take-off, the other the droop which is a similar set-up on the front of the wing, and it controls the flow of air over the leading edge of the wing.

Over the preceding months, there had been continuous cries in the press about noise abatement and it was pretty horrific. When you took off, you would have to pull the power almost back to halfway, which would cause the aircraft to wallow and slowly climb up to about 1,500 feet, when you would then open up the throttles and clean up by reducing the flap and then the droop at 210 knots. However, what seemed to have happened was that someone (and most people believe it was the Captain) moved the leading edge or droop lever up instead of the flaps so that the aeroplane lost all lift. They were in a left turn and the plane just went into a flat dive out of the air, crashing in a field just short of Staines. Obviously, nobody noticed that the wrong lever had been moved and the design of these levers made them appear virtually identical – one was on the left of the throttle quadrant and one was on the right. Someone moved the first one by accident and, this not having been noticed, there was really no way that they could control the plane. On top of this, the stick shaker went (this is to stop the aircraft stalling by shaking the control column – if no one reacts, it will push the control column forward). However, someone pulled the stick shaker override, known as the tiger's tail, thus disabling it – and from then on they were doomed. We later practised it on the simulator, but we were well aware of what was about to happen, and we could just about get the aeroplane to climb just before it hit the ground. If you didn't know what had happened and that the wrong lever had been moved, the chances were very slim that you could survive.

Everyone in the aircraft was killed. I met a police officer who was the first on the scene and he said he went into the aircraft – it had come down in a flat position almost vertically – and nearly all of the passengers were in their seats, but they were like dropped eggs, with everything broken. He claimed that the Captain was alive but died shortly after. Someone even claimed that there was a passenger who walked around or out of the aircraft but died in a very short time. There had been sixteen doctors and senior staff from the Royal London Homeopathic Hospital on board.

Jersey

On leaving the B&B, I managed to lease a flat on the ground floor of a small block. In the flat above me resided a doctor who evidently looked very much like me. During my time in Jersey I was often approached by certain women who began talking about their gynaecological problems, thinking that I was their doctor.

James, who had led a carefree life and really didn't worry much about what went on, was a Jersey-born pilot. At one point fairly early on in his career, he applied to fly the 707 and went to London, but failed the course. He was then sent back to Jersey where he stayed.

However, some fifteen years later the company was offering severance pay – in other words, any pilot who wished to go for early retirement could pick up a pretty sizeable lump sum. This guy applied, and when they received his application they did not know who the hell he was. On investigating, they found that he had completely and utterly disappeared from the books and didn't appear anywhere, except that the wages office had paid his full salary every month and his pension was building up and up. He was eventually paid off with a lump sum. If he had kept his head down, he would still have been paid to this day!

There were about twenty crews in Jersey. I came to know the Captains and their mannerisms – most of them had flown during the war, one or two were fairly new, but a couple of them thought they were the bee's knees. Dealing with the new ones, one of them just fancied himself something dreadful and the other one did nothing to encourage you as a pilot. Indeed, you were absolutely guaranteed that on every single flight he would tear you to pieces on some issue or other. It wasn't until a couple of months later that it was pointed out by one of the older co-pilots that, if you made a mistake right at the beginning of the flight, he would then tell you off and he would be perfectly happy after that and wouldn't bother you any more.

Another Captain was an engineer who ran his own heating and engineering company. He was basically a very good bloke – I liked him – but others did not as they thought he was a Walter

Mitty character because he had this business. He often explained it to me, and my father always said that the laugh must be on the other pilots because he was reasonably successful in what he was doing. He had an interesting notion that all central heating pipes should be on rollers so that there was no creaking and groaning when the heating system warmed up.

He also explained the unusual system in Jersey, were it was the norm for any bills that were submitted by a company always contained a clause that if the bill was paid within thirty days, you would receive a 2½% discount. He always claimed that paying his bills before thirty days made a difference to his company making a profit or loss. It doesn't sound like a lot, but many large companies in the country do not make much more than that.

Then we had another strange pilot. It was explained to me that he always had a chip on his shoulder because he was only a sergeant bomber pilot, and had never been made an officer. He was grumpy, grouchy and rude, and if you had completed the flight plan when he came into the flight planning room, he would push you out of the way, take the flight plan and go over to the hatch and order the fuel, with never a hello or thank you. When we started flying and were airborne, if he had given you the leg (flight) and you had not put the autopilot in by about 500 feet, he would put it in anyway. This is not good cockpit resource management, spelling possible danger due to the fact that you might not realise that the autopilot was actually on. On one night I remember two of us First Officers were playing poker with him in a room in Birmingham and I got four jacks but declared them as two pair. He just took the money and said it was illegal to call that way. I've watched this carefully in numerous cowboy films where people miss-call their hands – I must find out whether it really is illegal. I thought it was extremely unfriendly and we rapidly decided that we wouldn't play poker with him any more. It was pretty typical of his attitude.

Another pilot had flown Stirling bombers during the war – he was fairly quiet and docile, and didn't talk to us much. However, if there was even slight turbulence, he seemed to get twitchy. On the Viscount we had a set of four small switches called fuel trimmers, which were moved up and down to give slight changes to the throttle, which in turn moved the propellers through different pitches. This changed the noise of the engine a little and it used to give him pain. He would put his hands over his ears and would shake his head and have a real go at you for doing it. When we positioned as passengers, he would put his hands over his ears and appeared to be in agony as the engine notes changed. Later on, I believe he was sent to a sanatorium.

I felt very sorry for him as most of his fellow buddies on the Stirling squadron had been killed during the war. In just under six months, 67 out of the eighty-plus aircraft that were delivered were lost due to combat or training accidents. They used to get a briefing which told them to go up about 12,000 feet, and everybody except a couple of the experienced ones used keep to that height. However, the aeroplane definitely lacked power and he found that, if you whacked a bit of flap down in the cruise, the aircraft would actually go up about fifty feet, and if you kept operating a flap like that you could actually get up through 400 feet above the rest of the squadron. The German radar control ack-ack guns used to hit all the aircraft at 12,000 feet and he regularly managed to get back on the basis of being higher. I didn't take too much notice of what he said until I was reading Len Dayton's book *Bomber*, which actually explains that the Lancaster pilots had found the same system worked and managed to get above the main bomber stream.

Bomber is the most magnificent book I have read, and I thoroughly recommend it to everyone. However, the reason for Len evidently writing the book was that he had discussed with his brother as to what it was like to go to a pre-op meeting (where they were shown what their route was). His brother, who was a Lancaster pilot, said that when they had Stirling aircraft or Halifaxes, or even Wellingtons, accompanying the Lancasters, they would all give out a mighty cheer because Stirling and other aircraft were more likely to get hit, which would take the pressure off *them*. He said that it didn't appear very sporting that your own colleagues would be killed and not yourself, and that it was not a cheering matter. However, we were not there so it's not for us to comment.

Another had been a Pathfinder pilot who used to precede the bombers and mark the target with flares. We were flying from Berlin to Nuremberg one night. It was pitch-black except for a few lights on the ground, and he was looking down for some considerable time when I said to him, "A penny for your thoughts." He replied, "I was flying here once and I was looking out just like this, when there was a flash from the ground and I realised that it was a radar-controlled ack-ack being fired at me. I turned the aeroplane almost on its side and corkscrewed the aircraft when the aircraft directly above me got hit and went down."

Another man had flown Lysanders and used to drop spies in France in the middle of the night. He had a number of medals which he never wore.

The people who wore medals most were with Pan American as First Officers, which was quite interesting because most of the them had been in the Korean War. The young Captains who had missed the war and joined Pan Am had a considerable amount of seniority, giving them priority on the Captain's seat, but they had no medal ribbons whereas the First Officers had masses of them.

One of the Pan American pilots in Berlin owned a flat in London. His drains got blocked, and he was aware that there was a piece of kit in America which you could use to clear drains. He bought one of these back to England, unblocked his drain and started up Dyno-Rod drain cleaning. He continued with that company until fairly recently, when I understand he had an offer of £56 million but turned it down. In the meantime, he continued flying with Pan American for some considerable time.

The islands around Jersey had many multimillionaires as residents, one of whom I used to fly to Dinard in Brittany for lunch, and also to the occasional Grand Prix race at Silverstone. He had sold his family steel production factory many years ago to the government and made an absolute fortune, just before the whole industry collapsed. He was the only person I know that actually tipped me £5 at the end of a charter flight. The only other tips that I ever received in aviation was ten shillings (50p) from a little old lady whom I showed around the cockpit while we were waiting to start the engines, and also £5 from a football team. If there had been any other tips that were given to us through the cabin crew, they never got to us.

Another interesting character in Jersey was Leonard Matcham, whom I understand, at the end of the war, bought up all the .303 bullet-making machines and conveyor belts that produced the ammunition for the rifles. He bought them at an auction for virtually nothing, at basically scrap value, and then set himself up producing lipstick cases. To this day, I marvel at such a fantastic effort by somebody with such a futuristic view.

Another crash. A twin-engine aeroplane took off and climbed out towards the west when it lost an engine – I believe number two, the right-hand engine. However, as I have mentioned before, you do not turn onto the dead engine, but rather always towards the live one. This guy didn't get back to the field and crashed in the sea – all were killed.

On looking out towards the east and coming into land was an old four-engine Constellation freighter. It came in to complete its landing roll and was then parked far away at the end of the parking area, but it appeared to be dripping oil in several places. The engineers put chocks under the wheels and the engines were stopped. I walked towards it, seeing that it was a small charter freighting company run by a well-known fighter ace who had been the first Spitfire pilot to shoot down a 109 with cannon (the one mentioned earlier, John Wolferstan 'Pancho' DFC with 17 kills during the war. I had flown with him on Vikings).

Then I noted the First Officer descending the steps and coming towards me. He was the 'flying spanner' in the charter company that I worked for, that I have often mentioned before. He was wearing a brevet (a pair of wings). I congratulated him, saying that was fantastic. "How long have you had your wings?" meaning when did he pass his pilot's exams. At which point, he shushed me to one side and whispered quietly that the co-pilot had been sick for about a week and he was replacing him by simply using his jacket. Basically, he was a ground engineer pretending to be a pilot but nobody knew.

Finally, the Constellation started up its engines with masses of smoke pouring out the back of the engines. One engine wouldn't start, and whatever they did, they could not get it going. They taxied out to the end of the runway on three engines, held on the brakes, applied full power on the three engines and roared down the runway with the faulty engine windmilling. It started just before they got to the end of the runway – this is definitely not a normal procedure!

Golden Airways came in with their newly-acquired Trident, unloaded all its passengers, loaded up the return flight with passengers and taxied to the end of the runway. It received take-off clearance, turned onto the runway and went down it like a startled ferret, but barely got airborne at the end, knocking off the Instrument Landing System aerials. He was lucky to get away with it.

The local charter Captain had a fantastic rapport with his Dakota DC3, and everyone swore that, whenever he walked to the plane, it would talk to him. There's no doubt that, as he walked towards it, it would squeak and make all sorts of funny noises, almost as though it were excited that he was going to fly her.

I was sitting in the pilot's Crew Room on standby one Sunday, when there was a commotion in the corridor (the cabin crew rest room was on the other side of the corridor). Looking out, I found that a stewardess had turned up the worse for wear – she had been drinking heavily and had stripped off all her clothes – and I mean *all*. She was determined that she was going to go on her assigned flight. It being a Sunday, the senior management were not around and several of the operation staff tried desperately get her to go home, but she wouldn't. Eventually they had to report her and she lost her job.

On another occasion, there was a steward who was up to all the fiddles. He used to fly into Gatwick Airport and other places and have an arrangement with the ground crews and catering staff, leaving boxes of splits (a small tin for gin and tonic) such as tins of non-alcoholic drinks like lemonade, tonic water, ginger ale, etc. They tried to nail him for a long time but they never could catch him out. So one day the company made up a story that they believed that several cabin crew were stealing from the company. Saying that the cabin crew were thought to have drugs on their property, they asked the police to accompany them to the crews' houses at night. They couldn't just go to this steward's house because the union would have gone bananas, so unfortunately they went to a number of cabin crew houses to cover up who they were after. I can remember being in Guernsey at the time. We were all drinking at the bar in our hotel when the senior steward had a phone call that his wife had been raided and arrested. Like the others, they all had something in the house, although nothing worth raiding them for. She took the blame for all that they had in their house – blankets and other bits and pieces – so she lost her job and he kept his. Two other young stewardesses were perfectly innocent except that they had some Dundee cake in the house, which they used to dole out with a cup of tea to the odd pilot who might come past. They were totally innocent but were also fired – it was totally unfair. Ironically, many years later, I noted one of them in Terminal One working for the company again. I asked how she had managed to get back in. She took me to one side and asked me to keep very quiet about it, as they didn't realise and they hadn't checked the records out – she had managed to get a job in the company without telling them what had happened.

Lastly, there was an extremely efficient steward who lost his job because they found that he had sets of sheets from some of the hotels that we stayed in when on night stops. Evidently, what he did was to change his sheets with a set at the hotel and then continued over the years to take his dirty linen to any hotel and change the sheets over!

One Chief Pilot who is now long since dead was very, very intelligent and actually appeared on TV's Mastermind and did extremely well.

The most interesting pilot of the lot was a Battle of Britain veteran – evidently, he had once been one of the very youngest Squadron Leaders in the RAF. He initially got the job with a company called Railway Air Services and actually had a tent on the beach down in Jersey, where the original aeroplanes used to land. After a while, he decided to build his own house and immediately after it was finished, he sold it. I think he must have built sixty to eighty houses in Jersey and was a multimillionaire. He specialised in the stock market and had a great following from the rich and famous in Jersey. In actual fact, it was not so much that he was good at wheeling and dealing, but that he had a cold and a very clever way of doing business. He had some reasonably good inside information and would get the multimillionaires to go into a company and buy shares, the same as his, he having bought them slightly earlier. They would all buy the stock and it would go up on the basis of their money. He would then sell his shares, other people would hear about it, but in the meantime he told the rich people to pull out and all the poor suckers who followed (including myself) lost out. Everywhere you went, he would rush off the plane and be on the telephone buying and selling shares. When he eventually retired, they gave him an old telephone as a farewell present.

I can remember him specifically walking across the tarmac in Berlin with his hat in his hand as usual. When some bumptious high-ranking office manager shouted out, "Captain, put your hat on immediately," his only remark – without turning his head – was "F—k off." He always just walked onto the plane at the last minute, having just finished his phone call, signed the load sheet and the tech log, and started the engines to taxi off. He was a brilliant pilot and always allowed his co-pilot to take responsibility. I can remember coming in on finals on an easterly landing in Jersey, when we had to shut an engine down due to oil pressure failure or loss of oil, and he let me carry on and land the aeroplane – few other Captains would have allowed this. I was very impressed. He was a great squash player, but I understand that he 'wandered' and he and his wife eventually got divorced, which cost him a fortune.

One day I was leaving the staff car park, which was right up against the front door of the Jersey Airport terminal building, when someone went past with all their scuba gear. He was putting his catch in the back of his car and I asked to see what he had caught. He gave me a large rubbish bag holding the biggest spider crab you've ever seen in your life and charged me fifteen old pence. I took the bag home to the missus who put her hand in the bag to see what it was, discovering a ginormous spider crab. She put it in a pot and tied the lid down, but the legs kept coming out and falling off!

Buying houses in Jersey was a very interesting game. I moved from a flat to a nice semi-detached house in a horseshoe type of estate and had a beautiful fireplace built from the pink granite that was a speciality of one of the quarries in Jersey. I ordered several tons of topsoil to be delivered to the house and put it in the back garden but it ended up full of couch grass. I threatened to sue the garden centre to get it removed.

Jersey itself was a real cliquey place – everybody knew what everyone else was doing and everyone knew each other's business. I had to get a new driving licence, or a Jersey driving licence, on arrival. I went round to the senator at his farmhouse and he asked my background, and as soon as I said I was an airline pilot, he immediately seem to take to me. He asked me nicely what sort of driving licence I required and I replied just a normal car driving licence. He asked if I wanted a motorcycle licence as well? Answering, "Yes, I might use one," he replied, "Tell you what, I'll give you all groups." I walked out with a driving licence and I could have driven a tank, tractor and all sorts of other vehicles.

The one thing that you must remember in Jersey is that if you are not a local and have an accident and the other driver is Jersey-born and bred, you are definitely guilty. A couple of useful things on this: give way when you come to a small roundabout; at an intersection, always filter in turn – it works brilliantly, but some visitors don't quite understand it, but it certainly works well; in the winter, when there are no visitors or 'grockles', as we called visitors, the traffic flowed very freely.

Driving round Jersey is a major epic – some people have never left their home to drive to the other side of the island. To actually drive the ten miles to the other side or to go round the island (approximately fifty miles) would require taking at least a bottle or two of wine and some pâté and bread in case something went wrong. Normally people never usually ventured into St Helier, which would only be a distance on average of three to four miles from any point. The only time they would go was to pay their council tax equivalent, or to renew their driving licence, or something like that.

There was great excitement one evening during a spate of murders. The whole island was in terror for about two to three years until finally the police stopped a car, purely by accident, and found a hood and a knife. It turned out that the local butcher was killing women and hanging them up in his freezer compartments and then disposing of them. The real shame about this is that there was a very old chap who was thought to be the murderer, and in desperation he went to one of the tiny islands and set up all on his own. Occasionally, people would stop past on sailing boats and leave some provisions. It was only after they captured the real killer that he was able to return to Jersey.

One of our pilots (who was an amazing cartoonist) and I were staying in the Hotel de France, when Bergerac (from the TV crime series) came into the bar, and sat down at a table to have a drink. Bergerac had been trying to get Jersey residency and was having quite a lot of problems at the time. Our cartoonist drew a picture of him on the beach in a tent with all his belongings round him. Unfortunately, Bergerac had a complete sense of humour failure – I'm afraid we were not one of his best fans from that point onwards.

Jim was a nice young co-pilot, married to an attractive wife, but he went on an illicit liaison one day for about a week. When he got back, he found that the Duty Manager had slipped up and told his wife that they didn't know where he was, and that he was not on a trip. However, later on the co-pilot came up with an idea. When he was actually at home, in order to gain credibility, the

Duty Manager rang his wife and said her husband was on the trip and he would not be back for another day – at which point, she said that was stupid because he was there with her. He managed to worm his way out of that problem somehow.

Another was caught out when he spent a couple of nights with a girlfriend. His wife found out about it, so the Battle of Britain pilot decided that now was a good time to go in to console her – and he bedded her. Another man, a total womaniser, would chase anything that had a skirt on it. One day he was in the Crew Room when he heard that one of his fellow pilots was delayed and would not be home that night. He voluntarily went round to pass the news to his wife and ended up seducing her. It turned out that when she was a child, she had been raped and it had affected her and given her a bit of wanderlust. Another marriage on the rocks!

Another marriage broke up when the pilot was in bed with his wife. The mail arrived and she brought it up, and he said she could open it. When she did it was a 'Dear John' letter laying out his secret liaison with a stewardess.

In Guernsey, a relative of one of the stewards built himself a real biplane. However, he dropped it when lowering the parts out from the first floor at his house and had to repair it. After a fairly major repair, he took it to the airport, started it up and turned it onto the end of the runway. He applied full power and took off, only to find that the aeroplane would only turn left. Bearing in mind this was a small island, approximately eight miles by six, he managed to go round in a great big circle. When he got to the end of the circle, there was the end of the runway and he managed to land – a very, very lucky pilot. He also owned a Nord 1002 Pingouin 11 aircraft, a side-by-side two-seater monoplane, which can be seen in many films pretending to be a Messerschmitt 109 fighter. There was money in the family because before the war they had owned a very successful laundry business. By the end of the war, after the Germans had left Guernsey, there wasn't much left of the business, so some Americans with their money spread round Europe paid for a brand-spanking new laundry business for them.

Weather in Jersey is among the most amazing in the world. It is the only place where you could have fog and a Force 10 gale. We would regularly look down from the aircraft to see a 12,000-ton steamer coming across from the south coast of England, trapped out at sea for one to even three days in a Force 10 gale, because the visibility was so low that they could not get into the harbour. Personally, I hate ships and would prefer to be airborne rather than on the sea. It is quite something to be looking down on a 12,000-ton ship disappearing below the waves and coming back up the other side – the thought of sitting on the deck there with hundreds of people being sick is appalling.

As mentioned earlier, the best weather forecaster in Jersey was named Windless, whom we called 'wet and windy'. He could tell you when the weather would change to within ten minutes and I learned so much from him. It seems that all the knowledge of this older generation has been lost nowadays with forecasting done by massive computers, with all sorts of parameters built into it, which in itself must make it extremely unreliable. Weather forecasting is now a broad-brush approach. For instance, if you live somewhere between Guildford and Kingston in Surrey, your weather is totally different due to the Hog's Back and the South Downs – near the South Downs, you may get lots of rain with the south-westerly wind, but on the other side of the Hog's Back, not more than 25 miles up the road, you may get very dry weather.

The Pilots' Union sold our rights to be able to sit on the ground and have lunch – evidently, it was included with a small extra amount of money during a pay deal many years previously. It doesn't seem right that someone whose health is of vital importance could not sit quietly at the lunch table and digest food properly. Instead, we had to take meals in-flight, so on any flight that went over a lunch period, we were given a tray at some point during the flight, balancing it on our laps and bolting it down while flying the aeroplane. This happened to one of the Captains leaving Guernsey for London, but when he looked at the tray, there was no salt and pepper on it. So he actually turned his aeroplane round and landed back in Guernsey to pick up the salt and pepper, the argument being that others had been incompetent – it wasn't his fault! I never found out what happened to him. Another Captain was served a box with some salad in it and a couple of small sandwiches. He cut a hole in the bottom of the box and pushed his John Thomas through it, closed the lid and called the stewardess. When she came in, he opened the lid and said, "What do you call this in my food?" She looked nonchalantly into the box, picked up the fork and stuck it into his private part. She closed the lid and left the cockpit... which was an appropriate name in this case. Nothing more was heard about the incident.

I used to do marking for the Jersey Air Rally, an absolutely fantastic event with aircraft coming from all over Europe. Marks were given for different items – the aircraft's condition, pilot turnout, but in particular the amount of effort they had put into their planning and navigation for the flight. On one occasion, the aircraft for the film *Battle of Britain* arrived in Jersey. They had been sent by the Spanish Air Force, and consisted of a large number of Messerschmitt 109s and three Heinkel He 111s. People on the ground remarked about the wonderful noise the Spitfire's Merlin engines made, but I understand that they all had Griffin engines instead. With reference to the Merlin engine, there is a local legend which says that during the time of Camelot, King Arthur and the Round Table, it was said that when Merlin died, he would one day come back and save England. It is a real coincidence that the Spitfire engine was called Merlin and saved Britain again!

Old pilots have always said that, whenever you are trying to pass an aeroplane of the same make as the one you are flying, be careful, because it means your wing tips will be exactly the same height. Also another wartime tip... We were approaching Bournemouth, coming in from the east and were about to turn left towards Jersey when Air Traffic Control suddenly said there was an unidentified aeroplane ahead. The old bomber Captain merely flew straight ahead through the beacon instead of turning left. When asked why, he replied that if you start the turn, you cannot see what is underneath you – you could hit what was coming from the west, so go on until you can see him or get clear of him. Also, if you want to see where the aeroplane is, it is very difficult, but if you keep your eyes still, you will actually see it moving, immediately alerting you.

One night I had an unscheduled night stop in Bournemouth. I spoke to a guy who ran a large company in Jersey where he said he used to test Merlin engines, right in the centre of the island, although no one knew anything about it. He was concerned that they did not know, because once they did, they would probably complain about the noise.

There were two guys who owned a small charter outfit – one was an elderly, very pleasant guy and the other (I'm not sure whether it was his son Mark) was a fairly innocuous person who had a very, very attractive wife who had previously been a stewardess. I can vividly remember he told me that, every time he bought and sold an aeroplane, he would take his wife to bed with a bottle of champagne and stay there for most of the day and night. Lucky fella!

From my contacts in the Jersey area, I was offered the opportunity of flying an Apache twin-engine aircraft on charter flights. There was no money involved, but good experience of flying a twin and helpful towards my command.

One of the Apaches that I flew had a dreadful habit of the engines refusing to start when they were hot, and I can remember doing a long flight to Manchester and then down to Gatwick. At Gatwick, I was running out of time before Jersey Airport closed that night, and the engines refused to start. After many attempts, I became extremely worried about running the batteries down, until finally, at the very last chance, the engine spluttered into life and I set course for Jersey. By now it was well past the airport closing time. However, luck was on my side and a scheduled airline had asked for the airport to be kept open as one of their aircraft was running late, so I managed to sneak in just before him.

This aeroplane was often filled up with masses of luggage in the rear hold and solid in the nose cone, so it often took off with no load sheet. These were completed at the end of the flight when the aircraft was in the hangar, which is most definitely *not* the way to operate the system.

I have mentioned the Jersey weather before but it is quite amazing how it would close in almost every Friday and Saturday during the year. At the end of the runway was a 300-foot drop down onto St Ouen's Bay where you could sit on the beach all day long in beautiful sunlight, sunbathing and swimming in the sea, and looking up to the end of the runway but seeing no aircraft land or take off. When you went into the airport for your flight later on in the day, you might discover that fog had completely obscured the approach to the westerly runway. This was caused by westerly winds – remember a wind coming from the west, being pushed up over the end of the runway 300 feet up, turns into cloud or fog, forming a wedge of cloud all way back to long finals. This meant that no aircraft could get in all day long, although there would be beautiful weather on the beach.

This cliff face in itself caused some very unusual flying effects when landing towards the east. If the wind came from the east towards the runway and hit the edge of the cliff, it would fall down the cliff face and go back up again, and then go off towards the west. So when you came in to land to the east, you would start off with normal power and flap settings and a pretty standard approach until about 300 feet above the runway, when you would get an updraught from the wind. You would then pull the power back to keep the speed from increasing, and just as you did that, you got down to 200 feet where the wind was now pushing you downwards into the cliff face, so you now needed to apply virtually full power to hold on to the correct glide or approach path. Then, just as you went over the threshold, aiming for about 300 feet into the runway, you would end up with a normal straightforward wind and you'd have to whip the throttles back at the last minute, wrestle with the controls and make a landing.

It was fascinating to watch people coping with this, especially when they were unfamiliar with the Jersey easterly runway approach. Often you would be at the end of the runway, waiting your turn to take off with these aircraft passing you in all sorts of attitudes, often thumping themselves into the runway, or sometimes just overshooting and trying again. Remember, the runway was pretty short – landing towards the west naturally was short, but if you made a mess of it and overran you ended up crashing down 300 feet onto the beach.

Before the airport was built, aircraft used to land on the beach, and they needed someone to mark out the runway by sticking flags in the sand. No one was really interested in doing this job except one guy from the fire service who eventually did it on a regular basis. When they built the new airport in Jersey, he was appointed airport manager and served as such for very many years – the case of being in the right place at the right time.

In the old days, some of my Captains used to fly Dragon Rapides off the beach, and one of them always related tales over a beer. He had done so many flights back and forth to Southampton that he'd forgotten if he if was going to or from Jersey – he actually had to go back into the passenger cabin and ask the passengers where they were going, which must have filled them with confidence! Another Captain was well known for the fact that he didn't even have a uniform. He sat in a Rapide one day with the passengers, take-off time passed, and after about ten minutes he stood up saying, "If they are not sending a pilot, I will fly it," walked forward to the cockpit and started the engines. It was only later that he explained to the passengers that he really was the Captain of the aircraft as most passengers were shaking in fear.

Captains have varied – some were good and included their crew in their decision-making, although others were known as 'Atlantic Barons' because they would have no truck with anyone else making or helping with decisions. This often led to some of the worst crashes in the world. Believe it or not, many co-pilots will sit on their hands and make no comment and watch a Captain fly into a hillside or run out of fuel and kill them, rather than speaking up.

One day, one of the old Captains was not on the aeroplane. When he eventually boarded it, the Dispatcher, who gets everything ready for the flight, came up to him and told the Captain he had done this, this and this, offloaded some fuel, offloaded some freight and that the aircraft was ready to go. The Captain thanked him for his work, went down the steps and returned to the Crew Room. Walking past the crew report officer, he was asked where he was going – his reply was that he was going home as the Dispatcher was taking the flight for him. When he got home, the flight was cancelled. Remember, the Captain rules!

On another occasion, when he was on a Trident aircraft, a Captain was called to take a flight to Paris and had a bit of a run-in with another Captain in the Crew Room who was doing a flight to the other Paris airport at the same time. However, he went out to his aeroplane where the other one was empty alongside his with no sign of the Captain of the second flight. Being a bit of joker, he told his co-pilots to make his flight ready and in the meantime he went across to the empty aeroplane, stood at the bottom of the steps and welcomed all the passengers on board, aware that the Captain of this aircraft had not yet arrived. He then told each passenger as they came on that they were welcome to visit the flight deck at any time they wished – just open the door and come straight in. One presumes that the second Captain would have been inundated with nearly 100 passengers coming into the cockpit throughout the flight and he would not have been very amused. Of course, with today's massively increased security, such goings-on would be unheard-of.

This Captain existed only to fly aeroplanes at the end of his flying career. After his last flight and on his way home in Cornwall, he overtook a lorry and hit one coming the other way and was killed, just hours after he had retired. Many think there is more to this story than meets the eye. It was a shame, because although he was a bit of a dragon, he was one of the few characters in aviation who got away with murder.

I remember flying into London one afternoon and approaching the airport some ten miles away. (Keep in mind that the runway consisted of two very long runways parallel to each other and about a mile apart and sometimes if the runway was blocked you might be asked to switch to the other one.) On this particular occasion, a Japanese aircraft was approaching the left-hand runway. Now, at three o'clock in the afternoon they used to switch runways, mainly for noise abatement reasons – so before three o'clock you could land on the left-hand runway and take off on the right-hand one and after three o'clock they would switch over. On this occasion, Air Traffic Control came on the radio and told all the aircraft they were changing runways – would they switch to 27 right. To which the Japanese pilot, being first to land, said that he could not see the other runway. A broad American southern drawl suddenly came up on the radio and said, "You saw Pearl Harbor all right, didn't you!" Another day a Court Line aircraft landed. Every aircraft was in a different colour, and this one was brown and an American pilot radioed, "What have you been flying through?"

By now I was beginning to learn a few things about the airline business, which turned out to be pretty true. If you went to a dinner party, you could recognise the pilot because he wiped the bottom of the plate before he put it down – he did this because he was used to eating on his lap in the cockpit and would get his trousers dirty. He would also probably eat a three-course meal in something like three minutes flat, almost as if someone was going to take it away from him! If you want to know whether someone walking along the street is a stewardess, then just look at her handbag and you will see a normal company handbag. On the other hand, to recognise a pilot in civilian clothes, just look at his socks – if they are black, he is probably a pilot. It is always said that pilots break aeroplanes and engineers fix them.

George was one of our pilots. He had recently completed an exam where many people were seated at tables, completing their exam papers. Some students finished their papers early but others carried on up to the last second. When time was called, George just sat at his table and continued to work on his paper. Unbelievably, the invigilator just sat in his seat and allowed him to continue, just to see how long he would take to brazen it out. After nearly half-an-hour of extra time, he got up and walked towards the front desk where all the papers were stacked in a pile. He said to the invigilator, "Do you know who I am?" and the person said, "No, never seen you before" – at which point he lifted up a large chunk of the papers, slotted his in amongst them and left the room. The invigilator couldn't work out who he was and so he ended up passing the exam!

An African aeroplane was flying quietly along when the Captain decided to go back and have a short break and a cup of coffee, then talk to the passengers. He left the cockpit, shutting the door. Shortly afterwards the co-pilot, who was flying the aeroplane, decided that he was on maximum range tanks and desperately needed to go to the toilet. He was unsure how to do this because, of the two pilots, he was the only one left in the cockpit. However, it was an emergency and he left the cockpit and ran into the toilet. When he came out, he found that the cockpit door had locked and neither of the pilots could get back in. They then had to get the fire axe (which is usually kept in the back of the aeroplane) and smash the door to pieces in order to get in to save the aeroplane.

On another occasion, one of these charter outfits had a problem with their weather radar. The First Officer decided that he had some engineering knowledge and checked whether one of the cables had come off the back of the radar, situated just in front of the throttle quadrant. With the help of a spanner, he pulled the weather radar out, checked and found a wire loose, pushed it back in and then attempted to put the radar back into position. However, nothing that he could do would make the radar set go back to where it was supposed to go. After fiddling with it for several hours, they realised that they couldn't move the throttle, which was set at about halfway for the cruise. They couldn't get full power, and the more they tried, the worse the situation got. They had to get the fire axe and smash the weather radar to pieces so that they could continue the flight and land the aircraft.

I was carrying out my senior licence at this time in London, doing a crammer course, when I met an Australian pilot. He was a real character and really upset management. He was on the end of the runway when one passenger said that one of the fuel caps on top of one of the wings was open and that some of the fuel was dripping from it. He should have returned to the stand and allowed the engineer to check it. However, he removed the emergency escape hatch from above the wing, climbed out, walked along the wing and put the fuel cap back on again. He then came back into the aircraft, replaced the emergency escape hatch and returned to the cockpit and took off. One could consider that he used his initiative, but unfortunately Flight Managers never see things like this, and so once again he was threatened with losing his command.

Being in trouble with Flight Managers was a constant problem. Whenever you checked into work, you had a pigeonhole where there was usually some mail. However, the most wonderful thing about reporting for a flight was when the pigeonhole was empty – there was never any really good news in those holes or slots. However, it did not always go the way Flight Managers would have liked it to have gone. In an unusual situation, one was called into the Flight Manager's office and asked whether there was anything that they could do for you. This was unheard-of and quite chilling, although the reply of one stalwart was, "I would like a Tampax," to which the astonished Flight Manager said, "Why on earth would you want one of those?" He replied, "Well, anything that a Flight Manager gives you has strings attached, so I might as well ask straight off."

A First Officer was walking across the tarmac very slowly towards an aircraft quite a long way out on a stand, and as he walked past the halfway point, a Flight Manager going in the opposite direction stopped, looked at the co-pilot and said, "Next time you get a day off, get your flipping hair cut." The co-pilot didn't reply at all and the Flight Manager continued towards his office and started some paperwork. His secretary came in and he asked, "Is all going well?" to which she replied, "No, we've just cancelled the Barcelona." The manager asked why, somewhat puzzled. She said, "Well, you told the co-pilot of the Barcelona flight that next time he has a day off, he should get his hair cut. This was his day off – he was merely helping by volunteering to come in when one of the pilots went sick at the last minute. We were going to have to cancel the flight, so it was only out of his generosity that we were going to be able to operate." The embarrassed Flight Manager never got round to apologising.

Astro Navigation was no longer required on flights, due mainly to technical improvements in navigation aids. Some Captains used to keep their eye in, and renew their qualification by getting to the end of the flight and obtaining a blank Astro Navigation chart so that they could back-plot what they had seen on the flight and send it in to the Civil Aviation Authority so it counted towards their annual requirements to keep current on Astro Navigation. Astro shots were usually done through a bubble of Perspex on the top of the aircraft, and many a pilot has said that they sometimes have to spend fifteen or twenty minutes to take a shot while standing up on a stool with their head in the dome taking the shot – while it was quite usual for some stewardess to come along and pull his trousers and pants down, leaving them completely open to the elements. I have heard of a vacuum cleaner coming into a story. But think I better leave that one alone.

On one long flight to Glasgow and in bad weather, passengers were kept strapped into their seats. Eventually the lap strap sign was switched off and one of the male passengers who had been drinking fairly heavily made a dash for the toilets. He approached the toilet door, unzipped himself and exposed himself just before opening the door, which turned out to be the cockpit door and not the toilet. In extreme embarrassment, he then turned round to look for the toilet, still exposing himself to the full view of all the passengers, and then found that the toilet door was locked as one of the crew were using it. After a lot of fumbling, he was able to gain entry to the toilet and relieve himself.

An elderly lady, obviously from very good stock and breeding, was sitting in first class when she flicked her fingers and called the stewardess across and said to her, "Is it difficult in England to get staff?", to which the stewardess said, "No, Madam, I'm sure you'll have no difficulty getting a position."

One Christmas Eve in Jersey, the aircraft was delayed because there was no one to fly it. The crew that was supposed to fly back to London had been delayed and didn't seem likely to arrive in Jersey to fly the return flight. So operations pleaded with the previously mentioned Battle of Britain pilot to come in and take the flight, which he finally volunteered to do. When he arrived at the aircraft, the First Officer went up and started the checks as the Captain finished doing the outside checks. He then came up into the aircraft to find Diana Dors (a famous actress from the 1960s) was seated at the front, the aircraft being full. She shouted out in a very loud voice, "This is disgusting; you have been keeping us all waiting on Christmas Eve." He replied in a very loud voice (as usual with his cap in hand), "I'd like you to know, dear, that I have just come from a dinner party, leaving eight people sitting around a table, missing my meal and my drink, in order to take you to London. I do not have to do it, I only volunteered to do it, and I am more than happy to go back to my guests. What would you like me to do?" All the passengers shouted and booed Diana Dors.

We often visited night clubs in Germany, mainly in the Berlin area. In the very early 1960s, there were very few jobs in Berlin. The barmaids in these clubs appeared pleasant until about five or six in the morning when they seemed to get a blue stubble, and it turned out that they were men dressed as women, although not necessarily transvestites. It was the only way that they could get a job. Nowadays they probably *would* be called transvestites. The normal reason for going to the clubs would be that there was a new pilot or crew member that had never been to Berlin or visited any of these clubs, so we would use them as an excuse for a visit.

Jersey Airport

Dakota DC-3

Jersey Airways Rapide

OPENED ON 18TH JUNE 2004
TO COMMEMORATE THE

PAPA-INDIA
AIR DISASTER IN STAINES
WHEN 118 LIVES WERE LOST

IN GRATITUDE FOR ALL
WHO ASSISTED ON
18TH JUNE 1972

Chapter Eight
BAC 111 as Co-Pilot

Pan Am Flight 708 (PA 708) was a cargo flight that crashed less than ten miles (16 km) west-south-west of its destination airport, Berlin Tegel, in the early hours of 15th November 1966. The flight was operated by a Pan Am Boeing 727-21, registration N317PA, named *Clipper München*, routing from Frankfurt. PA 708 was on initial approach when the accident occurred. All three crew members perished. The cause was undetermined because US investigators were not allowed to survey the impact site near Dallgow in the former East Germany and only half the aircraft remains were returned by Soviet military authorities in East Germany to their US counterparts in former West Berlin.

After eight years in Jersey, my last flight was on Viscount G-AOHO Jersey-Southampton- Jersey on 30th October 1971). I was enjoying Jersey, but I was facing a dilemma: whether to stay there, flying propeller aircraft, or to move on and try and get a jet on my licence, which would help me move forwards to being a Captain. I decided to take the plunge and find a new opportunity. With hindsight, this was possibly a bad decision as, had I stayed two more years, I would have qualified for Jersey residency which would have entitled me to buy and sell property there. Naturally, this would have been at the very bottom of the ladder, but I could have retired there on a very low income-tax bracket.

However, I applied for a move to the BAC 111 aircraft. This was similar in appearance to a Trident or a Boeing 727, except that it had two engines at the back instead of the three on the Trident. It was originally supposed to have HUD (Heads-Up Display) showing flight instruments on the windscreen, but it was found to be unreliable in one way or another and was abandoned. It was a newly developed aircraft and its T-shaped tail plane had had a significant design fault which was exposed only on a test flight of the aircraft from Wisley Airfield. Part of the test involved running a stall procedure not unlike the one I described in my training on the Tiger Moth, except it started rather higher, at 16,000 feet. The aircraft was in level flight and the power was slowly taken off so that the nose came up and the aircraft speed slowly declined, until it reached its stall speed.

However, the designers had not realised that, once it was in the stall position, with the nose right up in the air, the airflow would be unable to go over the rear T-shaped elevator. The effect of this was to block off the flight controls, leaving the crew unable to get the aircraft out of its stall – it went into what we describe as a 'flat spin'. They called in frantically on the radio, saying that they needed to get the nose down to create airflow over the elevator and regain power. They tried to turn left and right, they tried to push the nose forward, they tried opening and closing the throttles, but in no way could they get the airflow to go over the tail. They were dropping at about 2,000 a minute, asking in desperation if there were any engineers there who could advise them on what to do.

They hit the ground eight minutes later and all seven on board were killed. With hindsight, the designers realised that if they'd had a parachute affixed to the aircraft tail as a precaution, they would have been able to deploy it, which would have solved the problem. This incident illustrates a universal truth: however much thought is put into the design of a new aircraft, there will always be something that is not right. In 2018 I attended a lecture at Brooklands Museum where I met an engineer who should have been on that aircraft, although at the last minute he had swapped with one of the other crew.

British European Airways had ordered eighteen BAC 111s (244 had been built), evidently on the assumption that they would lose two or three of them as they actually only required fifteen. But despite the rigorous partying regime which was integral to life in Berlin, my regular destination, we never lost any, so they always had a surplus. Other companies were less fortunate; in September 1971, D-ALAR was lost in Germany and crashed on the autobahn, though there were more survivors than one might have expected.

I landed in London on 10th January 1972 and turned up at the Training Centre in Heston the next day to start my 111 Ground Course. The BAC 111 version we had was specially ordered for the company. Initially, they had held a competition to decide on a new name for the aircraft and hundreds of people put in ideas, but they decided to ignore them all. The best one of the lot (which was not accepted) was 'The Backward' – a simple name based on joining two words together, 'back' for BAC, the British Aircraft Corporation that produced it, and 'ward' after the then company chairman who was called 'Millward'. Needless to say, they didn't accept this idea and instead came up with the blindingly obvious name of Super 111 which was a great shame as they missed a chance to raise morale in the company which, at the time, was abysmally low.

The course was following the old system of 'chalk and talk', a standard system of droning, lecture-based training. To our disappointment, most of the diagrams were in colour. In the Viscount training, which was similarly delivered, the only enjoyable part in the past had been colouring in the diagrams; now we did not even have that pleasure. The positive aspect of this, admittedly, was that it helped considerably in our interpretation of them.

I was very pleased to discover that one of the instructors with whom we usually had lunch had been a rating on a Royal Navy ship in the Yangtze Incident (Amethyst). (Briefly, in April 1949, with civil war raging in China between the Chinese Communist People's Liberation Army and Nationalist forces, the frigate HMS Amethyst was ordered up the Yangtze River to act as a guardship for the British Embassy in Nanjing. When it was about seventy miles away from Nanjing, Amethyst came under fire from Communist artillery batteries on the northern bank of the river, and while attempting to evade the shelling, it ran aground. During the incident seventeen members of the crew were killed and ten wounded, including the Captain, who later died.) By coincidence, my grandfather had served on the Yangtze River well before the rating (and had shown me a picture of a Chinese pirate being beheaded onboard ship). We spent much time discussing the activities in that part of China.[15]

At last, I completed the usual ARB (Air Registration Board) exams and had my licence stamped. Most of the flights on the 111 were to, or from, Berlin. It was an interesting aircraft though it had rather a slightly complicated list of rules and procedures which had to be religiously adhered to after an engine failure. The cockpit was smart, although it got castigated in the aviation magazines which said that the autopilot controls were dangerous. They were in a neat row of switches and looked fantastic – you had to move them backwards and forwards to import certain information to the autopilot. The aviation magazines disliked them ergonomically as the switches were identical; they said it was too easy to make a mistake and move the wrong one. In practice however, most co-pilots could play them like an organ and had no problem whatsoever.

My first flight was on G-AVMI Berlin to Frankfurt. Later, I arrived for a flight in Berlin Tempelhof, and the first thing that I was expected to do after flight planning was to go out and prepare a 111 by doing all the pre-flight checks. I duly went round the outside of the aircraft in the usual way, and then completed the cockpit checks, but was rather puzzled to find myself alone on board. There were no passengers, no ground crew, no Captain and no cabin crew – it was absolutely deserted. I looked out of the cockpit window but could see no-one – at first.

I glanced along to where the next but one BAC111 stood and noticed a considerable crowd of people hiding behind the wings and the fuselage, all looking in my direction. Bemused, I got onto operations on the radio and asked them what was going on – why was there no one on my plane and why were so many people skulking underneath the next but-one along?

"Where are you?" I was asked.

I told them the registration of my aeroplane. The answer certainly took me by surprise: "They are all hiding because there is a bomb on your plane."

Rather sarcastically, I thanked them for giving me the information and immediately went to get off. But just as I got to the bottom of the steps and was about to hurry away, all of a sudden, the crowd from the other 111 came running towards me. They rushed straight past me and started hiding behind *my* aircraft. In consternation, I asked them what was happening and they told me that they had got the registration wrong and that the aeroplane they had been hiding under was the one that was supposed to have a bomb on board. I couldn't stop laughing! After a while, they cleared the other plane – there was no bomb found. The airport returned to normal and, much amused, I took off. Passengers often phone in if they are running very late and say there is a bomb on board in order to delay the aircraft.

The 111 was an extremely noisy aircraft, and you had to be very careful on take-off that you did not get a noise violation against you. As I soon discovered, there was noise-measuring equipment placed round the airfields to which we flew – and not only that, but antagonistic members of the public were almost certain to report you if you deviated even slightly from your course and disturbed them. This happened to me on one occasion at Düsseldorf when my First Officer performed the take-off. There was a DME (Distance Measuring Equipment) beacon halfway along the runway and the procedure was to take off, fly past the DME and then turn right, carrying out the noise procedure when climbing away. This was my very last flight before I had three months off on unpaid leave when I travelled around the world in eighty days.

The First Officer shot down the runway and turned right in the usual fashion. But because it was a freezing cold day and we had virtually no passengers on board, the aircraft shot into the air like a startled ferret. We were up so quickly that he started the right turn earlier than usual – turning before the DME and not after it, which took us over an old man in the town of Duisburg. Shortly after levelling off at cruise altitude, only minutes later, we were asked to call Air Traffic Control when we arrived in London. Someone had registered us as a noise violation after receiving a complaint from an unbelievably persistent member of the public who apparently made it his business constantly to complain. I must admit that, whenever I read a book on bombing in Germany in the Second World War and it mentions bombing Duisburg, I rather lack sympathy.

Once at Heathrow, I duly made the call. The German controller was extremely helpful, especially when I explained that I was about to take three months' unpaid leave and that it would spoil my holiday if there was a complaint against me. Between us, it was established that I had turned early for the excellent reason that I was attempting to miss a nasty-looking cloud which might have created downdraught that would have endangered the aircraft and potentially create a crash. I never heard any more about the incident, but the First Officer was always highly embarrassed about it. I was not impressed with the resident on the ground.

At a later date in my career, we were generally chatting and I asked some people what they did if they received a noise violation – did they write a full report about it? One of the most senior Captains turned round and said, "No, the only thing you write is that, quote, 'I operated this flight according to British Airways drills and procedures'." That was all that he would write and at a later date I copied his advice.

Not everything that happened was predictable. On one flight back to London, we came to the top of the descent (the point at which drills are gone through to prepare for landing); I moved the appropriate control to set up the pressurisation system and, with no warning, there was a huge thump and all the oxygen masks fell out. There are various procedures which should be immediately followed on a move to oxygen and I put my mask on straightaway. However, I was flying that day with a Captain who was extremely large and he was either so manly or so stupid that he didn't bother with his mask. (The passenger masks had also been deployed.)

Certainly, breathing the oxygen was not pleasant; the feeling was similar to when I went to a dentist and had gas in order to extract a tooth, as though all the blood was draining out of your body. Perhaps my Captain saw it as beneath him. We descended as swiftly as we could to below 10,000 feet which was the point at which we could then come off oxygen and went on to land as normal in London.

The procedure upon landing should have been to ask any of the passengers if they wanted to go to hospital or see a doctor. The Captain had not been affected by it in any shape or form and had no interest in seeking medical help or offering it to anyone else. All he did was write something in the tech blog, a book where we have to report anything that goes wrong, and he then went home.

They never found out what had caused the thump; engineering naturally tried to blame the crew, but there was little if anything we could have done wrong. However, it was not the last we heard of the incident. Two days later, we were summoned into the Flight Manager's office and here they tried to trap me in order to get the Captain into trouble. I managed to bluff my way through the situation and nothing else was heard about the event, although I know that he was rebuked for not getting medical supervision for the passengers. Just after this, flight safety reports were introduced; this meant that the Captain had to report an incident, even if it could be used against him in a court case. Obviously, forcing someone to do something that could result in them effectively incriminating themselves or losing their job was always going to be difficult and some Captains had a clever ploy – the reports were on carbon copy paper, so they would write a report, destroy the top copy and keep the bottom copy. This way there was a good chance no one would learn about the incident, but if it came to light they could simply say, "I have a copy, you must have lost yours!"

At about this time, consideration was being given to the new large transatlantic jets and whether they should have two, three or four engines. They were seriously considering using twin-engine aircraft, which I thought was asking a great deal of them.

One of the parts of my navigation exam had been to work out the so-called 'critical point' of such a journey, also known as the 'point of no return'. When you pass this point, it means that you have to continue to your destination as it is quicker to go on than to go back. On this topic, a Captain was once heard talking to a young pilot who enquired how many engines he thought an aircraft should have. "Six," he replied, then hesitated for a short while. He then added, "On each side!"

As a twin-engine aircraft, the 111 was great – it had a reasonable range, although not fantastic, but I must say that I preferred flying the Viscount with its four engines.

Various aircraft manufacturers began to gather data on all of the three- or four-engine aircraft going across the Atlantic. There is one thing that has never been specifically disclosed to the public: and that is the way that this was gathered. It was fairly obvious to most pilots that someone had an axe to grind and was ensuring that it must be shown to be statistically acceptable to fly on two engines. In order to do this, pilots who reported an engine problem mid-flight were told not to shut it down (thus avoiding some reports), but merely to close the throttle. You would never normally have dreamt of doing this – the engine may be seriously damaged, so continuing to fly with it may result in it needing to be scrapped, or (even worse) the vibration caused by flying with a faulty engine could result in structural damage to the airframe itself. However, they got their statistics: this modification to the recording of engine problems showed that there were few, if any, engine problems on transatlantic flights and hardly any engine shutdowns. Speaking personally, having luckily avoided being in a Viking aeroplane on which both engines failed over Hamburg almost simultaneously for two unrelated reasons, I was sceptical then and remain so to this day.

I flew the 111 for about two years and thoroughly enjoyed it. It was a little like strapping on an aeroplane rather than flying in it – it felt rather like a sports car. It certainly had its quirks. One of which that did amuse me was that, when it was ordered, some bright spark had decided that, in order to save weight for the flight and make fuel use more economical, they wouldn't have automatic steps on the front door of the aircraft. However, if they had thought through the calculations correctly, they would have realised that omitting these admittedly quite heavy steps would make the entire aircraft out of balance. To counter the issue created by removing the steps, all our 111s then flew with a huge chunk of concrete in the gap where the steps should have been!

Trips on the 111s were not without incident. One 111 crew flew the Queen on a royal trip. When they arrived and started to offload Her Majesty's luggage, it all fell off the aeroplane and crashed embarrassingly open on the tarmac. They had visions of being put in the Tower of London!

Once, whilst standing at Manchester Airport, the refuelling bowser came steaming across the tarmac, the driver clearly not paying attention. It smashed straight into the trailing edge of the wing. This went into the bowser's cab and rather grimly severed the driver's head.

Skydrol is a fire-resistant aviation hydraulic fluid. It's important not to get it in your eyes as it could blind you. An engineer on my 111 got some Skydrol in his eyes – there were bags of first aid fluid on board which were used but I called up for an ambulance, only to discover that ambulances were no longer sent to aeroplanes. I was incensed at their refusal so I went ballistic on the radio, blocked the channel completely, and demanded that somebody be sent out. Eventually a medic arrived who washed the engineer's eyes out and he was then taken away – I hope they saved his vision.

I thoroughly enjoyed my 111 flying in Berlin; it made for some memorable times. On 9th November 1989, I was out having a drink with colleagues when there was a huge commotion out on the streets – it turned out that the Berlin Wall was coming down that very night. There was a tremendous frenzy; East Germans came ploughing through the Wall and rushing into the centre of West Berlin. Everybody was hugging, shouting and singing – it was simply amazing. They somehow managed to get lorry-loads of beer out into the street and everybody could drink as much as they wanted because it was free. East Berliners were given 160

Marks to spend – I noticed that many queued outside the sex shops to celebrate their freedom there.

Berlin was an island within itself. The legacy of poverty from the East/West divide lingered on for many years. Many of the German men had been killed in the war. On Sundays, some housewives often went to work in local strip clubs during the afternoon and also in the city squares where you could find a lot of them 'on the game'. It seemed to be an accepted custom for them to become prostitutes for the day. Of course, it must also be remembered that most women in Berlin were raped at the end of the Second World War when the frontline Russians came through. The mothers of a lot of the Berlin-born cabin crew had suffered this fate.[16]

One of my favourite ways to spend an afternoon off in Berlin was to go down by the bombed church at the end of the Kurfürstendamm and sit on a wall, eating ice cream and watching the world go by. You could eat virtually anything along that street – one of the best meals was Swinehack, basically a pork knuckle. There were many stalls dotted around Berlin where you could buy sausage, or 'wurst'. My particular favourite was the 'currywurst', a sausage with curry powder sold with a type of tomato sauce and potato salad – naturally followed by a beer. This was available at all times of day and night, or else you could go for the bean soup which was absolutely delicious.

If you really wanted to treat yourself, you could go to perhaps the most interesting shop I have ever visited. The Kaufhaus des Westens, usually abbreviated to 'KaDeWe', is a department store in Berlin. With over 60,000m^2 of selling space and more than 380,000 articles available, a huge store very similar to Harrods. The kitchen utensils were way ahead of ours, and the curtain material was just amazing – I specifically remember taking back huge rolls of beautifully patterned velvet. If I wanted to indulge myself, I would sit in the food section with something truly delicious enjoying it all with a glass of champagne.

My last BAC 111 flight was Manchester to London on G-AVMK from 1458-1533 for 35 minutes.

BAC 111

Berlin Tempelhof

Chapter Nine
Viscount Command in Glasgow

Iwas still a First Officer on BAC 111s, but at last I had my all-important command course interview. I spent several days brushing up on manuals before heading to the Queen's Building office at Heathrow. I then waited uncomfortably in the Crew Room until I was at last called to the Flight Manager's office (thirty years later, I discovered that he lived no more than 300 yards from me) and sat outside his door in trepidation, pretending to read an out-of-date safety magazine.

At last my turn came. I took my seat in his office, surprised to find only the Flight Manager present. He was studying a file on his desk in which he seemed absorbed. After what seemed eternity, he lifted his eyes up to me and asked the first question.

"Do you pay the voluntary contributions each month through the payroll to the pilots' retirement fund?"

This amounted to a mere 25p a week. I could only think that he must have been due to retire soon and thought that he would not get his engraved tankard or tie if they did not have my 25-pence worth.

"No," I replied hesitantly, realising as I spoke that this was not the required answer.

"Well, provided you sign here for the Pay Office, you have passed the pre-command interview. You will start on Viscounts." He stood up and I stood up; we shook hands and I left in a daze – 25p a week worse off, but with a skip in my step!

The first trip with a Training Captain was actually on my existing aircraft, a BAC 111, to get me ready for my command course on Viscounts. He smoked heavily, drank heavily and had projecting front teeth which we always said he had 'left out to dry'. The trip was to include a night stop in Hanover. We arrived in the transport at the usual hotel, which was of a fairly high standard. There was a large lake in front of the hotel which was built out of respect for Hitler, and at the far end was where all the German officers had met the Fräulein in order to produce babies for the Third Reich. I asked what time he would like to meet up in order to go out for a meal. His reply was, "When you have had a shower, come along to my room. We'll have a quick drink and chat."

I became quite nervous as I showered, assuming he would be testing me on all sorts of things to do with my command course. On arriving at his room, I found the door ajar. After knocking, I apprehensively entered. On the middle of the table, there was a very large bottle of whisky on it and two tumblers. I sat down and the Captain gave a toast to my success in the command. I really would rather not have had a drink just then, bearing in mind that I had not yet started the course properly, but I certainly did not want to alienate myself from a senior Training Captain, and there did not appear to be any way out. We proceeded to drink the whole bottle of whisky – irrespective of the fact that we had to be up at five o'clock in the morning and we had not yet gone out for a meal.

Having sunk the whole bottle, we took a taxi into town where I devoured a very tasty wiener schnitzel, along with a couple of steins of beer. I take after my father who could drink copious amounts without too much effect. I was pleased to find myself in a taxi after this, thinking it was definitely time to head back to the hotel. My Captain had other ideas: he asked for the nearest night club.

On arrival, we spilled out of the taxi and entered the club, passing the usual massive German bouncer. I said that I would order the first round of drinks, which went down very well with him. But at the bar I had a quiet word with the barman (who was obviously a transvestite), explaining my predicament. I said that I would be ordering gin and tonics and either my Captain or myself would be paying; what I wanted him/her to do was make sure that all I received in my glass was tonic water. Any extra money could go into his pocket as a tip.

I had made a friend – not that I wished to pursue the friendship. I think the reply in German was equivalent of "Thanks, Ducky". (Always remember you can get by in any part of the world if you say in their language 'My friend will pay'.)

The ruse worked well. It was late into the morning by the time we left (to be clear, the Captain and I, not the barmaid and I) and went back to the hotel. By then, I was recovering from the whisky and beers and was fortunately none the worse for my time in the night club. Several Alka-Seltzers seemed to do the trick and I was reasonably happy the next morning. When we started our flight, I ended up back in Berlin in the Crew Room. Someone who knew this Training Captain asked me how I was feeling, knowing that no one who flew with him ever felt very bright.

"Not too bad considering," was my reply. At this point, quite unexpectedly, the Training Captain became hopping mad with me and lectured me about not distorting the truth. He seemed to think that I was not being honest, perhaps because I felt better than he did.

We then took off to climb to altitude on our next flight and Air Traffic Control asked me one of their most irritating questions, wanting to know what height I would be by the time I reached the boundary of their control. There are so many variables on this – not least height, weight, air temperature and humidity – so I could do no more than make a guess. I made a stab at it and got it right, actually hitting the exact height, which I was pleased about since the Training Captain was with me. However, I have heard many pilots become quite annoyed with Air Traffic Control asking for information which cannot be given accurately.

I wouldn't want to give the impression however that there was friction with Air Traffic Control. Another charter outfit used to fly 111s, and quite often I used to hear them along the German airways using the term 'Chug-a-Lug' in their conversation. This mystified me a little; the term originates, I knew, from black-and-white cowboy films where a 'chug-a-lug' consists of a small wire cage on a pivot with dice in it – you spin the cage which twirls round and round; when it stops you then read the dice. It appears that some of these other crews had been to a huge party with the people from Air Traffic Control and they had played a game, using one of these incessantly. Between them, they had all agreed that, in future, they would identify that they had been to the party by using 'Chug-a-Lug' during radio conversation as a kind of code.

We started the next trip initially by going into flight planning to pick up our data and then on to Air Traffic Control to submit a flight plan. There were two other crews in the room, one of which was off to Greenland. One of their pilots asked the Air Traffic Officer where the box was to tick to show that they had life-jackets on board.

But the reply came from a German Captain of a crew next to them. "At this time of year, flying over the North Sea, you won't need life-jackets," he said gravely. It took a few minutes for the other skipper to understand the meaning of the comment. Crashing in the North Sea would give you a survival time of probably three to four minutes before you died of hypothermia.

This gloomy thought aside, it was quite pleasant to board the aircraft and find that the Training Captain had carried out the duties that I would normally do as a First Officer. I did the external flight checking for any snow ice or damage to the aircraft, and eventually sat back into the cockpit in the left-hand seat, which is where the Captains sit in all aircraft.

There were no problems in my supervision by the Training Captain, and a week later I received a letter containing my ground course date on the Viscount 800s. This had all happened after only eight years in the company, which was quite quick. I had left the Viscount as a First Officer two years previously for the BAC Super 111s and I couldn't help but feel that this should make the course easier as it was an aircraft I knew well.

The ground course was easy as it was little more than a re-tread on Viscounts; I did not even have to re-sit the technical exams. The whole experience was incredibly trouble-free.

Usually, as a Captain, you could nominate your preferred base on the grounds of your seniority (everything in flying is seniority-based), but on this occasion the only vacancy available was in Glasgow. Thus, straight after my London training course, I was posted there, where I would be until I was posted to Birmingham three months later.

I arrived in the Glasgow base for a look-see on 19th January 1973. Several crews were mixed together eating in the greasy spoon staff café under the main finger that led to the different stands. A well-turned-out Captain introduced himself to me and we chatted pleasantly about the base – he was one of those friendly men you take a liking to on first meeting. He then excused himself as he had been given an engineering test flight of a recently serviced Viscount 802, where the First Officer and himself would be joined by two engineers. They took off at 2.20 pm in G-AOHL and flew at Flight Level 40, or 3,850 feet for seven minutes before turning back to the field. But then they encountered a snowstorm and hit Ben More just 100 feet below the summit. No one survived. It was ironic as the Captain knew the area very well. He was sorely missed but he taught us, or me in particular, an early lesson: in Scotland, don't fly below 6,000 feet unless you really know where you are. The whole base was devastated.

Previously, in about 1971, I had applied to go and fly the Heron ambulance service aircraft out of Glasgow. This would have been quite a challenge, but would have given me an early command. The idea was that anyone who was sick or needed taking to hospital from the Highlands and Islands would be served by this de-Haviland Heron. I actually went on a look to see some of the islands, landing on several of the islands' sandy beaches. I was given an indication that I probably would have got the position, when the Flight Manager in Glasgow failed his check course in London. The only option he had was to take command on the Heron, so I lost the opportunity of command nearly a year earlier.

Later that day I boarded a Heron aircraft, which was an ambulance service that served mainly the islands in Scotland.

That day we went to Barra, a small island where one can only land on the beach – and only when the tide is out. The Heron had seen many hours of flying and it was kept airworthy through a constant battle by the engineers against salt-water corrosion. The police had all the Air Ambulance pilots' car numbers so that if they were seen driving at speed towards the airport, they would recognise that they'd been called to an urgent ambulance flight and either leave them alone or shepherd them along.

I was crewed up with a London Training Captain, and we went round most of the airfields on the Scottish islands on G-AOJF. The Training Captains were always looking to trip you up, so careful preparation was needed before each training flight, reading in advance and taking great care with everything you did. At one of the islands, we night-stopped and I spent a lot of time reading the small booklet that was in effect a guide to the airfield. I took particular note as to the taxi routes which led to the main runway; it clearly stated that if you went the wrong side of the Air Traffic Control building in a larger aircraft, you would not be able to get through. Next morning, we started to taxi towards the runway and the Training Captain pointed to the route behind the Air Traffic Control building and suggested that I took that particular route. Thank goodness I had read the book the night before or I would have been caught out as this route was too narrow for a Viscount.

My first flight in proper command on G-AOHG duly came and it could not have been more prosaic. The aircraft arrived late and the First Officer and I went from Glasgow to Belfast and back. It was not the most romantic of trips, but it was very satisfying.

This was followed the next day by Glasgow to Islay to Campbeltown to Glasgow, again on G-AOHG. The first leg was straightforward, but when the ATC clearance came through, I was instructed to set my course and 'reserve FL 50' (5,000 feet). I had never heard it said this way and had no idea what 'Reserve FL 50' might mean. The old, hairy-arsed First Officer had to explain to the newboy Captain that we would fly at 500 feet direct to Islay, but if the weather came down and we could not see, then ATC was keeping 5,000 feet clear for us – hence FL 50 was 'reserved' for us. As he pointed out, the local Radio Aids were not up to the standard for us to carry out a let-down. Many lower limits for let-downs were about 1,000 feet. We could see underneath at 500 feet, but if we went up into the cloud, we could not get back down legally to 500 or less to land.

Flying around these Highlands and Islands is a different world to flying normal scheduled flights to major airports. Not only was it dangerous below 6,000 feet due to a lot of oil company aircraft being around, not to mention mountains, but if you flew to somewhere like Shetland and you climbed up above 5,000 feet to take your rightful place on the airway, the weather was often so bad and the navigation aids so useless that you frequently couldn't get down low enough to actually land at the destination airport. The 'decision height' in Shetland at the time was something like 1,000 feet, but the cloud was often so low that when you reached 1,000 feet, it often meant that there was no way you'd see the runway. On numerous flights, you would have to divert and go back to where you came from.

Because of this, all the old local pilots, as I was encouraged to do, used to take off and fly at 200 feet above the waves, just missing some of the oil rigs and taking the chance of hitting seagulls whilst requesting Air Traffic Control to keep you clear up to 5,000 feet so that, if it became so foggy or so cloudy you couldn't see anything, you could climb up to 5,000 feet to continue the flight. Going up to 5,000 feet was usually pretty useless as you still wouldn't get into the airfield, but flying low was exhilarating – the waves seemed incredibly close at 100 to 300 feet and the passengers loved being taken for flights round places like the Old Man of Hoy where we gave them wonderful views of the rugged cliffs and beautiful sandbanks and sandbars and remote beaches that virtually no one ever went to. We operated on the Highlands and Islands like this every day.

Next, we flew to Shetland, noting that Wick did not have any fuel so we had to have enough to divert back to Inverness plus 45 minutes, if needed. On this occasion, the airport came into view and the weather required us to land towards the north. This runway was very short and required a reasonable headwind to use it at all; there is a lighthouse on the final approach at about three miles, so you have to aim at the lighthouse and turn on to finals, just missing it – it always feels as if your wheels are going to touch it. At the last minute, you swing the aircraft onto the centre line with a boot-full of rudder, pull the power off and you are down. There is no finesse – it's too short to play around. The passengers took this very abrupt landing in their stride, presumably being used to it, and I was simply relieved to be down. We taxied in and they disembarked. My father, who was stationed there during WWII, had described this to me – it was the one where the Polish Spitfire pilots, after tanking up in the bar, used to see which of them could take off and return to land the furthest down the runway. Some killed themselves.

We loaded up and were away, climbing over Fitful Head. It was here that my father, who had been collecting gulls' eggs from the cliff face, heard three bombers coming back from an attempted bombing of the *Tirpitz* (which was prevented by bad weather) circling overhead. Two of them crashed into the sea and one of them, Halifax R9438, crashed nearby into the cliffs – Fitful Head rises to 283 metres and is almost a sheer cliff by the sea. A memorial to the seven dead crew still stands nearby. I well remember my father saying that the ghosts of the dead radio operators were heard making calls for a year. He and the locals were utterly convinced that their voices were frequently heard on the airways. Should you wish to read the details of this crash and see pictures of the memorials, they are in the appendices.

We set course for home via Wick, confident we had sufficient fuel for any eventuality, though everything went very smoothly. Two weeks later, a Captain forgot that there was no fuel in Wick and diverted there. He was stuck for most of the day while a fuel bowser was sent from another airfield. He had to buy a round of drinks in the bar later.

The weather in the area was often bad. One Captain came back to Glasgow after a three-week holiday. He was running late and the

First Officer was on board with everything ready up to the engine start. The passengers were all publicans on a convention. He set course and was nearing Shetland when he called for a weather update, which was on limits. It was a strange phenomenon, but the weather could be very bad until you got near the airfield when you would hear that it was just on your limits and you would be able to land (with the help of Air Traffic Control as they knew the limits for us). The Captain spoke to the passengers on the cabin address in his Australian accent (though he was not actually Australian), and he kept it simple and to the point: "The weather is f...king awful!" Being publicans, they all appreciated his straightforwardness. He popped out of the cloud very low indeed and landed. The ground staff rushed over and congratulated him, which puzzled him at first but it turned out he was the first aircraft to land there for ten days as the weather had been so vile.

Since he was staying at the publicans' hotel, he joined them in the bar. They were only staying one night and were pleased to have arrived. The next morning, the weather was still awful and he thought he would be stranded there – you needed very good visibility for take-off due to the proximity of the hills. With the greatest good luck and the help of the Air Traffic Controller, visibility mysteriously went up just as he was ready for take-off. He flew back to Glasgow; again, it was several days before anyone could get back there.

The runways were short in this area and the let-down aids very limited, so landings were rather hit-and-miss. On one occasion, I flew into Orkney with Jo Grimond on board and a weather depression arrived over the airfield at exactly the same moment as us. The visibility was very good but the wind was very strong and kept changing direction. We had to fly round and round as the wind changed, working out landing weights for each of the four landing directions. Each time we lined up on one, the wind would change. Once again, the passengers were wonderful. Eventually, it all came together and we landed.

The local pilots who knew the area well had garnered all kinds of useful knowledge which helped them. When landing over Scapa

Flow,[17] there is a hill between the water and the threshold of the runway. In perfect weather, you can land visually with a steep approach, keeping the runway in sight all the way down to touchdown, but often the cloud is just above the hill. A pilot with local knowledge can fly below cloud at 300 or 400 feet, aiming at the flag that marks the wreck of the *Royal Oak* – this was sunk in 1939 by a German submarine with the loss of 834 lives (by coincidence, I know the granddaughter of the main assistant to Konteradmiral Doenitz who ordered the strike – I previously mentioned Rheims airport and Admiral Doenitz went to this airport, which was the headquarters of General Eisenhower, and signed a document for the surrender of all the German forces). Immediately over Scapa Flow, you pull up, close the throttles and push the stick forward and fly down the hill, and there is the runway straight ahead of you. Obviously, it would not be an intelligent manœuvre to try without that specific knowledge.

On take-off, we regularly took the passengers a little out of our way to show them the Old Man of Hoy. The local passengers on board would realise that, yet again, they had a brand-new Captain going sightseeing but blaming the passengers instead!

At that time, the IRA were very active in Ireland, which often affected our trips to Belfast and kept us on edge. On one occasion, after arrival, we were loading up for the return journey as usual and the Dispatcher emerged with the balance sheet for me to check and sign. As he handed it to me, there was an eruption of intense gunfire which continued with no sign of abating. My First Officer asked what it was, while trying to sound unconcerned. The reply, delivered in a dry Irish accent: "We're just getting rid of the over-bookings." He didn't know which way to look. It was actually the army on target practice.

A rather pompous Captain, not from our company, took it upon himself to test the security on the airfield. Having walked all the way round the inside of the perimeter barbed wire, he came back and demanded to see the Station Manager. He complained that nobody had challenged him at any time on his entire walk. The Station Manager, unimpressed, produced various clear photographs of him, all taken at different points round the airport. He explained that it was pretty obvious who he was, so they hadn't bothered him! Security was, understandably, a very high priority.

We were grateful for the high security as Belfast was another regular night stop for us. We often spent a standby at the airport in the Crew Room playing snooker, which was all very pleasant until one day the IRA sent over a load of mortars which messed up the table. The violence did feel close to home at times; we quite regularly stayed in a good hotel about fifteen miles outside Belfast. This experienced a bombing in which the bathrooms in rooms used by the crews were blown apart.

I thoroughly enjoyed my time being based in Glasgow. The flying and the crews were fantastic and I was genuinely sorry to move on. That said, the years in Birmingham were more fun still and were to eclipse them.

Near the end of my Glasgow posting, the Captain left the hotel to walk into town for a curry. On the way, some 'ladies of the night' offered their services but he politely declined. A couple of hours later, he walked back past them and they recognised him, beating seven bells out of him for not using the services.

Just after the last day of my son being at school, I took him to Glasgow as a treat. We stayed in the hotel and went down to the local gambling club where we played roulette for several hours and met several of the other pilots. I kept a note of what numbers came up each time and played with my son accordingly – we didn't win very much, but just as we were about to leave, one of the other Captains turned round and asked me to suggest a number. He had a single chip and didn't want to take it away with him, so I told him red 36, which he placed his token on, and it won. An Arab was standing next to the other Captain and picked up the Captains winnings, he was fuming – evidently, this Captain was one who could lose his temper and take a room apart, so I was getting rather worried. We called the croupier across and had a private word, explaining that we were aircrew and that there was no way we would cheat – rather, that other player was cheating. We told them to play the tapes back to see it was not us cheating. A short while passed before someone came down and said, "Look, this is embarrassing, the Arab loses loads of money here and we can't afford to upset him," so they gave us our 35 tokens back.

My son and I then went to leave and asked the receptionist to book us a taxi back to the hotel because it was a bit dangerous in Glasgow at that time of night – about two o'clock in the morning. However, we waited for nearly an hour and the taxi did not bother turning up for such a short trip (so make sure in future if you ever do things like that to tell the taxi you want to take a trip to the airport or somewhere a long way away, and then they will come and get you). As they didn't arrive, we had to start walking. As we stepped out of the casino, there was a rather nasty shady character standing just under a light – it was blatantly obvious that he was going to mug us. We were trying to work out what the best thing to do was when all of a sudden – thanks to the good Lord – a coachful of Chinese gamblers suddenly pulled up and all swirled round the coach. While this guy was trying to find his way through them, we did a runner back to the hotel. Previously, one of the pilots had actually won a Scottish £100 note and had been mugged on the way out, so it certainly was likely to have happened to us.

Chapter Ten
VISCOUNT COMMAND IN BIRMINGHAM

A t last my promised posting to the newly opened base in Birmingham came through. I took my fond farewell of Glasgow on 1st April 1974 and drove down to the local Redwing Hotel given me as accommodation for a very short period, until I could work out where I was going to stay. That evening, a special party had been arranged by the cabin crew to welcome all the new pilots to the Birmingham base. By this time, the cabin crew had actually been operating out of Birmingham for about a year.

The party was great and I could straightaway see that I was going to enjoy myself there. There was lots of free booze and fantastic entertainment put on by the cabin crew in the way of a show. They wore huge hats which came down to just above their navels, where they had eyes and faces painted. Great fun was had by all and it looked as if this was going to be the ideal posting for the future.

To my great surprise, at about 10.30 pm, the Flight Manager went round officiously asking everybody what time they were on duty in the morning. Those who were on an early shift were told to go home immediately. This was a complete damp squib for the party and revealed to me from then on his abysmal attitude to the crew. It really was counter-productive as morale suffered considerably.

The next morning, we were due to take off at 0720 on G-AOJD. I went into the airport toilets and found a drunk in there; I hoped he would not be on my flight as drunks get worse, not better, on an aircraft as the lack of oxygen allows the alcohol to get a better hold – especially if the cabin staff decide to give them more drink in order to make them sleep. Sometimes this works, but more often than not it backfires. I went to the Crew Room, carried out the pre-flight planning and passed the required fuel figure to the Traffic Officer, mentioning the drunk to him and expressing my hope he would not be on my flight.

It never ceases to amaze me how passengers will drink heavily before a flight. How they expect to get out of the aeroplane in an emergency when drunk, I have no idea. The problem is they will expect the cabin crew to risk their lives to help them. Drunkenness on board aircraft is a hazard in so many ways.

Naturally, the drunk *was* on my aircraft. I talked it over with the cabin crew but they said he was seated and was no trouble. We took off and he remained quiet. To my relief, we landed at Belfast without incident. The passengers started to get off and it was at this moment that a stewardess crashed through the door saying the drunk was threatening to hit her. I told her to stay in the cockpit with us and keep the door shut. I called security, put my jacket and hat on and went into the cabin, shutting the door firmly behind me. He was now the only one on board and he came staggering towards me. The doors at my end of the aircraft were closed; the rear port door was his only way out.

I asked if I could help and, as so often happens, he saw the uniform and snapped to.

"I only want to give the girl a tip," he muttered sulkily.

Having successfully managed to calm him down and convince him to leave the aeroplane, he was still a little unsure where the stewardess had gone. I don't think he believed me when I said that I had told her to lock herself in the cockpit and leave through a cockpit door. Of course, there was no door in the cockpit – the only way out of the cockpit is to drop a rope out of the rather small window and climb out.

However, at that exact moment, the silly moo opened the door and stood there, gloating. Her action in coming out of the cockpit and more or less laughing at the guy put me into some danger, but luckily he didn't turn round and attack me. This was at a time of high alert with the IRA and there was no way of knowing whether he was involved with the local problems or not. I put it to the girl that if I pressed charges for her, she and I would have to spend time in Belfast for the court case, and as we didn't know anything about the background of the person concerned, did she think it wise to continue? After some thought, she decided that two extra nights in the centre of Belfast being witness against some drunk on an aeroplane whom she knew little or nothing about, was probably not in her best interests. She had just missed the whole point and had no idea about the possible repercussions. He started to push by me but thought better of it. The next thing he was aware of was a shadow over him. He turned and looked into the navel of the biggest police officer I have ever seen. The police officer picked him up and, with his feet lifted clean off the ground, carried him off the aircraft.

The officer arrived back as I was telling the girl in no uncertain terms what I thought of her actions.

"What would you like us to do with him?" the officer asked.

I turned to the girl and asked if she would like to prefer charges against a possible IRA member. She went very quiet.

I turned and looked up at the officer. "Could you put the fear of God up him?"

His face beamed. "Captain, it would be my pleasure, Sir."

That was the last I heard of the incident.

A week later, in Glasgow, fortunately not on my aircraft, two drunks staggered from the main building down towards the aircraft on the stand. They made their way unsteadily towards the aircraft which had both of the engines running. The first walked straight through the propeller and literally cut himself off at waist height. The second put his arm out to try and save his friend and put it straight through the propeller, losing the whole arm. The ground was covered in blood, and the sky became dark as the seagulls swooped in by the hundred, screeching and fighting to clear the tarmac of any bits and pieces. Within seconds, the stand was virtually clear, except for the trunk and a writhing passenger.

One occasion where alcohol helped us was when I took the Leeds football team with Don Revie to the semi-finals of the

European cup in Liège. My crew and I were guests of honour at the match which unfortunately Leeds lost. I took the opportunity to ask Don Revie how million-pound players could be ten feet in front of goal and still manage to miss. He told me that there are only ten players in the world who could actually get the ball in the net every time. I do not know who the ten were, but they weren't playing for Leeds that night. I asked him (although I don't think he was amused) what would happen if I failed to hit the runway every time on landing. I think he got my point!

The point at which the alcohol helped us was on the (somewhat sombre) return journey. When we got out to the Viscount first thing in the morning, we found it smothered in snow. We were at a military airfield where they had no de-icing facilities, or at least none they were going to supply us with. So I raided the well-stocked bar and seized the strongest alcohol I could find. The footballers volunteered to go out onto the wing with a couple of brooms and the alcohol and they very effectively de-iced the wings for us. I dread to think what would have happened if one of the players had fallen off, but their sense of balance on the wing was better than on the pitch and we were able to fly home.

We often night-stopped in Inverness. Standard procedure after arriving at about ten o'clock in the morning, having got up at some awful hour, was to have a quick sleep and arrive down at the bar at about one o'clock. The customary order was three pints of beer each with whisky chasers, and with it the most fantastic bowl of soup that I have ever had – I can thoroughly recommend that you attempt to make it yourself on a really cold winter's day.

It could not be simpler: one takes a large tin of mulligatawny soup, a large quantity of prawns (which may at first seem strange because mulligatawny is beef-based), a large portion of whisky, and some cream. The whole lot is heated through and served piping hot. This incredible soup we usually digested looking through the window at the really miserable weather that always seems to dog Inverness Airport.

Another thing for which Inverness was notable, and in which alcohol no doubt also played a role, was cat-fights – not the type you might initially think. Whenever we went to the toilets in the back of any pub, there would be women fighting and tearing each other to pieces over boyfriends. It wasn't unusual to find large clumps of hair splattered about on the pavement the next morning. The police seemed to ignore it completely.

We certainly had fun in Inverness. Our favourite game in the bar was to take all the tables and stack them on top of each other, creating a frame on which we clambered to the very top. Once there, the aim was to lie on your back and put footprints on the ceiling. Naturally, this happened in the early hours of the morning when there was nobody about to witness it. The tables were then carefully placed back in position.

Another joy of Inverness was the large hangar devoted entirely to seafood (sadly, no longer in existence). On the way from the hotel to the airport, we used to call in, this being usually very early in the morning, which gave us the opportunity to buy huge bags of Scots prawns, salmon and baby kippers. One amazing sight was when a truck arrived with thousands of prawns on board which were then poured into a machine. The prawns emerged from the other end, after a lot of whirling and grinding, minus their shells and neatly frozen and bagged. We could never fathom out how it worked.

The problems with the Flight Manager in Birmingham did not, unfortunately, stop with his over-zealous approach to partying – to which, obviously, he was never invited. On a flight out of Belfast one day, a considerable number of unidentified bags were left. As a security check, all the bags were laid out in a line at the bottom of the aircraft steps and the passengers, as they passed them, had to point out theirs. Finally, there were five bags left, so I asked for it all to be done again before we left. The passengers were disembarked and asked again to identify their bags, with greater care. This time they were all identified so, rather late, we flew back to Birmingham. On arrival, I was called to the Flight Manager's office and reprimanded most severely for delaying the flight. I should, I was forcibly told, have just left the bags behind.

Well, fair enough, I thought to myself. One has to live and learn, and although the reprimand was needlessly heavy-handed, I was happy enough to comply with the policy. About a week later, a letter appeared from the Chief Security Officer (no less) saying in black and white that 'it is our policy not to do the second check'.

Less than a week later, back in Belfast, a similar thing happened. This time, there were even more unclaimed bags on the tarmac. And then somebody rushed across the tarmac, grabbed one of the bags and disappeared into the building. You must understand that this was the height of the IRA troubles, so someone running off with one of the bags seemed highly suspicious. Anyway, I told the Duty Manager just to leave the other bags behind. The result: he exploded and said that this should not be done as it was normal procedure to have a second check.

I still had the letter from the Chief Security Officer (no less), saying exactly the opposite, so I produced it for him, and with no further checks, flew back to Birmingham, leaving the bags behind. Obviously, it was frustrating for the passengers but that would have to be that; it would equally be frustrating to be late.

On arrival at Birmingham, I immediately received a summons to the office of the Flight Manager. On arriving there, with a sense of déjà vu, I was then given a severe rollicking for leaving the bags behind and told that this was a serious error as it cost £100 each in order to get them to their destination. I asked him about our previous conversation on this matter (less than a week ago) – he utterly laughably denied that he had said this. I then produced the letter from the Chief Security Officer as final and undisputable proof that I had followed the correct procedure. He went berserk and refused point blank to admit he was wrong.

Why was this man like this? I'm sure I cannot say. The Birmingham base was split into two fleets, BAC 111s and Viscounts. I was in command on Viscounts, and as far as he was concerned, we were the troublemakers to whom he was determined to give a hard time. The opposite was clearly the case for the BAC 111 pilots – the sun shone out of the proverbial place for them and, in his eyes, they could do no wrong. He frequently changed his mind and had no idea what he had said the last time he gave any of us a dressing down. I don't think he was particularly intelligent, but I don't think stupidity was the issue. If anything, he simply enjoyed destroying people's confidence where he could and had taken an exception to our fleet for an unknown reason. Some people are simply like this and there is no rational explanation for their behaviour. Needless to say, I had no respect for him whatsoever. He constantly criticised new Captains, never supported them and was constantly changing his mind without remembering that he had done so.

Lost bags cost companies in the region of £100 each to deliver to the owner's homes. One base suffered a problem whereby the Duty Manager and his wife used to delay in delivering bags for, say, a week and then deliver them in one hit, but in the meantime claim for several trips. Eventually, they were found out. They used to offer some pilots on a night stop use of a free car if they would deliver some of the bags, giving them yet another saving for themselves.

One of my friends had flown out of Glasgow, and during the flight, a stewardess came to him, saying that one passenger who seemed drunk was swearing at her and insulting her and, astonishingly, actually threatening to hit her. The Captain went back to the passenger and told him in no uncertain terms that this should cease immediately – which it did. The passenger then wrote in and complained, saying he had been threatened. This resulted in the Captain being called to the office of that same Flight Manager who lambasted him for his actions, telling him how he had acted was 'insane' and totally out of court in what he had done. His defence, that he had been protecting his crew, cut no ice at all. He was told that he was grounded with immediate effect and was to report to him on a fortnightly basis, which was an outrageous response. My friend went to see him on more than one occasion again but could get nowhere.

Eventually, in sheer anger, he left his office and sat outside writing notes. The Flight Manager emerged and, seeing him there, asked him what he was doing.

"I'm writing notes," he replied.

"Notes about what?"

"Notes about what happened in your office. I'm writing down absolutely everything that you said to me."

Alarm spread across the Flight Manager's face; he realised that this could be used for evidence in some form of case or industrial tribunal at a later date. He returned a few minutes later. "I've thought it over. You can go back online."

Sometimes he was chastising us with good grounds, of course. On one occasion, one of the pilots had to get to the Channel Islands where he was on a cert with a stewardess, but there were no seats available. Rather stupidly, he asked the skipper (Willy – mentioned earlier at my interview) if he could sit on the toilet for the flight – which was only short – who, also stupidly, agreed. Really, he should just have stood in the cockpit so that passengers could use the toilet. Perhaps unsurprisingly, one of the miserable female ground staff reported them both to the Flight Manager and they got a really serious dressing down, nearly losing their commands.

The Flight Manager certainly did everything he could to make life difficult for us. He used another favourite tactic of those in power – that is, the 'divide and conquer' rule. He was constantly trying to get people to shop others to him so that he could tell them off. I once had the dreadful situation of the Assistant Flight Manager, who was cut from the same cloth, calling me into his office and stating that he had been at the local pub when one of the other pilots had said that I had been badmouthing the Flight Manager. Luckily, I was on the ball at the time and I quickly thought how best to respond to this bullying behaviour.

"That's fantastic!" I said to him in reply. "Now at last we know who's been passing all these rumours round. You name the person to me and I will go straight to my solicitor. I've really had enough of all this, I will take him to court. You can be the main witness against the guy and we can finally stop all this happening!"

His face dropped; this was not what he was expecting. He thought he had got me into trouble. He was totally lost for words and blinked and swallowed. I repeated it enthusiastically and with a show of great sincerity.

"So," he said after a while, "you would agree that there's nothing wrong with the Flight Manager and people shouldn't criticise him?"

"Naturally," I said, nodding.

At this point, the whole conversation was dropped. It was like living in a Nazi state that was watching what was said and to whom it was said.

We continued to have a very good time in Birmingham despite the Flight Manager and his cronies. One night in the company club during another riotous drinking session, at about ten o'clock the police arrived with the Chief Inspector. We all looked around guiltily, thinking that we'd been doing something wrong – but as it turned out, that was very much not the case. The officers explained to us quietly that it was the Chief Inspector's birthday and that he wanted us to keep the bar open!

We said that that would be highly dangerous as we would need an extension of the licence.

He and several other officers wrote on a beer mat that we were allowed an extension for this particular night and signed it. The drinking continued and a great night was had by all. It was about three o'clock in the morning that the Chief Inspector said that he was feeling hungry; the other officers agreed, so one of them was told to get hold of one of their contacts in town who ran a curry house and he rang him straightaway.

The owner, woken by the phone, answered, no doubt wondering who on earth was calling at such an hour. He was told that he needed to get out of bed and organise a meal for twenty for a birthday celebration. We then had a police escort down to a top Birmingham curry restaurant where we enjoyed a fantastic meal. He must have been a good contact; as far as I could see, it was all on the house.

Since I needed digs in Birmingham, I got together with two other pilots and the three of us rented an old Victorian-style house in which we bounced around very contentedly. The garden backed onto a large reservoir, the top-up lake for the local canal system. People fished there and you would often find huge pike thrown in the bushes. During a dreadful drought, the water level dropped considerably and one morning we saw the police very busy at the water's edge. It turned out they had been called when a saloon car had been seen looming out of the water; when it was dragged to the side, they found a body cemented into the car – a murder from a gangland hit. Despite the passage of years, a lot of his clothes were still intact in the mud and I can remember identifying with them in terms of era and style; I could reasonably have dated the time of the killing!

The water was still low when we hired a barge for a canal party. The bar was at the back of the boat, and when all the pilots congregated round it as normal, then the boat would cease to chug along and come to a halt, its propellers stuck in the mud. We were then moved forwards and encouraged to spread the weight evenly, but ten minutes later we were all back in the same place and it would happen again! We ended up that night playing 'boat race': a race begins with all competitors placing their drinks on a shared table. When a referee begins the race, the first drinker on each team is allowed to pick up their drink and start drinking. Once a beverage is consumed, the drinker must invert the empty vessel on their head. This is done to ensure no cheating occurs. The next team-mate cannot touch his or her drink until this has occurred. Empty vessels must be kept on the competitors' heads until the race is over. It was great fun; naturally, this was another party to which the Flight Manager was not invited.

I seriously considered building myself a barge by buying a metal hull (these were very easy to come by at the time) and constructing my own, but this came to nothing. I changed digs to a more modern house with different friends. We got on extremely well. One, a smiling, balding pilot called Eric who always seemed to have women throwing themselves at him, was friends with Engelbert Humperdinck and Tom Jones, amongst others. He would regale us with stories of his times with them which included going through a celebrity's wine cellar and the wine racks to choose a £500 bottle of red to drink with a vindaloo curry. He was always off with the rich and famous though couldn't manage to keep up with their spending power. He did, however, have an astonishing wardrobe crammed with thousands of shirts and pairs of trousers. Jeff, our third resident, used to sit on his bed and stare in amazement at Eric's fantastic array of clothes.

Jeff got rather irritated with Eric for being slow paying his rent; on one occasion, when he had disappeared upstairs with a rather beautiful lady, Jeff, in his annoyance, crashed into his bedroom to lecture him about his rent arrears – which did not go down very well as Eric was comfortably curled under the bedclothes while the girl lay there listening!

We lived quite riotously in that house: Jeff once impressed me by consuming a whisky upside-down with his head in a fireplace before taking off his four Captain's epaulettes and putting them down the front of the dress of a buxom young lady Eric had brought home with him – before, a minute later, retrieving them. Jeff had his own girlfriend, a tall American blonde. I remember walking into the cockpit on one occasion and finding her in with him; he was playing a game with her, seeing how far she could get the lipstick marks on a banana. I was, I admit, rather impressed. He then slapped her hard on the back and she spat banana all over the instrument panel.

One night, Jeff was at a pub near the Excelsior Hotel for an evening with two stewardesses, a Queen Bee and a younger girl. They downed many pints of beer, and went to the hotel bar for one last drink. It was there at the bar, all sitting on bar stools, that the younger stewardess was violently sick. Her beer-laden vomit ran the entire length of the bar. All the businessmen, in finest English fashion, politely ignored it and pretended it hadn't happened while it slowly dripped off the far end into an ice bucket.

Eric had driven down one night to meet his girlfriend in the Skyways Hotel – he was married, so was keeping things secretive. He had a great time there that night but awoke to find that someone had stolen his car. This was of course reported to the police and he spent several months trying to keep it from his wife. A similar thing happened to anther pilot who had the wheels pinched from his Ford Capri 3000 whilst visiting somewhere he shouldn't have been. Another pilot was one day cleaning his car when he found what he thought were an incriminating pair of knickers in the boot. He quickly disposed of them, congratulating himself for having found the evidence in time. A week later, his wife asked if he had found them – they were her spares! It is not beyond some stewardesses to leave their knickers under the bed as incriminating evidence, or to pour perfume over a jacket for a laugh.

With the possibility of staying there permanently in Birmingham, I looked at quite a few properties and went to view a house at Henley-in-Arden. This was an old farmhouse dating back three or four hundred years; the floorboards up in the top floor must have been two feet across and fifteen long, and there was a fireplace that was simply magnificent. Looking out of the kitchen window, one could see the part of the farm where all the cows were put before they were presumably taken away to be milked, and there was a superbly beautiful barn at the other side of it which would have been perfect as an artist's studio. They wanted £35,000 for the property so we went to make an offer, only be told that the area with the cows, which was literally touching the side of the house, was not included. We said we were prepared to offer £30,000 if they included it but they refused. This put the kibosh on the purchase; we decided that it wasn't worth the risk and backed out.

About five months later, my wife and I were walking through Henley-in-Arden when we noticed a sign indicating a property auction actually in progress. Out of curiosity, we went in to watch. The first item to come up was a stately old house; the bidding began but nobody put their hand up. The auctioneer tried and tried but the only bid that he got was for about £8,000. There was nothing more, so after a while the immortal phrase, "Going, going, gone!" was said and he brought the hammer down. There was a squeal from the back of the room.

"You just sold my £50,000 house for £8,000!" Someone was in agony.

The auctioneer replied that since the vendor had not put a reserve on it, this was how it had to work. The poor chap was nearly in tears and left the room.

The next property was, by quite a coincidence, the old house that we had looked at – now including the area with the cows. We had now lost interest in living in Birmingham as I was looking at moving on to Tridents and going back to London so it wasn't of interest to us any more, but to my surprise, the bidding started slowly at £10,000 and the hammer fell at only £13,000. The vendors had seriously lost out.

One aspect of captaincy that did not sit particularly well with me was having to write reports on people. It turned out that the path to further promotion lay at least in part through writing negative reports on one's colleagues. I discovered this in Birmingham on one boringly dull, drizzly Sunday when I was either on standby or sitting around in the Crew Room with nothing to do and no one to talk to. It suddenly occurred to me that someone had said in passing that the key to the filing cabinets in the Flight Manager's outer office where all pilots' records were kept was in a certain drawer in the secretaries' office, at the back and on the left.

I strolled innocently around the different offices, as if looking for company, and there was no one to be seen – so I took the chance. I went into the Flight Manager's PA's office and opened the drawer that had been described. To my surprise, at the back and on the left, there was indeed a filing cabinet key. I went to the filing cabinet, unlocked it, went through it, pulled out my file and disappeared quietly off to the toilet where I could carefully look through it.

I must admit, it wasn't actually too bad – but there were two items in it written by Training Captains which had been written before they became Training Captains. It was rather obvious they'd used me in order to enhance themselves and promote their chances of promotion by making it look as though they were advising me on all sorts of aspects of flight. I was absolutely amazed; I thought the two guys were very pleasant but they certainly had been two-faced to write such things without telling me. Technically, they were not allowed to write reports without showing them to me – obviously, they hadn't had the guts to do this. Anyway, I needed something to wipe my backside with; a short while later, the two reports, having been torn up into small pieces and used to serve my immediate need, were flushed away and I was sat feeling happy with myself.

I have only once written a bad report about a co-pilot, which was, I felt, richly deserved. We had a couple of retired RAF Squadron Leaders; I used to say to them (and indeed any First Officer) at the beginning of a flight that I didn't want them trying to be high or fast, or to try to prove to me that they were fantastic pilots as I knew they were better than I was anyway. One of them, however, was so high and so fast on landing that we only just made it back into the airport in one piece, scraping in on the runway by the skin of our teeth. We were due to go straight on to Glasgow and I was fuming, so I told him in no uncertain terms that he had been out of order; he should have gone around for a second attempt. "I'm going into the building and I'm going to come back in ten minutes' time," I told him. "I want you to think this over as I think you owe me an apology."

In the event, he came up with every excuse in the book as to why the landing hadn't been his fault, refusing point blank to accept any criticism. I was so annoyed that I put in a report saying that he had shown no interest in listening to any feedback and that the flight had not gone well. It was not complimentary. The Flight Manager's reaction was rather interesting.

"I got your report," he told me later. "It's fantastic – this is just what we want. You write me a couple more like this, and you'll be a Training Captain in no time."

I never ever wrote a nasty report about anyone again!

Later in my career, I was approached by a pilot who was recognised as probably the worst pilot in the whole company. When we got into the aircraft and did the checks, he turned to me very openly and asked me if I would put in a report on him at the end of the flight. "I am coming up to my command," he said, "and I am having a great deal of difficulty in getting them to accept me."

My reply was simple and straightforward: "I will write you a fair and honest report."

In the flights we did that day, he didn't put a foot wrong; he was first class the whole time and I had not a single problem with him. In consequence, I gave him a glowing report and put it in the voyage report box.

Two days later, I was summoned to the Flight Manager's office yet again.

"What the hell do you think you're doing?" he said. "How can you write a good report about this bloke? He is no good whatsoever and you have put us in a very difficult position as to whether or not he should have a command. What have you got to say about that?"

When I'm trapped in a corner like this, I actually quite enjoy it and often come up with the right answer.

"So," I said assertively, "what you're saying to me – and let me get this straight – is that this guy is highly dangerous and you don't think he's fit to be a Captain, and yet you have not seen fit to warn me? So, you have happily put me in danger and you've also endangered my passengers – is that the way I should read this?"

He nearly choked and did not know what to say. Finally, he simply said, "Will you withdraw the report?"

"No!" I said, annoyed. "He was perfect on the day; he never put a foot wrong and the report says it exactly as it was. He deserved it. And if you wish to push it further, I will happily fly with him again and report accurately on him." I never heard any more about it but some time afterwards, for better or worse, he got his command. Certainly, from what I saw on that day with me, he deserved it.

On the subject of reports, if you are on staff travel as a passenger, it was well known that if you were ever thinking of writing a less than complimentary report about the cabin crew on an aeroplane, you would potentially get yourself into hot water. If they have any inkling at all that you will be writing to complain to the company about them personally, you have two problems. The first is that the name tag that they have on their uniform is probably one that belongs to their friend, as they swap them around constantly, so you may well be getting the wrong person which will make you look incompetent. The other is that they will write a nasty report about *you* as a passenger when you have been on a flight somewhere, not as crew, describing you as drunk and abusive. You may have been docile and not said a word all flight, but that doesn't matter – they will get their story in first; when your letter arrives, they will turn round and say, "I told you so." Discretion is almost always the better part of valour here.

I had many happy times in Birmingham – some of the happiest of my career. I was then posted to Tridents in London.

One of the famous reports on a co-pilot was as follows: "He sets himself an abysmally low standard and constantly fails to achieve it."

Viscount

Viscount Cockpit

Chapter Eleven
THE 'ABBEVILLE HARD'
AND RELATED MATTERS

There were many occasions which I remember during my career as standing out for their sheer human comedy. One of the joys of aviation is that you are always dealing with people, and people never fail to surprise and entertain you.

On one occasion, we were three hours into a flight, navigating from beacon to beacon, and approaching the Abbeville VOR (Vhf Omni-directional Range) beacon on frequency 118.45 (designated on the chart as ABB, beating out constant Morse Code ·- ···· ···· dot dash dash dot dot dot dash dot dot dot). It was dawn and the sky was lightening in the east. As I listened to the steady Morse of the signal, my eyelids got heavier and heavier and conversation between the co-pilot and I stalled. Our minds began to wander onto other things. Occasionally, the steady drone of the engines was disturbed by radio calls from other aircraft. To old, experienced pilots, Abbeville has significance during the night and particularly first thing in the morning – it is well known as the 'Abbeville Hard'. Without dwelling on it, certain parts of the male anatomy tend to rise on early morning occasions after flying all night, particularly on long flights.

The door to the cockpit crashed open and one of our well-known 'queen bees' (mature, older stewardesses, also known as 'wrinklies' or 'crinklies') blurted out, "Captain, you have to come immediately – there is an emergency." The usual policy for this would be for the co-pilot to go back and see what was wrong, leaving the Captain to fly the plane. However, the stewardess was most insistent that I should go personally, without explaining exactly the situation that I was expected to deal with. So, unbuckling my seat belt, I attempted to get out of the seat – remember that the control column sits between your legs with what we call the 'yoke' or 'spectacle', the part that you control the airplane with. I managed to disguise my 'Abbeville Hard' predicament and, pulling on my Captain's jacket and hat, I followed her from the cockpit door into the bright cabin lights, leaving the controls in the safe hands of my First Officer.

My First Officer at that time was in fact completely dependable. He was well-built with light, short-cropped hair and his natural charm made him a real ladies' man. He bore a certain reputation from his military career: before becoming a pilot, he had served in the Royal Navy as a submariner and had left with the somewhat uncomfortable fame of holding the record for the largest peacetime tonnage of shipping damaged since the war. He had been a War Officer on nuclear submarines, responsible for launching torpedoes during fleet manœuvres. Whilst practising firing against the French fleet, he had successfully launched a practice torpedo but failed to adjust its depth so that it would pass below a French destroyer. Although there were no explosives in the torpedo, nonetheless it struck the destroyer amidships with considerable force and almost sank it. He was dismissed from the service and ended up as a co-pilot in our company.

Once we were out, she blurted out, "What are we going to do? He's stuck firmly." She pointed to where four of our stewardesses were gathered around the door of the forward toilet, all talking excitedly at the same time. It never ceased to amaze me how four stewardesses could converse simultaneously with each knowing exactly what the rest were saying. I pushed my way firmly through the throng where I was met by the sight of a rather swarthy gentleman with jet-black, brylcreemed hair, looking not unlike Clark Gable (the well-loved actor from the 1960s). He was standing wearing a T-shirt on his upper half and no trousers (or 'pants', for our American readers) on his lower half, and with one foot planted firmly inside the toilet bowl. Most eye-catchingly of all, and exposed to full view, was a certain part of his body – it was clear that I was not the only one affected by the Abbeville Hard.

I looked at him in amazement. He looked back at me, and all four giggling girls, in various pitches of voice, began to chorus at me: "Captain, he was standing on the seat and his girlfriend was performing an act on him when he lost his balance and his foot jammed in the toilet."

I looked from the girls to the young man and back to the girls. At that moment, a female passenger joined us – an attractive blue-eyed, blonde who was wearing a tight-fitting pale blue blouse which rather accentuated her considerable bust. Her flared designer skirt and overall appearance indicated she was definitely well-off, but she was in a rather distressed state.

She looked at me pleadingly. "We were trying for the 'Five Mile High Club', but he lost his balance before we joined it, Captain. Can you help him get his foot out of the toilet?"

I decided to exert my authority as Captain – what else could be done? – and decisively delegated the task to the four stewardesses, instructing them to do what they could to remove the stuck appendage. But it was a difficult problem. The girls were eager to lean over to exert pressure on his foot, but another offending appendage, which was obviously enjoying the spectacle, was somewhat in the way.

The oldest stewardess, claiming seniority, volunteered to try first. However, whilst she grasped his leg, something else pressed firmly into her left ear. She clearly put considerable effort into pulling his foot out, though I was not sure that her exertions required quite so much in the way of head movement. However, it was to no avail. She reluctantly admitted defeat and each of the other girls enthusiastically tried in turn. One, enterprisingly, asked one of the others to hold the appendage up out of the way so that she could get more leverage, which she most enthusiastically did, but this also yielded no results. Face cream, mayonnaise and liquid soap were applied in turn – to the foot. But nothing helped.

We were by this time approaching our destination, so I had to remove myself away from the admittedly enthralling spectacle. "We shall be landing in about forty minutes' time," I said, trying my best to conceal my smiles. "Can you all look after him?" Just at that moment there was a rumble and a shake as the plane clipped the top of a cloud, forcing the young man to extend his hands left and right and brace himself against the walls of the toilet so that he didn't break his ankle – or anything else.

Gravely, I took the opportunity to point out that descent and landing would potentially be rather bumpy. "Someone will have to hold onto him," I said authoritatively. "We don't want him to fall and break anything." I was nearly killed in the stampede of volunteers from the young ladies, and after heated discussion, one was elected to stand in the toilet during the descent and hold onto him. The sole male steward on board popped his head through the throng and offered his assistance – to the obvious horror of the trapped young man. He was, however, quickly ushered to the back of the aircraft with a look of great disappointment on his face, but not before he managed to whip out a camera and take (without showing any faces) several steamy shots.

The gentleman's girlfriend seemed a little less keen on my plan and offered to relieve him so that he wasn't such a spectacle. However, the volunteer (or, winning) stewardess said, with a perfectly sincere expression on her face, that the appendage might be useful to help hold him upright. I'm not sure that the girlfriend was too happy with this but she had little say in the matter. The toilet door was duly shut and a notice put up indicating that it was out of order due to 'a passenger in a distressed state'. I could have thought of a better form of wording! It looked to me as though the passenger was rather enjoying himself and was in no way distressed. I removed myself to the cabin and performed the gentlest landing I could manage. Having radioed a request for the company to send us a couple of engineers on landing to assist with an 'on-board issue', we turned off the runway and parked on the stand.

The main doors were opened, the passengers were disembarked and the Customs officers boarded to do their checks and searches in the galley. A female member of the Customs staff was first onboard and it was she who queried the closed toilet door. It was duly opened for her, revealing the stewardess still dutifully holding the gentleman's appendage. The Customs officer made no effort to keep a straight face and called over her colleague to see this spectacle for himself. The engineers boarded behind them, but they had to wait their turn. Eventually, after several camera flashes from the Customs officers' camera, they were allowed to get to work. An enormous hairy engineer, holding a large monkey wrench and a three-pound hammer, elbowed his way into the toilet and closed the door behind him.

Muffled thumps and bangs ensued and the large crowd outside (no one was leaving) waited with bated breath for the outcome. Eventually the door opened. The engineer strode out. Following dejectedly behind him, hobbling awkwardly and still naked from the waist down, the passenger emerged – with the toilet bowl still attached to his foot. He clattered slowly and awkwardly out of the aircraft and down the steps to the tarmac from where he was given a lift over to the engineering base. I am told that photographs of the incident are regularly used in training for engineers and Customs officers.

My final action on this incident was to fill in the 'voyage report' – any incident on the flight would generate a long form which were a nuisance to fill in. This one, however, I quite enjoyed writing, though I left out a few details which, although they had not escaped my attention, did not seem strictly necessary for the official record. I did not include in my report that the gentleman's appendage had two distinct rings of lipstick upon it, nor that – intriguingly – they were of different colours; nor that whilst one was a short distance from the top, the other was breathtakingly far down.

The final detail I elected not to mention was that there was a Customs seal tightly wrapped around the appendage's base with a tag number on it – these are a distinctive yellow and are (usually) used to seal boxes of duty-free items. A possible explanation to this rather mysterious aspect of the event was given to me some time later when my wife and I were having tea in Jersey with a couple we knew. The wife, who had been a nursing sister at the local hospital, informed us that by putting a tight elastic band around the base of the male appendage, an erection could be maintained for a considerable time. I can only assume that the Customs seal served the same purpose!

It must be said that there were incidents of a somewhat bawdy nature from time to time amongst the pilots and crew. When we were staying over regularly in Belfast, one of the pilots used to frequent a local bar where he got very amorous with the local landlord's daughter. He in fact got her 'in the club'. The landlord came out one day with a shotgun and asked him his name. On the spur of the moment, he came up with 'Nigel'. This was not his real name and he managed to get out of a tight situation and never returned there again. From that day onwards, all pilots were known as 'Nigels'.

Various people were at times caught in compromising situations, one way or another. One of the stewardesses in Birmingham was known as the station bicycle. One of the Captains caught a nasty dose from her. I never heard it called Birmingham flu, which perhaps it should have been, but it was often known as the Luton flu.

Two of the cabin crew were caught out having sex in a small room. They had actually finished but decided to have a cigarette. They set the fire alarm off and were caught *in flagrante*.

Amorous couples regularly used the toilets in order to become members of the so-called 'Five Mile High Club'. Alternatively, they could be found under a blanket on regular occasions. There is clearly something about flying: the rare atmosphere mixed with alcohol seems to act as an aphrodisiac to some passengers.

These misdemeanours were a stock part of the trade and a frequent talking-point. Aviation was full of rich tales of bawdy behaviour. It was part of the comedic and light-hearted nature of the daily experience.

Flying back from Berlin, a First Officer had a bottle of Scotch and went to the Flight Manager's office where he had been summoned, only to find the Flight Manager had gone home. The

Flight Manager's PA was a very attractive woman who should have been on a hen night as she was getting married the next day. The First Officer sat on the side of the desk and gave her a couple of drinks to celebrate the coming wedding. This continued until most of the bottle had disappeared, when they then moved into the Flight Manager's office where he had his evil way with her across the Flight Manager's desk, at which point she was sick over all of the paperwork dribbling into the drawers of the desk and over the carpet. I never heard the end of the story.

I heard a shocking story that, at the end of the war at Northolt Airport, a load of Mosquito aircraft had landed and an engineer was instructed to go along underneath the wings of each aircraft with a fire axe to smash the fuel tanks, allow the fuel to run all over the ground and then set fire to them, destroying every one. They would have been worth a fortune now.

Chapter Twelve
TRIDENT 1, 2 & 3

Another course, another ARB (technical paper). I passed and my licence was stamped Trident. Unlike my previous aircraft, we no longer needed to do six take-off and landings. Unknown to the travelling public, these were all completed on normal passenger flights with passengers on board. Yes, we actually flew the aircraft for the first time with passengers on board. It is not as bad as it sounds – all the practice on the simulator makes the whole exercise very easy.

The Trident was a prime example of a company mess-up. They had a research and development department who came up with a great idea, and after operating it a while, they would ask for a stretched version. In the case of the Trident, some bright spark somewhere decided this was not a good idea, and that they could save money by reducing the size of the engines and thereby reduce the requirement of extending the aeroplane. However, the aircraft, although very fast flying at almost Mach One (the speed of sound), it did not like leaving the ground. It was termed the 'gripper' – indeed, many thought that the only reason it got off the ground was because of the curvature of the earth. However, occasionally on training flights at RAF bases, it was known to out-perform most of the current fighters anywhere, certainly within the circuit of the aerodrome. The Americans were delighted and had a ball with their Boeing 727s.

What a Trident could really do was to descend really fast. You could actually put the two outboard engines into reverse thrust in flight and pull 10,000 revs on the thrust levers – and at one point you could even drop the nose wheel and come down at a frightening rate of descent, still with high speed. However, one Flight Manager made a mess of the whole thing and nearly hit the ground. Probably in order to save his job, we were no longer allowed to drop the nose wheel as a speed-break. Just because he made a mess of it, we all had to suffer – typical schoolboy attitude by the teacher.

The Trident had a very sleek fuselage and a 'T' tail plane with three engines in the tail. It was a delight to fly, even on your very first flight. Never having landed in real life, it was amazing how realistic the simulator training was that had prepared you, so that the first landing didn't present any problems whatsoever. From the Captain's point of view, it was great. You had two highly trained First Officers to look after you and the Captain naturally sat in the left-hand seat. The First Officers swapped around each flight or, as we would term it, take leg and leg about, one sitting in the right-hand seat and the other sitting on the instrument or engineer's panel. (In helicopters the Captain sits in the right-hand seat.)

When on the engineering panel, lazy First Officers used to sit back with their feet up on the right-hand windowsill. If you go to a museum and manage to look into a Trident cockpit, you would find it is completely dented by the co-pilot's heels on the panel. Just under this damaged area (in other words, behind the right-hand seat on the right-hand wall of the aircraft) you would find a box which comes out and contains all the manuals required to fly the aeroplane. If you pull this box out and look behind it, you will find that it's used to store pornographic material for the P-3 or third pilot to read during the cruise!

For our logbooks, a First Officer doing a flight and acting as a Captain would be called a P1 U/S. If he was not flying it but merely acting as a First Officer, he would be designated a P2. One Captain, known for his rudeness, used to refer to First Officers as P1 or P2 instead of by their first names. On one occasion, the Captain referred to the P2, asking him to do a certain task. The First Officer replied, "Captain, don't be so formal – why don't you just call me P?"

I finished the Trident course and had only a final check flight to pass. It was set for London to Edinburgh and back to London. As the Trident has three crew, I had two seasoned First Officers and a Check Captain to pass or fail me. The company training was great – they really trained you and did not aim to just chop you, so if you failed, they genuinely felt they had let you down.

The system was for the crew to check in one hour before take-off to brief, flight-plan and do the checks. As it was a check flight, I naturally came in an hour early so I could mull over the weather and other data, and then appear brilliant when I repeated it again in front of the Training Captain. The best advice I ever had in my life was to take all the paperwork into the toilet, lock the door, and study it in peace. Then go out and dump the paperwork, having made your plan. When the others come in, you go through the whole thing from scratch. When you go on holiday next time and you check in for the flight, and you are standing in the queue wondering why everyone else did the same, spare a thought for the Captain probably sitting on the toilet planning your flight.

Princess Diana visited the Crew Room once and needed to go to the toilet. However, there were no female pilots, so no ladies' loos. She used one of the male ones and later a very crude pilot went in to smell the seat. A similar thing happened to the Queen Mother when she visited an RAF station in Rhodesia. They had to build a special toilet just in case she needed to go. Naturally she did, and was away for some time. Later, above the RAF bar was placed a large bottle with a royal turd in it!

Back to the check flight, my early arrival was a good move. The Edinburgh weather was blowing a gale as usual from the south-west. The only runway then had been built on the headings 310 and 130. They could not have chosen a worse direction, as the wind was always directly across, especially if it was strong. The maximum crosswind component allowed on Tridents, like most aircraft, was 30 knots. It was blowing 38 knots across and the runway was wet. As I was new on this type, I should have taken a little off the component and a little off for the wet runway – 20 knots was about right. Not a hope at this stage, but there were two hours to take-off and an hour in flight, so there was time for an improvement. The last thing I wanted was to have to cancel the final check.

I rang through to Edinburgh Tower to get an on-the-spot report. They said it had stopped raining but was still windy, with the runway drying a little. It was never clear at these times where you stood with a damp runway, wet or dry. It probably would not bother us normally, but it's different on a check flight. If you had an accident, then they would go through everything with a fine toothcomb. The controller was going to be on duty when I was due overhead. I explained that it would help if he gave the runway as wet or dry, not damp. He said he would bear it in mind.

The correct report time was one hour before, and on time I briefed the co-pilots in front of the Check Captain. I had to be seen to cover weather, passenger loads, diversion airfield, aircraft defect and anything else relevant to the flight. We arrived at the aircraft 35 minutes before departure, and the co-pilots checked the inside of the aircraft while the Check Captain followed to watch me check the outside and liaise with the appropriate ground staff, usually through the Dispatcher. Everything went well and we arrived over Turnhouse Edinburgh Airport and established contact with the tower. (Turnhouse was the destination of the first flight I ever had as a passenger when I was about eight years old on a Viscount 700.) The tower said they were awaiting the latest official weather report and would pass it on when it came in. We were cleared to finals on Runway 31.

I turned finals but no weather was forthcoming. I could see the runway ahead as the cloud base had lifted to about 3,000 feet. At the outer marker at 4½ miles out, I asked for the weather again, being really interested in the state of the runway. They delayed and at three miles said the wind was gusting 25 to 30 knots across, with runway damp and some standing water. Normally this was not a problem, but what was the Checker thinking? At two miles, the wind was 28 knots across the runway, still the same. I decided to be cautious and told the tower that I would go around but check the runway as we passed it. A gentle application of power calling for the go-around drills and we climbed ahead. The runway looked dry to me but with a few large puddles. I elected to come around and land, which I did. The approach was very rough but I carried out a good landing and taxied to the parking space and shut the engines down.

I honestly did not know what the Checker would say. He would either chop me straight away or say it was a good decision in the difficult weather conditions. After a pause, he congratulated me on the way I had handled it. A straightforward flight back to London and he was congratulating me on passing. Another course passed.

As I mentioned earlier, the Trident was a Rolls Royce to fly: it was fast – very fast. It had three pilots, and in our case that meant that the Captain had two very experienced co-pilots to look after him and peel his grapes. It had three engines instead of two, even a fourth on the Trident 3, which was used mainly for take-off. The cabin had a first class section and the cabin crew were of the old school. In some cases, there was an emphasis on the 'old', but they were good. Later, they took out the first class, which had a knock-on effect for us – up to then we always had first class food, but now it did not exist, so the union protected our right to it by getting a large cheese board with our food.

Pre-flight checks are certainly important. You have to check against a checklist, and the outside check is carried out with an eagle eye looking for anything out of place. We used to fly both the Trident 1 and 2 (and later the Trident 3), which were virtually the same. A crew carried out the inside and outside checks, and waited for the cabin crew and passengers. After some time, no one had arrived. They called ops on the radio and they were told that they were on the wrong aircraft, and everyone was waiting for them on another. The funny thing is that they were sitting on a Trident 3, which they had never flown. It had a fourth engine and some extra gauges, but they had not noticed. They were very sheepish and were ribbed for many days about it – they had not realised that the aircraft was twenty feet longer.

On one flight, I invited Selina Scott (a British TV presenter) into the cockpit and she stayed there for the landing. She was an absolute beauty and spent most of her time on the fourth seat with her legs crossed in a most casual position. She was obviously a natural flyer and was most certainly the pin-up girl of all the pilots. Another time, a TV news reporter was on board to give a broadcast in Glasgow and she developed severe toothache. We called our operations room to arrange for a dentist after landing. We also told her that the tooth would probably be OK on the ground, because such aches were often caused by the aircraft pressurisation.

During my simulator training, I had the great pleasure of meeting a test pilot, the most fantastic character I think I'll ever meet: Richard Walter Millward (Dickie). Richard was a great guy, and although he was not one of our pilots, the safety branch of the company had just employed him. He was a fantastic pilot and had been a test pilot in the RAF where he had flown the Fairy Delta 2, the prototype small fighter aeroplane built to help with the design of Concorde.

He had flown many other aircraft. Once he was flying the latest fighter in Germany, and one night he left the local RAF station to go down into the town to have a beer when someone hit him over the head, knocking him out. It was believed that they were checking for documents in case he had taken some with him. Anyway, he was very badly injured and was never allowed to fly again as a pilot, which was a great loss. He later flew the Trident simulator with me and was the best I've ever seen – an absolute natural.

Richard told the story one day of how he was in the Farnborough Research Establishment when they were doing the final plans for Concorde. He was quite scathing about Harold Wilson's government when Denis Healey was the Minister of Defence. One day, there was an order from high up in the government that there was a Russian contingent being sent over, and that they were to be shown anything that they wanted to see on the defence side. They were particularly interested in the new

Concorde plans. All the people in Farnborough were absolutely horrified at the security risk. However, there was no way that they could not obey a direct order which they believed came from Wilson's government.

Someone had a brainwave. They had a lot of plans for the original Concorde which basically contained a lot of flaws, so they deliberately took these into the room and exchanged them for the latest ones. When the Russians came along, they told them all about the new aircraft. They then arranged a deliberate phone call, designed to make out they had to leave the room to take the call, so that the Russians were left alone – during which time they naturally believed that the Russians photographed all the plans. Presumably they took them back to Russia because the Concordski was then built which, as everyone knows, was a pretty disastrous venture and included all sorts of faults of the original design, including the way the engines were placed, allowing debris into the engines, etc. One of them crashed at an air show and the aircraft was relegated to a transport aeroplane or freighter. Anyway, the Russians were sent on their way.

Richard joined our company's air safety branch but, sadly, I learned that about two years after I had trained with him, he was in a restaurant having a meal when he collapsed over the table and died, due to the head injuries that he had originally received in Germany.

When we used to fly down the Berlin corridor, we often took RAF staff on a look-see basis so that if the balloon went up, they could step into our planes and fly them for us. It would certainly be rather daunting for us to fly aeroplanes – if the Russians were at war with us, we would not last more than five minutes in our airliners. Remember that a Russian Yak aircraft rammed a British Airways Viking shortly after WWII during the Berlin airlift, and all on board were killed. The 1948 Gatow air disaster was a mid-air collision in the airspace above Berlin that occurred on 5th April, sparking an international incident. A British European Airways (BEA) Vickers VC1B Viking airliner crashed near RAF Gatow air base, after colliding with a Soviet Air Force Yakovlev

Yak-3 fighter aircraft. All ten passengers and four crew on board the Viking were killed, as was the Soviet pilot. The disaster resulted in a diplomatic stand-off between the United Kingdom and the United States on the one hand, and the Soviet Union on the other, and intensified distrust leading up to the Berlin Blockade in the early years of the Cold War.

A colleague decided to leave the company and go to Cyprus where his wife was already living. He called a removal company who loaded up a container with all his possessions. Just before the flight, he received a phone call, and when he took it, was informed that the ship with the container on board had sunk with no hope of ever retrieving his items. Mysteriously, this happened in the deepest part of the sea in the area. He then rang his wife saying, "You know that cherry wood sideboard that we cannot decide where to put in the house? Well, you haven't got that problem any more." She asked why and he said, "They lost it." She then asked about the container, to which he replied, "They've lost that as well. In actual fact, they've lost the ship, sunk with everything in the deepest water between Athens and Cyprus." Luckily, he was fully insured for the same amount as his house insurance, but he lost everything that was dear to him.

One bar room story mentioned a ship coming across the sea during the war with 600 soldiers on board. There were four vicars, all with life-jackets on, but many of the soldiers didn't have any. It was torpedoed, so a soldier was given one of the life-jackets by a vicar who drowned. The soldier survived to tell the tale, and apparently the other three vicars also gave their life-jackets away and drowned.

On the Trident you got some stewardesses who were called 'stiltons', after the cheese – the reason being that they're old and had veins. Alternatively, they were called Italian road maps, because the veins on their legs looked just the same.

What is the difference between a cowpat and a stewardess? None – the older they get, the easier they are to pick up.

We are a very safe Airline, see how old the Stewardesses are!

I needed to go to the bank at Terminal 3 at Heathrow in order to get some money and I queued behind an attractive young blonde who eventually stepped up to the desk and asked for some money, presenting a Coutts Bank cheque. The bank teller remarked that he required a supporting bankcard, to which she replied, "Daddy owns the bank." She got her money.

In the same Terminal 3, a man was arrested for stealing baggage off the shuttle luggage carousel which served shuttle services to Glasgow, Manchester and Edinburgh, so not within the Customs area. This guy evidently stood on the first floor overlooking this carousel and when he saw that there was a bag that was not being claimed, he grabbed the bag and ran off with it. He was finally caught.

Jack was a new Assistant Flight Manager on the Trident and I had known him well in my private life as an antiques dealer. He was a womaniser and would spend any amount of money on wining and dining a woman on the off-chance that he might score. I had reason to go into his office because I decided I wanted to grow a moustache, and also to get permission to officially own an antique business. He just turned round and said, "No problem – just go ahead with both of them." I then grew my moustache and at a later stage another more senior Flight Manager asked how I'd got permission to start a business. I merely referred back to Jack on both counts and I never heard another thing about it.

To start a modern aeroplane, you don't need a ground truck or electrical supply. Instead you have an APU (Auxiliary Power Unit) which is a little jet engine just by the tail. If you start this thing up, it will then supply electrics and the air you require to start the main engines. It's very noisy. One of the First Officers went to a museum where there was a Trident with all the droop on the leading edge of the wing and the flaps hanging down. The people who ran the museum could find no way to put them up and it looked very ugly. The First Officer offered to fix the problem. Slightly with tongue in cheek, he then got into the aircraft and pressed the APU start button. Even though the aircraft had been there for about two years, the APU started immediately. Large bellows of black smoke with a tremendous noise followed, as it roared into life. The First Officer then selected the flaps and droop up, and all were cleaned up within seconds. He then switched off the APU. The staff looked dumbfounded but it did the trick!

I flew to Istanbul on quite an uneventful four-hour flight, picked up my usual cheap Lacoste T-shirts and Turkish Delight, when Hannibal the Duty Manager came to me, asking for a favour. Not wishing to upset him, I agreed. He told me that an engineer had been sent over two nights previously, in order to change the engine of an aircraft. Lifting the engine up required what might be call an X-lift gantry – if you can imagine it, it is manœuvred under the engine and raised, with the top of the platform going up higher, depending on how you adjust it. Unfortunately, when the lift was lowered, the engineer had his foot in the way and it was virtually cut off. Although he was rushed to the local hospital, they merely wrapped it up in a sheet (which rapidly filled up with blood) and gave him a couple of aspirins. He was desperate to get back to London, as the poor fellow was about to retire that week to take up a job at Blackbushe Airport as an engineer.

I took him up in the cockpit and allowed him to sit on the fourth seat behind me, his foot stretched out alongside me with the bloody sheet still wrapped round it. This was the best seat in the aircraft. Eventually we arrived at London where he was met by an ambulance and taken to hospital. I never found out whether he kept his foot or not.

The Istanbul flight was not very popular as the allowances were very low. However, in the departure terminal you could buy all sorts of cheap Turkish items, including fake T-shirts, Turkish Delight and many more items. We were about to depart one time when the stewardess came rushing into the cockpit and said that we could not leave because there was a discrepancy in the bar. I called the Station Manager and the girl explained that she had ordered 24 miniature whiskies, 24 miniature bottles of gin and 24 miniature bottles of brandy, plus a few other things. However, they had delivered 24 litre bottles of cheap Turkish brandy and she wanted them taken off the plane. I asked the Station Manager where we stood, and he said that there was no way they could be removed from the aircraft – if they were, we could end up in prison. I asked the stewardess if she had ever seen the film *Midnight Express*, which she had not. I said it was the most horrific film and that there was no way I was going to go into a Turkish prison and suffer what had happened to the hero... so she inherited 24 bottles of brandy and we took them to London.

The next flight out of Istanbul, a poor Turkish baggage handler drove up to the plane on a flat conveyor belt truck which had no brakes or rubber guards on the end. He ran into the side of my aircraft, cutting two holes in the fuselage. The poor guy was sacked immediately, and I pleaded on his behalf, but they would not listen to me. We were now in a position of not being able to pressurise the cabin, so we sent the passengers back by another airline. We night-stopped and they plugged the holes, allowing us to fly back the next day unpressurised and below 10,000 feet, taking the long way round past the Alps.

Another Istanbul trip and halfway through the flight, the stewardess came up and complained that there was a passenger sitting in Club who had invited his son from the third world end of the aeroplane to come and sit next to him. The Club Class passenger refused to tell his son to return to the back end of the aircraft, so I sent my First Officer down to sort it out – he was at least 6′ 6″ and built like an ox. He wandered down the aircraft and I could feel the thump of his feet on the floor actually resonating into the cockpit. He went up to the passenger and said to him, "Sir, do you have a problem?" to which the reply was, "No, my son is just going down the back to his seat."

Another flight to the same place, and I was just pushing back from the jetty in London when a passenger came to the end of the jetty and banged on my window, signalling to me frantically. I stopped, signalled to the Dispatcher to get on the headset and talk to me, and I pointed to the jetty entrance. The Dispatcher said that the passenger was late and asked me to put the steps down and allow him on board, which we did. Halfway through the flight, the stewardess came into the cockpit, saying that we had a problem with that late passenger. Evidently, he was supposed to go to Oslo for a wedding and somehow he was on our flight instead. I invited him up to the cockpit and he explained about the wedding. I pointed out that he would most certainly *not* be going, as we still had two hours' flight to go, an hour turnaround and four hours back, so he would miss the last Oslo flight. He then rather stupidly told me that he was on a free ticket paid for by his air miles. Apparently, he fitted kitchens, but when he was supposed to give out free air mile vouchers, he kept them and was using them for this flight. Anyway, when we arrived back at London, I reported to security so I think he may have had a problem over and above his original one.

We had a First Officer who, when on standby, used to spend his whole time at Brentford car auction, ringing in occasionally and not admitting where he was. They never caught on, and he rarely ever got called for a flight, probably because someone else got called in his place. This was all long before mobile phones. Most pilots had two different phone numbers at home, so they knew if the wrong one rang that they were likely to get caught if they answered it!

Flash Harry, one of the pilots, was full of himself. He used to ride motorcycles and really fancied himself. One day (probably due to this other guy being at Brentford) he was called in from Maidenhead. He reckoned his average speed into the airport was about 115 mph, including going through the tunnel at Heathrow Airport. He used to race a motorbike and sidecar at different events and his girlfriend used to sit in the sidecar, leaning in different directions in order to help round the bends. Unfortunately, she fell out once and was seriously injured

Tom was also a bit of a tearaway. He kept snakes, which readily escaped from his flat and ended up going under the floorboards and appearing in other people's units. This failed to endear him to his neighbours. If you ever visited his house, he would delight in asking you to feed live mice to his snakes, which

I would rather not have done. He told a very long story about having gone to India on holiday, where he went off up into the hillside, miles and miles from anywhere, and became very ill. It took several days before a doctor got through to him. It turned out that he had blood poisoning, and despite his state he was told to drive back to a railway station and get a train back to the airport.

Tom eventually arrived at the railway station and boarded a train, which chugged off into the night, but after about six hours it came to a halt. He was feeling like death warmed up, the toilets were full, and there was no food or water. When he looked out of a window, he found that an elephant had died on the track and that a herd of elephants were all standing around it, wailing and crying. Nothing they could do would make the elephants move, and under these circumstances the animals could be extremely dangerous. Later the next morning, they finally moved off the track and the train moved off and arrived in the city. At the airport, he went to the Duty Manager, expecting to go on the next flight back to London. However, there were no seats available. Tom replied, "If you don't put me on, I will die here – the amount of paperwork you would need for that will keep you here for about three weeks." Seeing his argument, the Duty Manager put him on the flight and he eventually arrived back in London – although not a happy Duty Manager, as he had had to bribe a passenger in order to get Tom on board.

Finally, Tom went to his flat to find that there was no food whatsoever, so despite feeling like death warmed up, he decided to go to the local pub. He went up to the bar, managed to climb up on the bar stool and sat there feeling really really sorry for himself. A couple of city gents came into the bar and started telling him all about their day's problems – they had lost some money here, the train was late, they hadn't got the right wine when they had lunch, etc. Tom sat dying on his seat, listening to all their minor problems. This just shows how minor things in life are viewed as very important – the guy next to them in the chair nearly died while he was in India and was still feeling awful

We flew off to Athens on an uneventful flight. The stewardess said that there was a very pleasant businessman sitting in first class and he would like to visit the cockpit. We got chatting and he seemed very sociable, and was staying in the same hotel as us. He invited us for a drink with him in the evening and offered to take us all out for a meal. He eventually arrived in the bar, but he couldn't take his eyes off one of the stewardesses. He gave each of us a present (and to this day, I've still got the designer wash-kit bag that he gave to each of us). He was obviously very wealthy and spent much of the time having drinks, basically trying to get into the stewardesses' knickers. However, she wouldn't play ball and we were all very disappointed – if she had sacrificed herself, we would probably have received much better presents. We thought it very selfish of her!

Having a very flash sports car can have its advantages, but sometimes people don't notice it. One of the guys had a habit of going to his local pub, leaving his Porsche outside with its headlights on, so that people would come in through the front door and ask who owned the Porsche – to which he would put his hand up, to then be told that the lights were on. He would wander out, switch them off and then look the bee's knees in the bar, increasing his chances of scoring.

Another tale is about a classic Italian sports car. A chap in Chelsea had advertised it for sale and took a guy out for a spin. Somehow this man had checked the keys to the ignition and had been able to get the key number and a duplicate set. He returned during the night and stole the car which was never seen again.

We lost some more fellow pilots and crew. On 10th September 1976, British Airways Flight 476, a Hawker Siddeley Trident G-AWZT en route from London to Istanbul, collided mid-air near Zagreb, Yugoslavia (modern-day Croatia), with Inex-Adria Aviopromet Flight 550, a Douglas DC-9 en route from Split, Yugoslavia, to Cologne, West Germany. The collision was the result of a procedural error on the part of Zagreb Air Traffic Controllers.

All 176 people on board both flights were killed, making it, at the time, the world's deadliest mid-air collision. It was, and at the time of writing remains, the only fatal accident to befall an aircraft operated by British Airways (not counting BA's predecessors), as well as the deadliest aviation accident in Croatia. A ground controller had allowed another aircraft to fly straight up through his level, and sod's law – of all the sky in all the places, they had to hit.

On a night stop somewhere behind the old Iron Curtain (it could have been Warsaw), I was on my own walking round the town which was drab and miserable, to say the least. I came to an area where the building from the first floor upward overhung the pavement and was supported by pillars – it was rather dark and formed a passageway. I wasn't too happy about walking down it, although I did so to avoid walking in the road. Just then, from behind a pillar, stepped a guy in a dirty raincoat who came up to me. He ascertained that I was British and spoke to me in quite good English, asking me if I wished to buy some currency. I told him in no uncertain terms that I wasn't interested but he kept on pestering me for probably forty yards, still under the building.

Just then, from behind another pillar came two guys dressed in black leather coats with black hats on, typical Gestapo-style officers. They stopped both of us and accused the two of us of dealing in currency. I said to them that I was an airline pilot and I had ample allowances for the night stop, and anyway there was no way you could spend money in this town. In any case, if I needed any more money, I merely had to go back to the hotel and just ask for it. I also said, "Could you not see by my body language that I wasn't the least bit interested in dealing with this guy?" They rather begrudgingly agreed and sent me on my way, but the other guy was bundled into a black car and disappeared.

You do have to be streetwise when you go to these places, or you can get yourself into serious trouble. Some of the crew were mugged in Prague on three separate occasions. On the first occasion, a girl had £400 stolen with her handbag, which seemed a ludicrous amount of money to have with her. The second time, the stewardess had a handbag stolen with all her credit cards and money in it. And a third, when the whole crew (including me) had gone to Wenceslas Square in the centre of town and had had a meal, we returned to the tube station when two guys in long raincoats pushed through our group onto the tube. The stewardess at the front was apologising to one of the guys holding onto her handbag – she genuinely believed that she had pushed into him. She thought the guy was objecting to her pushing her bag into him – in actual fact, he was grabbing hold of it and trying to steal it.

It is difficult to know what to do in these circumstances and it had happened so quickly. Being at the back, I was not able to do anything, but you have to remember that it is quite possible that these people may have had a knife or an infected needle to stick into you. In the confusion, they must have been frightened off – the two decided not to continue into the tube and disappeared down the platform. We entered the train and sat down, but it became blatantly obvious that an elderly guy in a boiler suit who sat opposite us was part of the gang. I have a feeling that if they had got hold of the bag and her wallet, they would have passed it to him. When we arrived at our destination, he got out and followed us for a considerable way, until finally turning back towards the station and disappearing.

I mentioned the hypodermic syringe because on another occasion someone had their car stolen near London Airport. After a couple of days, the police called up and said they had found it. However, when the guy got into the driver's seat, there was a hypodermic syringe propped up under the seat which had been deliberately positioned to stab him..

I thought the tube stations were great in Prague – they all had names like ours, but they had great big square tiles, about two foot square, and each station had its own colour. This meant that if somebody was a foreigner or dyslexic, or just could not read, they would know exactly which station they were in or going to – I really think we should adopt this policy. Similarly with our banknotes – Dutch banknotes have indentations on them so that people who are visually impaired can just feel or know what the note is, but all the American notes are exactly the same size and colour, so I do not know how people know which is which.

Another car was stolen from one of the First Officers. It had been parked in London Airport car park. An old Morris Minor with a totally clapped-out engine on its last legs, it was stolen from the staff car park. The officer actually hoped he would never see it again and made a claim on his insurance policy. Within the claim date limit, the police found the car in a back street in London and asked the man to pick up the keys from the police station, which meant that he would have to pay the money back to the insurance company. He rather stupidly said to the police officer behind the counter, "You couldn't say you found it in two days' time could you so I can claim on the insurance?" At which point, the huge Chief Inspector grabbed him by the collar and dragged him into a room, sat him down and threatened to arrest him for fraud and trying to get the police officer to commit a felony. He came away very sheepish. However, the insurance company inspected the car and found it in such a state – particularly the engine – that they assumed that the thief had trashed it beyond repair. He managed to keep the full amount of the insurance money!

The old Brabazon Aircraft hangar, which is now a Grade 2 listed building, was a strange sight. There was a car parked there in brilliant daylight, with the sun shining, but it had its headlights on, passenger doors open and the windscreen wipers going with the radio on full blast. I asked what was going on. It turned out that the Captain, who was going on the flight, had parked his car outside the hanger, quickly ran in and picked up paperwork but became distracted and had forgotten that he had left the car outside. He had gone off on a two-week trip. When he returned, he was amazed to find that security had set the car up as a good joke.

A Captain on an Oslo night-stop talked to a well-known and extremely attractive Duty Officer. He enquired what people did in Oslo during the middle of winter and her reply was, "In the winter we ski and make love; in the summer we don't ski." He took this as a come-on and that evening he managed to persuade her to go out for a meal. Having downed many glasses of wine and schnapps, he managed to get an invite back to her house, where he was very successful, despite the fact that he had continued drinking until a very late hour. He had driven to her house in a hire car, and went outside to look for it to drive back to the airport hotel early for his flight home – only to find the place and his car surrounded by thousands of police and police cars. His car was now parked between probably twenty or more police cars, right in the middle of the main road. He managed not to slur his words (they didn't think his English was that good) to ask what was going on. He was told that the President was going to a state occasion and all traffic was barred from the road. Being in somewhat of a predicament, he managed to persuade a police car to take him down the road which he followed, zigzagging all over the place and finally returning to his hotel. He has no idea how he got away with it.

Several of us were discussing this issue in the main Crew Room back at Heathrow when we were joined by a Scottish skipper whom nobody particularly liked. As usual, while we were talking, we started to criticise the management. This man went very, very quiet and said we had to be careful because the Crew Room was bugged. He was an extremely strange guy whose surname was Hugh, and many of the pilots used to joke that this was 'Captain Hugh welcoming you on the Trident Two'.

We had an early flight to Amsterdam and the rest of the day off where we visited the Heineken brewery. We sank many litres of free lager and took part in a competition at the end where the answer was, 'It is my birthday today' – and we were given a super-duper tankard. A local bar in Amsterdam was half-a-mile from the hotel and served the most fantastic spare ribs. They were reasonably priced and you could have as many racks of ribs as you wished, as long as you finished all of them. They also had A1 sauce, which was brought in from America by the Pan American crews – if they brought enough bottles in with them they could get their ribs free.

A business guy from America got in with some English chaps and drank virtually through the night with them, although he consistently slagged off England. When he was so drunk that he eventually passed out, the guys took him down to the local tattoo parlour and got a huge union flag tattooed right across his chest. I've no idea what his feelings were about England from that day onwards, but every time he looked in the mirror or had a shower, he was reminded of our Queen and country!

We had a great night in Hanover. We went to the local bierkeller (beer hall), where there was a jazz band, and the leader of the band was a local chief of police. We had a ball – everybody was singing, and one of the other crews arrived with a skipper who was fantastic on the piano and could sing as well as anybody. He joined in with the jazz band and led many of the tunes, playing with all his might and thoroughly enjoying himself. It was at this point that he started playing the German Second World War tune, 'Deutschland über alles', without them realising it. It is illegal to sing the first verse of the German national anthem – the verse begins with, 'Germany, Germany above everything'. – because it was made the national anthem by the Nazis during the Third Reich. This first verse was banned at the end of WWII. It was only when we got halfway through the tune that they realised that all of them, including the chief of police, were singing it… but what the hell, they continued to the very end and just ordered more beer!

Always be careful when you go to a beer hall in Germany. If you are asked to conduct the band, there will be a catch. This is at the end, when you would have to buy every member of the band a stein of beer. Also be careful about making advances to the girls when they are serving you. You will see that they can carry seven heavy steins in each hand and they have extremely powerful muscles, and so can give you a whack round the ears. If you push your luck, you may have the delightful experience of being taken outside by a bouncer, grabbed hold of by one arm and spun round and round until you lose control. One thing you have to remember is not to go down – if you fall down on the pavement, you will get your head kicked in. All you can do is to hope that at some point the bouncer will let you go spinning off into the distance.

The favourite beer halls were the ones with telephones where you could all sit round a table which had a large number over it. You could then phone any one of the tables and talk to them without them knowing which table you were on, unless you chose to tell them.

In the morning, the First Officer suggested we go sailing. We went down to a huge lake in front of the hotel which had been built specifically for Hitler. It was extremely long but not very wide and was full of large carp. We easily sailed down to the very end of it where the SS had had their camp and where they were encouraged to meet women. By the lake, a green VW Beetle police car turned up. Police got out and hid behind the car, shouting at some yobs to halt. At first they did not, but when they turned round, the police were aiming their pistols at them which got their attention. We had the problem of coming back and had to tack all the way up the lake which took forever. The pick-up time for the crew transport from the hotel got nearer and nearer, and in the end, in sheer desperation, the First Officer let me off the boat and I ran like hell to the hotel where I explained that there was a problem and they had to delay the departure of the crew transport. The First Officer eventually arrived and got to the aeroplane with about ten minutes to spare, but we managed to get it ready to take off quickly and on time.

One pilot took his wife to Germany for the first time and left her in the hotel while he carried out his day's flying. He was exceedingly mean and did not want his wife spending any of his allowances, so he cooked up a story and told his wife (who enjoyed her food) to always ask a taxi driver for a good restaurant by saying, "Take me to an Imbis." (This is German for a street vendor in a caravan or street corner stall.) He then made it worse by saying that when you get the menu always ask for 'wurst' which is usually the best thing on the menu and at a special daily rate. She fell for it, and it took several visits before it dawned on her that she had been set up.

A pilot had crashed on the runway. When the fire crew went across to him, they were very eager to show their expertise and immediately started to try to get the crew out by releasing the canopy, which turned out to be stuck. So they started smashing it with a fire axe, when one of them put the axe right through the canopy and struck the pilot very heavily on one shoulder. They then managed to extricate him from the cockpit and laid him on the wing for a short while, while they waited for the ambulance to arrive. Just before it arrived, he rolled off the wing onto the tarmac and fell extremely heavily, banging his head and exacerbating the wound to his shoulder… at which point the ambulance came roaring round the aircraft and ran him over! They always say things come in threes, and every pilot believes this.

We had all been complaining at how dirty the aircraft were becoming, particularly on the outside. About this time an aircraft aquaplaned off the end of the runway. Aquaplaning is when you land so lightly on a wet runway that the wheels still think they are airborne and do not start to spin. You can get it in a car. When the runway is wet, you are expected to do a firm landing in order to spin the wheels up – if you do not and you apply the brakes, the wheels could be about a millimetre off the runway locked solid and will just burn and get red-hot until the tyre is either scalded or bursts. Whichever way, you will get no grip on the runway, and if there is a crosswind, you are likely to slide off.

Anyway, this aircraft slid off the end of the runway into the mud. No one was hurt except the Captain's pride, but the aircraft had to have a major inspection before it could be flown again. Some days later, the company had obtained a transcript of the cockpit voice recorder (a thirty-minute continuous loop audio tape, recording everything said in the cockpit). The transcript should have contained the last words of the crew as they went off the end, with the Captain calling various commands, including a call to the co-pilot to action or carry out the imminent overrun drills – this is to stop the aircraft catching fire – and also starting the passenger evacuation drill, again in case of a fire. However, all the tape contained was the Captain saying, "That's ruined my f...king day," followed by the co-pilot saying, "Now they will have to wash the bloody aircraft."

The management did not see the funny side of it.

An aircraft arrived from South America and landed at Heathrow, but whilst there, the crew had suffered food poisoning. On arrival in London, the Flight Manager was not amused to learn that the Captain and the First Officer had decided to fly back, even though they were in much pain. What made it worse was that the flight engineer had severely damaged his leg during an accident but also wanted to return to London.

A crew arrived at Heathrow, having called in to the Duty Manager to say that they had a very violent passenger on board. They had had to use restraints, which were like large cable ties, around the guy's wrists and strapped him into the seat. Unfortunately, they had to take these off for landing in case there was an accident, during which he would not be able to get out of the aircraft by himself. When they had landed and were met by the police, the passengers all disembarked except the culprit who remained sullenly seated. One of the policemen was huge and came on the aeroplane first. He walked down the plane – you could almost feel it – but as he went down, he leant over the passenger and whispered something in his ear (which I assume would be totally unprintable), at which point the passenger lunged at him and head-butted him right on the nose. He was frogmarched down to the front of the aircraft, down the steps and into the back of a van, which then drove off rocking all over the place... presumably they were 'entertaining' him, I do not think he would have done that again.

My next-door neighbour had regularly seen a ghost. He used to walk from his house, which was next-door to ours in Camberley, up to the hotel at the top of the road, and on his way out with the dog, the animal regularly cowered into a corner with all its fur standing on end, refusing point blank to go forward. He had to lift the dog up and carry it up the road – the dog quite convinced that there was a ghost in the area.

The crew hotel in Rome had originally been used by the Gestapo as a torture centre. Many of the stewardesses were seen to come out of their rooms almost hysterical, so that many of the male crew members offered to look after them for the night. Many parts of Tempelhof Airport were also considered to be haunted – just round the corner had been the main torture chamber for the SS and many had also been tortured underneath the airport. People often said that they could hear screams and yells when they walked down some of its corridors.

As I mentioned before, Flight 401 crashed on 29th December 1972, and was the biggest example of ghostly apparitions. Many crew members have experienced ghosts during a flight and have usually found them to have been very helpful to them, but they fail to report anything in case they might appear to be stupid. Often the ghost will be helpful during a flight, either by pointing out things that may be wrong, or even correcting them. One ghost on our Tristar is reputed to be that of the flight engineer from a Tristar flight in the Everglades, No 401. Evidently, the aeroplane tried to come into land but could not get a green light on all three undercarriages and the nose wheel appeared to be unlocked. The flight engineer went down into the holds below floor level to investigate. In the meantime, something happened in the cockpit which appeared to be as follows: the Captain was playing with the undercarriage lights on the front panel and leant on the control wheel or yoke. The autopilot was in but there are three different settings for an autopilot – one being off, two being the normal controls, and the third (rarely used) whereby the autopilot can be selected so that, whatever position you put the flight controls in, they will obey it. It seems that it was in this position when the Captain, without realising it, was leaning on the control panel. The aeroplane very slowly descended in the dark, unnoticed by the other crew members, until it crashed into the Everglades. The flight engineer was down below, 101 were killed and some possibly got out but were eaten by the alligators. 75 survived.

The flight engineer (or ghost thereof) was often seen on a particular Tri-Star where some of the galley equipment had been used from the wreck of the original 401 aircraft. Those using the lift down into the current Tri-Star galley would often see his face looking out from the lift itself through the glass panel, or experience him in the galley where he often helped solve problems in one way or another. On top of that, he was often seen when cabin crew were resting between flights in the seats of the cabin where he would sit next to them. He was very friendly and never gave anyone cause to fear him. However, the hostesses demanded all of Flight 401 items be removed, which solved the problem.

It was also recognised that people did not report strange or alien encounters. The biggest one was across the Atlantic when one of the crew looked down and could see the largest spaceship you could ever imagine in your life, up to half-a-mile long. When the pilot asked on the radio if anyone else had seen it, the others on other aeroplanes within the sky just merely said yes but made no other comment. Sightings that I know of from other pilots consist of items or spaceships coming up out of the sea, but without making any particular splash or disturbance to the water. There are occasions when people have been lost above cloud and a spaceship has come alongside and led them to an opening in the clouds, leading them through it for a safe landing.

The co-pilot with the most northern accent was sitting in an aircraft when it was pouring with rain. The pushback driver was pushing the aircraft with a long tank-like vehicle attached to the nose wheel. An engineer was standing alongside with a headset, communicating with us in the cockpit, but he was absolutely drenched and it was freezing cold – he almost had icicles on his chin. The First Officer called down to him and said, "Hello engineer, what's it like out there?" to which the engineer said, "Absolutely dreadful." The First Officer's reply was, "If you had worked hard at school, and got all your exams, you would be sitting up here at the moment drinking coffee and tea with a stewardess behind, instead of freezing to death." Everybody liked this guy – he was not worried whether he hurt people's feelings or not. However, not long after this, we got the message that he committed suicide because his girlfriend had left him – he put a shotgun under his chin and blew his head off.

The regular taxi driver in Scotland attempted the same thing. He now had a beard to cover the wound. Many cases exist of pilots dying or committing suicide, and at one point we had five cases in a very short period, followed by other incidents – like the First Officer who was on board a cabin cruiser with his girlfriend, but they had a gas fire going which suffocated them with the fumes. Three others merely sat in a car with a bottle of whisky and fed a tube from the exhaust pipe into the car and passed away. Some others just drank themselves into an early grave.

An old Captain who had retired always wrote something in a book or diary before he set off to fly. Many years went by and people always wondered what he had written. One day, on his very last flight, he left the book on his seat while he went back to say goodbye to the cabin crew. The First Officer grabbed the opportunity and looked in the book. There was written in big bold letters, 'Left port, right starboard'.

The cabin crew used to stitch each other up, because if there was a flight without good allowances, they would tend to go sick. This particularly applied to the Moscow and Istanbul flights. There was also another flight aptly named, "What has three legs, and f..ks cabin crew"? The answer was the London – Sofia – Bucharest flight.

I overheard a couple of stewardesses having a very heated conversation which went something like this: First stewardess: "What's your problem?"; Second one: "We were discussing our ages, and when I told her mine, she said, 'Blimey – you're older than my mum!'" Always be very careful if you decide to banter with a stewardess because they know all the answers and put-down statements.

One passenger called the stewardess over by flicking his fingers, which they hate, and said to her, "I am not eating this food; it is not fit for a pig." So the stewardess called the steward over and the man repeated what he had said. The steward shouted very loudly to one of the other stewardesses, "Can you bring me some food that is fit for a pig?"

Once when I was disembarking the cabin crew and standing at the door saying goodbye, an objectionable passenger came past them and said, "I'm never gonna fly with your airline again," to which the steward replied, "It's no good you being nice to us now, Sir."

The SAS soldiers used to use the Trident aircraft for training, and occasionally they would require a standby crew to come and sit in the cockpit while they practised boarding the aircraft during a terrorist scenario. Whilst being with them and sitting quietly in the Captain's seat they would come crashing through the door and throw themselves onto the central throttle quadrant with their back towards the instrument panel of the aircraft, looking straight at and pointing guns at the crew. It was quite frightening and though we had nothing to worry about at the time, I assume that it would be quite daunting for a terrorist. After one of the incidents, they forgot to remove the dummy bombs that they had planted in the back of the seats for sniffer dogs and others to find and dismantle.

By the way, never put your hand down the back of an aircraft seat pocket where the airline magazine and sick bag are kept. This is a favourite disposal place for hypodermic syringes, and most cleaners will wear thick pairs of gloves. One jab from one of these needles would give you several years of heartache until you knew whether you had AIDS or not.

The SAS soldiers went through a large part of the course for different aircraft like the Trident. One day, one of the instructors was fuming when the SAS guys appeared to be taking no notice whatsoever of what he was saying during the chalk and talk lesson that he was giving them. In the end, he said that he was going to pack it up and leave the classroom because they were throwing paper darts round the room. He said to one of them, "What's the point of talking to you? You don't listen to anything I've said, and you don't know what I've said." The guy said back to him, "On the hydraulics you said the following…" and he repeated virtually word-for-word everything that the instructor had said over the last thirty minutes, proving how intelligent these people were.

Some of the RAF pilots were also trained on 737 aircraft, with the specific role that, if the 'balloon went up' in Berlin, *they* would fly the aircraft into Berlin – and not us airline pilots. Don't know what the pilots who were actually in Berlin would do, but it would certainly not be a good idea to try to fly the aeroplane out whilst being pursued by a Russian fighter.

You could always recognise Russian civilian aircraft on take-off or final approach because they usually had black smoke coming out from the engines – we referred to them as 'coal burners'. Basically they were not tuned or serviced properly; this was rather similar to the black smoke you see coming out from behind an old diesel car.

Timekeeping is vital so that all flights leave smack on time. One nice thing about flying is that everybody can be pretty well guaranteed to turn up on time. It takes nearly fifty people all working together, either directly or indirectly, to run an aircraft, and it is rare that anyone purposely causes a delay. However, if you do, you will be marked down by the Dispatcher and the delay will be put down to your department. Every morning there would be a meeting of the management (called 'morning prayers') which would discuss any late departures.

A rumpus was caused on one flight. The stewardess was having an affair with a married pilot. The pilot was married to another stewardess. The rumour had got round and back to the wife and she made every effort to get crewed up with the offending stewardess, hoping to be able to check out whether it was true or not. (During night stops, the amount of gossip that takes place is just unbelievable, and many a nice young girl is ruined by the old re-treads, all wrinklies and crinklies who had been dumped by some male. A large number of them have the trait of hating men.) Anyway, on the night stop, the married stewardess started up a very innocent conversation, asking the other one where she lived, how long she'd been there, whether she had any friends... and the stewardess fell for it. She mentioned the name of the other guy, at which point she was set upon by the stewardess and the cat-fight took place until they were dragged apart. Eventually they were kept at opposite ends of the aeroplane for the return trip and disciplined.

A stewardess on my flight had eight husbands and none of them were hers.

The losses on airlines often come from shrinkage – in other words, cabin crew taking bottles of booze and catering off the aircraft. A favourite with some of the stewardesses was to take the internal silver balloon out of the wine boxes, fill them with brandy and put them under their clothing. They would then walk through Customs as if they just have a big stomach.

Halfway through the flight, a male passenger had a heart attack. His wife didn't even call the stewardess, but the cabin crew noticed and realised what had happened and tried to revive him. They made several attempts but his wife turned round and said, "I wouldn't bother, he's had a jolly good innings anyway." We never did work out what she meant and what her intentions were – they never did manage to revive him.

On one occasion, there was a bomb in the back of a seat pocket in the passenger cabin of a Trident. A bomb disposal officer came on board the aircraft at the end of the flight. It turned out that a female IRA member had got on the aeroplane with a baby, then gone to the toilet and left a dirty nappy there. Other members of the team went back with bits and pieces and put a bomb together which was then stuck in the back of the seat. However, it failed to explode – basically because they had forgotten that the watch that they were using had luminous paint on it and the detonator failed to make contact through the paint. The bomb disposal expert came on board with the dog, searched the aeroplane and found the bomb easily. There was no sign of any others. The dog grabbed hold of the bomb in the dirty nappy and the officer departed the aeroplane rapidly, followed by the dog with a bomb in its mouth. He was last seen running for his life across the airfield with the bomb neatly tucked in the jaws of his dog, with him shouting, "Go away." (We have special places on the aeroplane to put bombs or suspicious items where they are less likely to cause structural damage to the actual aeroplane. A bomb going off and blasting a window could suck anyone out of the aircraft, and this has happened on occasions.)

Two co-pilots were walking so slowly across the tarmac in Bucharest, making their way towards the aircraft from the main building, that even the passengers were catching them up. The Captain was fuming as he had to carry out their checks. At the rate they were crossing the tarmac, there would be a delay in departure. The Captain leant out and shouted, "Move yourselves, you bastards!" All the passengers started to run and passed the co-pilots, getting to the aircraft steps before them.

We were waiting for take-off from the main airport in Israel when a jet fighter aircraft landed. As it touched down, it deployed its parachute to slow it down. Eventually it disconnected the parachute which drifted gently to one side onto the grass. The controllers cleared our 707 to take off immediately. It started down the runway when about halfway down the parachute was caught by some wind and blown straight across the tarmac. It went straight into the number two engine of a departing aircraft, and there was virtually nothing left within the engine itself. The aircraft aborted, came to a halt and taxied off, having to go back to the hangers for a new engine.

Another incident took place but this time it was in Beirut. There was a charter outfit operating out of the city, and one of the ex-company guys was now a Training Captain with them. He had been there for a couple of years and it was his duty to pass or fail people for command courses. There was a stocky local Arab co-pilot coming up for his final command check. At the briefing, the First Officer turned to the Training Captain and said, "I will be doing my command check tomorrow with you, and I feel pretty certain that I am going to pass it." At that point, he let his jacket fall open where the Captain could see what looked like a .357 Magnum revolver. The co-pilot nonchalantly mentioned that his friends manned the roadblock that was just down the road from where the Training Captain lived. He said, "If I am right, you live in the block of flats near there, meaning you go past that checkpoint every day." He added, "You do know that someone got killed there the other day, don't you?" The Captain thought long and hard about this and the next morning, despite the fact that the chap was not competent to be a Captain, felt that he had no option but to pass him.

Two pilots at Gatwick wandered across the tarmac to an aircraft bound for Amsterdam. It was only when they landed there that the Duty Manager came into the cockpit and asked them what the hell they were doing. They were a bit taken aback, but asked why. The Duty Manager explained to them that they had got on the wrong aeroplane and basically had hijacked it with all the passengers and crew and flown to Amsterdam when it was supposed to go to Stockholm.

It is amazing how pilots, particularly American pilots, can come up with fantastic quips. A hilarious situation took place when these guys had flown from Istanbul, landed at London airport and taxied onto the stand. The ground controller called to them, "You're on the wrong stand – you are on C14 and you're supposed to be on C12." The Captain replied, "I have just flown 2,500 miles and I'm twenty feet out – that's not bad, really."

We were due to position to Paris to bring an aircraft back, and were airborne when a very pretty girl was invited into the cockpit. Often a good steward would pick a very pretty girl out and arrange with the Captain to invite her up front. Some of them must have wondered why they were selected. However, on this day the aircraft was flown by a God pilot (our name for a born-again Christian). After some persuasion from the second co-pilot the Captain, with some reluctance, allowed the steward to bring her up. She was a cracker, and asked several flattering questions. She was invited to sit on the extra fourth seat for the rest of the flight including the landing. They arrived in Paris and taxied to the stand where the engines were switched off. All the passengers left the aircraft for the terminal. The girl was just unbuckling her seat belt on the fourth seat and stood up in her miniskirt, pulling it down as best she could within the cramped cockpit. Her handbag had been placed between her seat and the side of the aircraft. This spot is carefully designated by First Officers – as was apparent at this point when the girl now standing had to bend over the seat and feel for her bag. The co-pilot not being a gentleman, did not avert his eyes. She retrieved the bag and said farewell to all of them and then went to join the rest of the passengers. The co-pilot grabbed the seat cushion that she had been sitting on and placing it to his nose he took a deep breath. The Captain turned and said – the way only a born-again Christian could – "How dare you". To which the co-pilot said, "Sorry, Capt – after you."

St Peter at the pearly gates said to a recently departed pilot trying to gain entry, "You have been very good, you can have a Rolls Royce"; to the next pilot, "You've been fairly good, you can have a Ford Escort"; the last pilot had been drinking and generally getting up to mischief, so was given a moped. Later he saw the Rolls Royce driver crying, and when he asked why, the man said, "I have just seen my wife go past on a skateboard."

Our resident comedian was in a holding pattern north of London, in an area where delayed aircraft are put into a racetrack pattern and held at a certain height to be lowered down by 1,000 feet at a time, until it is their turn to land and get picked off by the controller from the bottom of the holding pattern. After a while, an Arabian aeroplane came roaring into the beacon and was given permission to go in and land immediately. Being very annoyed, the skipper asked Traffic Control what was going on. The controller replied, "The aircraft had three princes on board and therefore had priority." To which our skipper replied, "That is nothing, I've got three queens down the back – I beat him, so let me land first." Needless to say, he didn't succeed. He was later seen in the crew restaurant ordering a cup of coffee when a Flight Manager came in and approached the serving area. Slapping him on the back, the skipper shouted in an East End London accent so that everyone in the room could hear, "That was the best bollocking I've ever had."

Later in a flight, the stewardess came up and said a passenger had died – this happens quite often on flights when elderly people decide to over-extend themselves to visit their friends and relatives, sometimes as far afield as Australia. Some modern aircraft actually have cupboards specially for storing bodies in flight – they used to be put in a first class seat with a blanket over them. Anyway, I made an announcement that, if there was a doctor present on the plane, would they make themselves known, which one did. The stewardess explained to them that a passenger had died. The doctor got out of his seat, walked along the aisle and went straight up to a passenger and thumped him really hard on the chest. The stewardess asked, "Why did you do that?" The reply, "To get his heart to work." She replied, "But he's only asleep – that's not the passenger; he is in the row behind."

Pan-American flights were renowned for the stewardesses being rude to passengers. In one case, a passenger got on board having been allocated a row that was smoking. He complained like mad to the stewardess saying, "I was promised that I would be given a no-smoking seat," to which the stewardess replied in a very loud voice, "They lied." I actually experienced this myself on a short hop flight or feeder flight from New York to Columbus Ohio. When the aircraft was climbing, the stewardess went along the aisle at a pretty fast rate, slinging white cardboard boxes with a sandwich and a fruit drink in it saying, "Wanna snack? Wanna snack?" to all the ninety-odd passengers on board. That was about as civil as it got!

It was about this time that we got the first lady co-pilots. We had never had any in the company's existence. The excuse had always been that they failed the test because they had no spatial awareness. When a certain Captain was crewed with this female pilot, he eventually ended up with a hernia trying to carry her suitcase down the stairs. He also remarked that, because ladies did their shirts up the opposite way to men, this was good because he could see their bra if they had one on.

Another skipper took the wrong suitcase back home (most people had Delsey suitcases). When he arrived home and opened it up, it was full of women's clothing, which took quite a lot of explaining to his wife. Another lady pilot found that somebody had been into her room and stolen a lot of her clothing – mainly underwear – and when in the cockpit, she promptly felt the Captain's leg to see whether he was wearing her suspender belt.

Going through 10,000 feet, a female pilot violently pushed the stick forward, almost throwing everyone out of their seats, because she had thought that she had gone through the assigned flight level.

One of the pilots was a transvestite, and whenever he arrived at the destination, he would go into the toilet and dress up as a lady and then go down the steps to the taxi. He was known to appear at the bar dressed with make-up on. At least one First Officer actually made advances towards him (or her) without realising it was his skipper. This guy was actually married to a lady who dressed in white leathers and drove a bike with a sidecar (which is where he was usually put). She was one of the most butch people that you could come across.

Then there was the case where the skipper was making advances towards one of the stewardesses and she gave him the go-ahead. She went up to her bedroom and got under the sheets, with another stewardess pretending to be stripped naked but having the blankets just above their breasts. The man ran into the room, pulling his clothes off, and was stark naked when the rest of the crew jumped out and generally took the piss out of him.

Early in the morning, after a really heavy night of drinking and eating a large curry, I got down to the lobby before anyone else. After a short while, the lift door opened and a very sheepish-looking First Officer came out, followed shortly after by two very attractive blonde stewardesses from another airline. After they'd left, he explained that, it being so early in the morning, he didn't expect anyone to be getting into the lift, and as he passed the third floor, he let out one of the loudest farts he'd ever done, which disgusted even him. At which point, the door opened and these two gorgeous blondes got in on the second floor. The door shut before he could do anything about it and so he had to ride all the way down to the ground floor with them and had no chance of denying that it was him.

During this period, the whole of aviation management were particularly keen on twin-engine aircraft. They considered that they were much cheaper to run and everything was done to prove that two engines were perfectly safe, despite the fact that many of the old Captains would not accept this. Many of the companies told Captains who had lost an engine in flight to merely throttle the engine back. However, in actual fact, this would probably severely damage the engine, as it was normal to shut it down, but then the statistics would look bad – so for a long time you had aircraft running around with damaged engines which had been throttled back, just in order to get the statistics correct for all the new twin-engine aeroplanes which were about to come out. This was referred to as the EROPS which the pilots translated as 'engines running or passengers swimming', but which should have been 'Extended Range Operations'.

An Australian skipper with another airline was having trouble with a very bolshie steward. The steward kept interfering till the Captain got fed up and said to him, "Look, sonny, I'm fucking this cat, your just holding its tail." The steward got the point.

A crew were flying to Italy. It was the First Officer's opportunity to do the flight and he told the Captain that he was going off the air to talk to the passengers and the Captain surreptitiously listened in. The First Officer said, "Ladies and gentlemen, I hope you're enjoying the flight. I really do wish I'd bought my Fiat car with me, because we are now passing over the Fiat factory and I could have dropped it on them from 30,000 feet. However, we will be landing in about twenty minutes' time and the weather there is fine – please adjust your watches by one hour."

At the end of every flight, the Captain was expected to make a report on the First Officer. Very few ever do it, and those that take the trouble to do so normally end up as Training Captains who are despised, despite the fact that most Training Captains think they're wonderful and everybody loves them.

The company opened the brand-new new hangar; it was an enormous place and referred to as 'the cathedral'. They had to carry out tests in it for fire drills, so they cleared the hangar and set off the fire extinguishers to check what would happen. The fire extinguisher went off with no problem, filling the hanger with about six to eight feet of foam. The problem was that it was made from bull's blood, and despite hosing it down with heavy fire hoses, the blood got into every crack and cranny so that the hangar was full of flies and bluebottles which bred like mad.

Just alongside this was a large building where engines were run up and tested. Oil was regularly lost from these engines and slowly seeped into the ground. Many years later, when they decided they wanted to knock the engine maintenance building down, they found that the oil had seeped twenty to thirty feet into the ground, and huge excavations had to be made in order to take it away and clean it for new EEC regulations.

At this time, at the end of runway 28 right at Heathrow, you would have seen a large lake, several hundred yards long by about fifty yards wide, with several heavy ropes strung across it, fitted with sheepskin dangling from them. This was where they drained all the de-icing fluid, oil and everything else that ran off onto the ramp from the aircraft when they were parked outside the main building. The drain ran into this pool and as it was taken away, the ropes with the sheepskin on absorbing most of the oil and the de-icing fluid.

We did not fly that day, but eventually travelled by taxi to our Glasgow hotel. After such a hard day, we changed, showered and went back to the 'Bon Accord', which still had sawdust on the floor. My First Officer was about 6' 8" tall. We were not the first in the bar but we were three or four pints ahead. A Glaswegian was drinking alongside us. He was much the worse for wear, and after a while he turned and said to no-one in particular, "Someone's stolen my jacket." It's a bit like calling someone a cheat in a Dodge City poker game. Luckily, he was pissed to the eyeballs, so no-one took any notice. He hunted round, and feeling sorry for him, we helped him – until his jacket was found, exactly where he had put it an hour before. Typical of Scottish hospitality, he offered to buy the two of us a drink so we had a pint of Heavy. He then told us his life story up until that afternoon, which appeared he had spent at a wedding reception on a boat sailing up the Clyde.

He looked up from his 5' 2" height to the top of my accomplice at 6' 8". "You could help me," he said (except it was said in a drunken Govan accent, much like Rab C Nesbit). "I got greens from a waitress. She said I was on a promise if I met her behind her flats. The only problem is that her old man is a bastard and is good with a knife. Now, if you two could come with me and keep a look-out for him, I can take her round the back for a quick one." He could not understand why we did not think it a good idea. Finally, he got the message that we were not going with him and he staggered out mumbling something about Sassenachs.

The pub was jumping when a stag night bunch arrived. Many pints of Heavy were poured onto many pints of Heavy, followed by whisky-chasers all round. Then someone had a great idea. The 'Bon Accord' was on a quiet road outside which there was a twenty-foot drop onto a dual carriageway below. The groom had temporality passed out, so they dragged him outside, stripped him naked and then handcuffed him to the railings between the quiet road and the twenty-foot drop. They all then proceeded to be sick all over him and washed some of it off by peeing on him. He was then abandoned while they all went for a curry!

Strange that flight crew are so keen on curries – we were always told by the medical staff that if you wished to pass wind when you're in an aeroplane, there was no way at all of stopping it. The women passed just as much wind as the men. A female doctor also said that pilots usually had daughters rather than sons.

Always remember when you get to your hotel room that all sorts of things could have gone on before you arrived. In particular, I advise you to be very careful on the use of the kettle, as many a steward has used the kettle rather than bothering to use the toilet! When in Edinburgh, I was told that one of the stewardesses who was always very game had invited three of the stewards to her room where she allowed them to perform sexual acts on her – all three of them at the same time. Somehow she managed to have an arm free and actually took photographs of herself. I believe she married into the airline.

When a flight was over and whilst walking back to the car park, you regularly had passengers asking you if you knew where they had parked their car. Not only do we not know which car park they would have been in, we certainly didn't know what their car looked like, but somehow they expected us to know exactly where they had left it. Indeed, pilots always make a point of writing down where they leave their car before they go off on a couple of nights stops – it is extremely easy to end up wandering around the car park for a long time trying to find your own car.

One crew were followed back to the car park after coming in from Istanbul. It turned out that drugs had been planted in their suitcases and the information passed to people in London who followed them out to the car and stole the bags.

A First Officer was invalided back from South America and came through the Crew Room with his leg in plaster. He had been a gentleman and taken one of the stewardesses out to see some of the local dancing, and on the way back they were approached by someone who asked them for a cigarette. The stewardess told him to get lost, at which point the local kicked the First Officer in the leg. He knew what he was doing because he didn't kick fore and aft on the leg, but kicked it sideways on the knee bone, which makes a dreadful fracture. The man was in agony for months and months, and it took nearly a year before he got back to flying.

At this time, again in South America, one of the skippers came across a new dating drug. They had gone out on a drinking session when they met up with some locals, both men and women, who fed them drink. Later they found when they woke up that not only had they been robbed, but all of them (including the men) had been raped. The skipper didn't think that they should fly the next day, but they were in such a dreadful state that they asked the other cabin crew to cover for them. They were allowed to go back into the tail of the aeroplane, sleep in the bunks and keep out of the way as their colleagues carried out their duties. I can only advise you to never, ever accept a drink from someone – and never to leave your drink unattended, particularly in Latin American countries.

In South Africa, one stewardess took all her clothes off in the hotel bar and performed an erotic dance on the top of the piano. She actually got fired, but we think this was due to the fact that it was so early in this date-drug situation that the management hadn't actually heard of it or understood what it consisted of. It was most unfair that she lost her job.

A crew went out to the Latin American bar and had a wonderful time with the locals drinking and gambling, playing cards, singing karaoke and whatever else you can think of, until it came to the time to go home. The locals said, "Can we just give you a little bit of advice – would you put your camera, your money and your wallet on the bar and just say goodbye?" They looked puzzled and the locals said, "Well, we've had such a wonderful evening and thoroughly enjoyed meeting you, so we do not want to have to mug you on the way home – this way we will not have to hurt you." They put everything on the bar and left.

Holidaying in America and the West Indies also needs a bit of care and attention when you have your young children with you. I say this without apology, as a couple of skippers have actually lost their children in the USA.

One of the crew and his wife were sitting around the pool with their two young children, about seven years old, when the little boy disappeared. They asked people sitting next to them to look after their daughter and they rushed off to look for the boy – they never found him, and when they came back, the daughter was missing. The skipper resigned, and as far as I know spent many years hunting around America, never getting his children back. Something like three million children go missing in America at any one time – so be aware. If you look at the milk cartons in America, you will usually see pictures of missing youngsters with pleas from the parents for any information.

Another thing to be cautious of is sailing in a yacht around the Caribbean. One of the crew was with four others – two men and their wives – when they were attacked by pirates. The pirates were about to rape the women and throw the men overboard when another more salubrious yacht came past. The pirates all got into their small boat, leaving a guard on board and disappeared off to attack the other boat. Luckily, one of the guys manage to get free and overpowered the guard, throwing him into the water, after which they managed to sail off and get safely back to dry land.

In Amsterdam that morning, the senior stewardess came up to me. She said, "I think you ought to know that there was a problem last night." The new young steward had an early night. At about two o'clock in the morning, there was a knock on his door and the night porter asked if he could come in and have a talk to him on the issue that the porter thought that he might be homosexual. The steward stupidly allowed him in and as the night wore on, one thing led to another, at which point certain acts were performed on the steward with his permission. Unfortunately, it somehow weakened or released his bowels and having a dose of diarrhoea, the entire bed was smothered in excreta.

At this point, the night porter did a rapid departure stage right and disappeared. The steward spent the whole night trying to wash the bed sheets in the bath. Not being streetwise, he did not realise that the chambermaid would have no idea as to why his sheets were smothered. All he only really needed to do was to leave a couple hundred guilders by the bedside with a note saying that he'd had an accident. However, by the time he came down to the crew transport, he had had no sleep whatsoever and looked like death warmed up. Thankfully, the stewardess had told me and we managed to cover up for him.

British Airways Trident 3

Trident Flight Deck

Chapter Thirteen
737

The First Officer and I decided to take a trip out to Dachau concentration camp. I was actually with the guy mentioned in the previous chapter who blew his own head off with a shotgun. The amazing thing was that the bus that took us to the camp and back could not have been more than three seconds out from the scheduled time of departure. It was typical Germanic efficiency.

It was most moving to walk round the camp itself and we went to the building which contained the ovens and where most of the bodies were burned. It was an extremely moving experience – in particular, where there were three nooses made of thick wire hanging from the ceiling where three extremely brave female undercover agents had been hanged on wires. This was so that they did not die immediately – indeed, it took some time – and during this frightful period they could see bodies being put into the ovens. (The bodies were laid on metal stretchers and then slid into the ovens.) We also looked in the shower area. Although they did not gas people in the showers unlike some other camps, it gave a very distinct impression as to what the facilities were like in other camps.

Between the two of us, we were disgusted at how clinical the whole camp had been at that time. You couldn't hear any birds around and it was easy to sit there and let your mind wander to try and imagine what it must have been like then. The other thing that really upset us was the Dachau holiday brochure for the town. Remember that the people in Dachau at the time denied any knowledge of what went on in the camp, and after the war was over, or at least when the camps were liberated, the locals were made to come in and view atrocities. However, the holiday brochure claimed this was a great area for hill walking, beautiful scenery, fishing, beer halls and many other wonderful facilities. There was no mention, other than one very short paragraph, that nearly a quarter of a million people had been killed in the camp, either being shot on the rifle range or dying of hunger or maltreatment. I thought it was dreadful that it was all glossed over.

We took a hot-air balloon to Berlin Tempelhof Airport where we boarded our own aircraft. Thank goodness I was a passenger, because we had a fantastically large complimentary bar on board to look after local dignitaries. Naturally, the hot-air balloon had to be tethered, otherwise it would have floated off into East Berlin, and anyone on board would have probably been put in prison – assuming that you were not shot down for spying.

The guys operating the balloon were a bunch of dedicated pilots from all walks of life, including one man who was a farmer. He was hobbling around with a severely damaged back which he got from lifting heavy bales of hay and putting them into a truck. He had been lifting much more than the younger members of his party, but unfortunately, in lifting the heaviest bail as he walked back into the truck, the wooden floor of the truck gave way and he fell straight through and straddled the back axle of the truck. You can imagine how painful it would have been and the damage that it did to his spine. However, this in no way affected his sense of humour and he was a great character all round.

We had many photographs taken with the balloon and eventually went across to the tanks that were there with the army, which they allowed us to climb all over and take photographs inside. We were talking about what would happen if the 'balloon went up'. We didn't consider it very sensible for us to try and fly our slow aeroplane out of Berlin, down one of the air corridors, when there were fighter aircraft around. They said that their war would last less than fifteen minutes, enough time for the German fighters to take off, do a circuit and then run in and fire their rockets and cannon at the tanks. That would have been about as much of the war that they were likely to see.

We used to get fed on the aeroplane, but the First Officer and the Captain always have different meals. We always said that the chicken that we were served had had more flying hours than us.

One evening, the aircraft toilets were blocked, and the engineers did everything they could to clear them until one of them decided that it would be a good idea to connect up the Copco (the air start system), which was basically a truck with a large engine on it which blew copious amounts of air in order to make the aircraft engine turn before it was started. Alternatively, it could be used for air conditioning. So one engineer coupled that (or at least held it) to the side of the aircraft at the vent for the toilets. The other engineer went inside the toilet cubical just to check the operation was working, and on his radio he told them to start the Copco up and then give it full blast – which it did, emptying the entire toilet contents over the engineer and the whole of the inside of the aircraft. It took weeks for the smell to go, and certainly most of the night for the engineers to try and clear the mess up by first thing in the morning. A great idea, but I don't think anyone's ever tried it again.

In a Munich restaurant, Sonia, the Russian waitress, liked our pilots but disliked the American ones, so we always got the best tables in the house. When in Germany, try the Hungarian Goulash Soup – it is out of this world.

Boeing had a stupid idea of making sure that anyone who flew their aircraft talked about left and right rather than port or starboard – I'm sure this caused many accidents, and in particular the Kegworth 737 crash, which is a very good example of the stupidity of this policy. First, you must remember that the stewardess or steward welcoming passengers on board the flight will look at their seat number in order to indicate which side of the aircraft each passenger should sit. So if you are given, say, seat number 23D, you would be sitting on the right-hand, or starboard, side of the aircraft, which means that you're on the right-hand side looking towards the nose of the aircraft. The stewardess however is pointing to the left-hand side of the aircraft from where she is standing, looking towards the rear. It is therefore vital that one uses port and starboard – if you don't, the following could happen.

At Kegworth, it is my contention that a passenger pointed to an engine and said that the engine appeared to be on fire. The stewardess then went to the Captain and First Officer and told them that the left-hand engine appeared to be on fire. The Captain asked the First Officer to carry out the fire drill closing down the left engine. However, it was the right engine which was actually on fire. More power was now naturally put onto the right engine which was actually on fire. The aircraft continued its flight using full power on a damaged engine and it was only at the last minute on finals that the engine packed up. The aircraft had been flying with a perfectly serviceable engine shutdown. The aircraft crashed short of the runway, having crossed the M1 motorway at 90°, and hit the bank on the far side, breaking its back and coming to rest just on the top of the embankment. Many of the passengers were killed, but it is interesting to note that the only reason some of them escaped was that there was a group of SAS soldiers passing at the time who managed to get them out. This accident need never have happened and I am convinced that I am right as to the cause.

With typical humour, when the crashed aircraft was eventually lifted, there was a dead hedgehog underneath it, which resulted in a cartoon being posted on the wall in our Crew Room. It showed a poor hedgehog's footprints going right across the motorway without being squashed, climbing the far bank and then being hit by a crashed aircraft. You would be surprised at the black humour and cartoons that appear after accidents – one would assume it's because pilots have to think in this way in case it happens to them. As I've mentioned before, it is quite sobering to go through the lockers of pilots who have died to make sure that there is nothing incriminating about a pilot's life which could upset the family.

It was found that an awful lot of stuff on one airline was being thrown away – for instance, during a turnaround, the cleaning staff would go through and take all the blankets that had been used and stuff them into black binliners, along with all sorts of other bits and pieces. When the truck pulled up, the black sacks were removed and thrown away with the rubbish. One day, the new bright spark manager, known as 'manager of knives and forks', came up with a great idea. He took all the skips from one or two days' operations and asked travellers if they would come to a field where they were offered the contents of all the bags, if they helped sort, which they gladly did. All the items were spread out over the field and put into individual piles so people could see what was there. There were piles and piles of blankets, piles and piles of teapots, knives and forks, and goodness knows what else... all about to be thrown into the tip. The travellers left with all the items and the airline came up with a very simple idea – that in future, all bags would be clear plastic, so that you could see what was in them.

We had a report from the steward that he had seen a female passenger going to the toilet who had been in there for quite a long time – so much so that he went in to inspect the toilet. Toilets are popular places to dispose of passports for passengers applying for political asylum. The airline gets fined £2,000 for every illegal immigrant, so people need to be on their toes to protect the company. The steward noticed a small piece of passport floating in the bottom of the toilets. I called up the company and asked them to call Immigration as we knew who the passenger was. Immigration were the first on board, the cabin crew had asked the lady to remain seated. They kept her there until someone had got a large pair of marigolds (thick rubber gloves) to search around in the toilet, until they came up with all the pieces of the passport, then put them in a bag and left for the immigration office.

I was listening to cabin crew discussing reincarnation and what they would want to come back as. One said as a Concorde sink, as all the champagne was poured down it. The other said she would like to come back as a dog, to which a steward said, "You already have."

The Queen was going to visit Berlin and stay at her hotel. There were many Union flags put up ready for the visit, but the crew used to taunt the concierge as to whether they were the right way up. They got the concierge to take them down, turn them upside down and raise them several times.

British Airways 737

Chapter Fourteen
CONCLUDING REFLECTIONS AND MISCELLANEOUS MEMORIES

There were various other memories of aviation which are bitter-sweet or stay in my mind for one reason or another. For example, I was very fond of the Viscounts, and I remember positioning Viscount 800 G-AOHW for its last flight. It first flew on the 18th July 1957, and I took it on the 18th May 1976 to Newcastle. It was subsequently given to the Fire Service and eventually broken up for scrap in August 1983.

Flying long haul always created scope for problems because of the sheer length of flights. On one occasion earlier in my career, a staff passenger (who worked for the company but who was flying for free as a passenger) complained bitterly about the behaviour of another staff family. They were in the front of first class and their children were behaving terribly, screaming and shouting and throwing things round the aircraft. The Captain decided that the best way to deal with this was to impose some order. He came down in his full uniform and spoke to the offending family. He said sternly to the father that his family's behaviour was completely out of court, and that he was going to report them to the company and say their staff travel perks should be removed. But the man looked puzzled.

"What do you mean – staff passenger?"

The Captain snorted at him. "I know you're staff passengers, a staff family, and I will get your staff travel taken away."

"I do not know what you're talking about," was the unimpressed reply. "I'm a businessman. I paid full fare for this flight."

The Captain nearly died of embarrassment and gave him a couple bottles of champagne in an attempt to brush the whole thing over.

On another long-haul flight to New Zealand, on which I was a passenger, there was another issue in first class. There was a couple who had paid a normal first class fare and near them were four 20-year-olds who initially sat quietly but, as the flight progressed, they drank more and more heavily, becoming increasingly the worse for wear. I asked the cabin crew who they were, as they did not look like normal first class passengers, and I was told that they were travel agents on a free trade look-see to find out how the first class passengers lived. The full- fare lady passenger looked particularly unimpressed with one of the female travel agents and ended up complaining about their behaviour, putting the steward in a difficult position as to whom he should upset: the travel agents, or the paying passengers.

However, the decision was at that moment made for him: the female travel agent was violently sick all over the lady passenger. The woman was in an absolute rage and stalked out. The cabin crew washed her down as best they could and gave her a couple of bottles of champagne and the complaints form. The steward was still in a difficult position, but I wrote a nice report saying that he had handled the situation as best he could; it was definitely the travel agents who had behaved badly, and it was not his fault at all.

Most members of aviation crews were good, solid people with whom one could have a good laugh and a drink, but there were exceptions or those who took you by surprise. Occasionally we flew out of Gatwick, which seems to be a mysterious base on its own, and we referred to the staff there as 'the boat people'.

Having said that, another skipper always changed into his slippers for the flight and made himself comfortable and at home. I always thought it would make rather a bad impression if passengers saw him in them. Another had a young child's satchel instead of a flight bag.

Many passengers objected strongly to having a female pilot when they were first introduced. We had to deal regularly with people saying that they did not want to fly with someone who might have PMT. I personally had little or no problem with any of them and found them fantastic colleagues. However, considerable resentment was caused in the Crew Room when the crews were told to remove from the walls the many pictures from Playboy magazine which splattered the walls, including the famous one of a girl walking towards the tennis net with no knickers on. I couldn't understand why they couldn't just put up their own pictures; the female pilots were by no means pristine pure in conversation and outlook. In fact, the reverse was usually the case. There was one female pilot in particular who sat in the Crew Room in Berlin and really didn't care where her skirt was. She would swear and exchange dirty jokes as much as any flight engineer.

Travelling round as we did meant that we stayed in a lot of hotels. Mostly, these were very good but we learned to be careful if ever complaining about noise in them. In one of the Glasgow hotels, a pilot who was trying to sleep in the afternoon got fed up with the noise from the neighbouring room; he went and knocked on the door to ask them to be quiet but there was no answer, so he rang Reception to complain but again there was no answer. He was so vexed he decided to go downstairs in person. He got into the lift and, just as he did so, the people from the room making the noise got in with him and beat seven bells out of him.

A pilot had his face slapped by a stewardess when he asked her name, completely forgetting that he had bedded her the month before.

When we returned from viewing this entertaining incident, we found Billy Connolly in the bar. He seemed a genuinely likeable character. It was quite late but we all decided that we would go to a local curry house – not with Billy Connolly, unfortunately. One of the First Officers there that night was a heavy supporter of the National Front. We sat down and were served huge soup plates full of curry. This place specialised in having Indian girls serving the table and we asked the First Officer how it could be that, when he didn't like foreign nationals, he was quite happy to be served by them.

His reply was blunt: "I don't mind f...ing them – I just don't like living next to them."

Travelling all round the world, we became wise to the safety issues different places raised. Girls who were with us learnt always to keep their handbags between two or three of us, as it was so easy for a motorcyclist to go past and grab it. We also, in some parts of the world, each rolled a couple of one-dollar bills around a matchbox and put an elastic band round them. We would all keep one of these in our pocket in case we were mugged. Then we could just throw this down on the floor and run, leaving the mugger to pick up a couple of dollars.

On one occasion, the crew on taking off from the Shetland Islands, hit so much turbulence that the toilet actually managed to empty itself in the toilet area, even leaking under the door. It took weeks to get rid of the stench. Though this at least stopped passengers sneaking in there in order to have a crafty smoke, which in the days before smoke detectors used to happen frequently.

'Honker' was a nickname given to one of the co-pilots who, after an exceedingly heavy night out, felt a desperate urge to be sick before the passengers arrived on the aeroplane the following morning. He dashed out of the cockpit, threw open the toilet door and proceeded to be extremely sick into the toilet – unfortunately, the Captain was sitting on it at the time. He never managed to shake off the nickname.

We once carried the Queen and Prince Philip on board one of our aircraft. Prince Philip visited the flight deck and clearly had a genuine interest in what was going on. When he excused himself to leave, the Chief Pilot asked him whether Her Majesty would like to come up and see what was going on. Prince Philip replied: "If it doesn't eat hay and fart, she's not interested!"

A pilot's advice to new cadet pilots: "If you are having drinks and you are going to make advances to a stewardess, do not pick the one on orange juice as she may have Luton Flu (i.e. be on antibiotics)."

If someone in another hotel room has been noisy and kept you awake during the night, make sure you bang your suitcase against the door when you leave very early in the morning!

One time myself and a couple of colleagues went to meet the new cadets; they were all embarrassed that the mums had turned up because they thought they were rather old, but we told them that to us they were just 'Dolly-Birds'.

On holiday in Hong Kong I visited a good friend and his wife. They lived in a walled estate, where she spent much of her time around the pool with the other wives. None of them wanted to be the first one to leave as the others would have been talking about them. She always said there were three things you did in Hong Kong as a wife – played bridge, became an alcoholic or took a lover – and she didn't play bridge! One of the residents was a top footballer that joined a Chinese football team but the whole concept fell apart and he ended up more or less stranded in Hong Kong.

A Dan Air pilot was at a meeting with senior management and they warned the crews that British Airways was like a load of circling sharks. A pilot immediately left the next day and said, "I would prefer to be on the side of the sharks them being eaten by them."

A First Officer was doing the control checks when he caught the Captain's shirt in the yoke and broke his nose on the coaming panel.

The company operated a London – New Orleans – Mexico – New Orleans – London service, and the accountants were looking for a way of saving money, so they cancelled the whole service for good. However, it turned out that they had made a mess-up because they assumed that the Tri-Star was a four-engine aeroplane when it had only three engines, which meant that the fuel cost was considerably less, and there would have been a profit.

On night stops it was quite usual for the stewardesses to say they were not coming out. The usual excuses were, "I am waiting for a phone call from my boy friend"; "I went to a party last night and have to get some sleep"; "I have to wash my hair"; or, "I have to shave my legs." Ether way it is better that they say something instead of just not turning up. Many times we have all been waiting for ages only to find they have not had the decency to let us know.

On one trip the girl said she had just come off holiday and needed the sleep. Some of us went out shopping and then on a boat trip down the Po River. It cost about £3 and they served beer during the two-hour return trip. Afterwards we went out for a pizza and a couple of bottles of wine. We went down town to a cathedral-looking building that was full of restaurants down either side. We were nearly finished when a black car drove into the building and cruised down the centre between the restaurants until it got to ours. The car stopped and someone leaned out of the window and pumped six shots into some guy about three tables away! As they finished, a police car came screaming in the way the other car had entered. Seeing that they had caught up with the black car, they braked hard but the black car then sped off. When there was no hope of catching the other car, the police sped up and left the building as well. We decided it was time to leave and eventually found a quieter watering hole.

In a slightly more subdued mood we turned out thoughts to the stewardess in the hotel. One of the stewards had bought a vibrator, supposedly for his girlfriend, to keep her amused when he was away. We hatched a plan to play a trick on the girl who had stayed in. In the morning while awaiting the van that took us to the airport, one of the girls would say there was a phone call for her. While she was away we would slip the vibrator into her case and when we went through UK Customs someone would go ahead and tell the Customs Officer and get him to play the big bad official. On the day all went well and the Customs Officer was briefed and agreed to play the game. We were all stopped and the girl was asked to open her case. The customs officer rummaged around in her bag and pulled out the vibrator, much to her embarrassment!

We would often all play tricks on new cabin crew. When the tug pushed us backwards off the stand, the third pilot would open the door and call out to the new person,, "Could you ask the rest of the cabin crew to stand to one side so that the Captain can see when we push back?"

First Officers were called 'Andrew' – this came from the stewardess saying, "What would you like to drink Captain?" then turning disdainfully to a young first officer adding, "And you?" (Andrew). Later they were known as 'Nigels', resulting from a series of cartoons from one of the pilots.

I was wandering around the cabin with a First Officer when I overheard a short conversation between him and a stewardess. He asked the stewardess her name and got his face slapped. On asking why she had slapped him, she replied, "You slept with me for two days about five years ago."

On an African aircraft the Captain went to toilet. The first officer had been waiting for a cup of tea and got fed up waiting so he went back to the Galley, but the door slammed shut and locked them both out of the cockpit. There was no option but to get a fire axe and smash the door down to get back in – the doors cost about £5,000 each.

A pilot took his wife to Madrid for a night stop, and feeling rather tired from the night before, decided to have a sleep in the afternoon. His wife said that she was just going out for a stroll. When she came back she had a paper bag and when she opened showed him a beautiful jumper which she said she had paid £40 for. Bearing in mind this was a long time ago, when he got his bill she had put a decimal point in the wrong place, so the jumper was £400 – which he could ill-afford.

A stewardess was standing at the door saying goodbye to all the Spanish passengers, when one person came past with a full sick bag and handed it to her. The Stewardess enquired, "Calamari?" to which the passenger replied, "No, Benidorm".

One of the skippers had a name very similar to a club, that being the Duet Club. He was finally invited onto the stage to perform with one of the girls – we were all a little startled but he entered into the spirit of the occasion, taking his trousers and underpants off. While she bent over, he performed an act on her – he was a pipe smoker and proceeded to get his pipe out, tapped it on her backside and proceeded to fill it with tobacco, after which he lit it, doing all this while they both proceeded to perform and while he smoked his pipe, which got a fantastic amount of applause throughout the audience.

Another lady performed a fantastic act with full bottle of champagne and lost it completely out of sight.

At a Hamburg Club on one occasion we took along a brand spanking new co-pilot, who after many beers was persuaded to partake in an act. He was put at the top of a ramp, stark naked, and on roller skates at the bottom of the ramp was a naked girl touching her toes facing away from him. Somebody gave him a push and the rampant male roller skater went perfectly down the ramp towards the girl who sidestepped at the last minute, the curtain was pulled aside and the stark naked guy on the roller skates ended up out on the road, being photographed by everyone in sight. He was eventually returned to the club and given a couple of free beers for his performance.

If you think that while you are on a flight that you want to complain about a stewardess and the way she has treated you, think again. It's well worth knowing that it is a regular feature among stewardesses to change nametags, so each nametag is on a stewardess who is on a totally different flight or schedule – so if someone ever complains about the stewardess, she can just say she was never there. They also swap credit cards, they take credit cards on different flights, use them heavily and then ring up and deny any knowledge of the credit cards being used!

At one time the cabin crew were offered a reward by credit card companies if they could discover a stolen credit card. However, this soon stopped when one was found and just one stewardess got the reward and the others who were part of the team that discovered the theft got nothing, so in future they never bothered.

A new story was going around the crew room, in that the head of catering at Heathrow had had his first day off sick in 15 years – he hadn't even had a day's holiday. When he was eventually sick and the normal catering supplies arrived, a large truck full of dead chickens appeared at the back of the catering centre and the truck driver asked where they wanted them put. They said, "We assume the kitchen," but he replied, "No, I usually have to put them into another truck which took them away, where is it?" It then transpired that for the last 15 years the head of catering had something going on with the suppliers, whereby he managed to make a huge profit – I don't think he had his job much longer.

One poor soul was driving into the airport in a standard Vanguard while wearing his pilot's uniform. On coming down the hill and before entering the tunnel at Heathrow, he made a slight mistake in stopping at the intersection and a police van full of police officers crashed into the back of him. There was not much damage to his car and the driver of the police van jumped out and started swearing and cursing at him. He said it was not his fault, as they had hit the back of his car, at which point the police driver turned round and said, "I know you, the make of your car and number – the next time you come into the airport I will fix you for speeding, parking or some other offense, just you wait and see." The pilot immediately went home, got his logbook for the car and took it out and sold it. Some poor soul would have gone to the airport in his standard Vanguard and got booked.

Another story with the police…. In Camberley (which was considered the dormitory of Heathrow airport, where a huge majority of the workers actually live) a pilot was sitting inside his car parked outside his house cleaning it. Having recently finished washing it, the next thing he knew a police car came down the road and crashed into the back of his parked car. The police realised that there was little they could do about it, but they all scattered out of the car and started searching in the grass. After a while one of them said, "I found some," and lifted up some dog poo which they smeared all over the brake pedal. It turned out they had just joined the Chief Constable at the golf club. On returning to the Police station the driver would have been taken off traffic duties and not allowed to drive – he would then have been put through all sorts of tests and be in serious trouble. So their story was that the driver and the other policeman had been up on the golf course where the driver must have trod on some doggie poo, and that his foot had slipped off the brake pedal and therefore the accident wasn't his fault. It gives you great faith, doesn't it?!

We then ended up in another pub, which was generally known as 'Jack's Bar.' It got its name from a pilot who had a long-term girlfriend in Berlin and was also married. His retirement date had been two to three years previously. His wife suddenly worked out that he was packing his suitcase with his uniform every week, saying that he was going to Berlin. He would then go to Berlin to be with his girlfriend and appeared five or six days later back at home – he spent most of his time in the bar, which is why it was called 'Jack's Bar' after him.

The bar had a very interesting roulette wheel, which instead of the normal table was based on blackjack (i.e. twenty-one), so they would spin the wheel twice and you had the total of two balls together and had to see how close you could get to the figure.

We had three cars in Berlin belonging to all the pilots, all VW Beetles, which we had paid for by pouring some money into a kitty. The advantage of these cars was that they had the BFG number plates – military plates. Remember, Berlin still hadn't really got over the war. After visiting pubs, invariably some drunk driver drove back to the hotel or onto another watering hole. If the Berlin police stopped us, they couldn't touch us because we were driving with British Forces plates. Additionally, if the MPs came, they couldn't touch us either, because we weren't military. We were just civilians, so we had the best of both worlds!

On one occasion they were driving back from a pub when it came to roadworks… or rather, they didn't see the roadworks and drove straight into an area where the road had been dug up – about a foot deep and about 20 feet long. The car fell into the middle of the depression so they were unable to get it out – they couldn't lift it out, and they certainly couldn't drive it out. Anyway, they abandoned it and went to another pub, eventually heading home to bed forgetting all about it. The next afternoon when someone came down to take the car out, they found the car in the garage car park with its headlights on and windscreen wipers going with a notice on it saying, 'Compliments of the Berlin Police, we think you lost your car last night'. We never heard any more about it.

There are many well-known exchanges between cabin crew and passengers. On one occasion there was a very rude and domineering white South African couple in first class. They had a baby and were forever asking for different things, either for themselves or for the baby, creating a considerable nuisance in the cabin. The steward became irritated with their rude attitude. The woman flicked her fingers at the steward and handed her baby to him saying, "Change it." The steward politely took the baby and wandered to the back of the aircraft, whereby he returned several minutes later with a black baby. The other passengers thought it was funny but not the mother of the child. It is thought that the steward was unfairly fired for the incident.

Captains came in all sorts of shapes, sizes and temperaments. One laid-back Captain called the stewardesses and said to them, "I would like 80 cigarettes and half a bottle of whisky." The stewardess asked, "Why do you want them at this time?" He replied, "We have an engine fire so I'm going to close it down and we're going to divert for a night stop." Probably the coolest way of telling the cabin crew that something was wrong.

What is the difference between a Rottweiler and a Stewardess? The Rottweiler doesn't wear lipstick.

Pilot to stewardess: "Where have you been all my life?" Answer: "I was not born in the first half."

What's the difference between a terrorist and a stewardess? You can negotiate with a terrorist.

A brand-new stewardess and an older 'queen-bee' stewardess were chatting when the queen-bee explained that she had recently come on the fleet, having served in Gatwick for some length of time. She explained that most of the stewardesses at Gatwick were lesbians. The new girl said innocently, "I've never met a lesbian." The queen-bee replied in a deep husky voice, "Haven't you?" and the innocent stewardess nearly jumped out of her seat.

A Captain started to doze in the cockpit when the third pilot craftily tied his wig to the window catch. When the cabin crew came in and asked if he wanted a coffee, the Captain moved forward, pulling his wig off – much to the delight of everybody.

To Conclude

I never lost my passion for aviation. However, my career as a pilot, which spanned 35 years, was brought to an abrupt end one day during a mundane journey to work. I was stopped at traffic lights when, with no warning, the car behind smashed into me at nearly 50 mph. My back was sufficiently damaged that I could not sit still for long periods of time without intense pain. When it became clear that this was a permanent condition, I was invalided out of the industry and could fly no more.

END NOTES

1. Under the auspices of the Society, in 1959 the industrialist Henry Kremer offered the first Kremer Prizes of £5,000 for the first human-powered aircraft to fly a figure-of-eight course round two markers half-a-mile apart on the condition that the designer, entrant pilot, place of construction and flight all be British. A Kremer prize of £20,000 for speed was won in 1984 by a design team of the Massachusetts Institute of Technology for flying their MIT Monarch B craft on a triangular 1.5 km (0.93 mi) course in under three minutes (for an average speed of 32 km/h (20 mph)).

2. Gustave Albin Whitehead (1874 –1927) was an aviation pioneer who emigrated from Germany to the United States where he designed and built flying machines and engines. Controversy surrounds his own claims that he flew a powered machine successfully several times in 1901 and 1902, predating the 1903 flights by the Wright Brothers His reputation rests on a newspaper article which was written as an eyewitness report and described a powered and sustained flight by Whitehead in Connecticut on 14 August 1901, a report which was repeated across the US and the world. The designs and experiments were mentioned in contemporary *Scientific American* magazine articles and a 1904 book about industrial progress. His public profile faded after about 1915 and he died in relative obscurity in 1927. A 1930s book asserted that Whitehead had made powered flights in 1901–1902 and included statements from people who said they had witnessed various Whitehead flights decades earlier, triggering debate among scholars, researchers, aviation enthusiasts and Orville Wright as to whether Whitehead was first in powered flight. There is no known photograph showing Whitehead making a powered controlled flight, although reports in the early 1900s said such photos were available. Researchers have studied and attempted to copy Whitehead aircraft.

3. On 25 March 1946 Lord Winster, the Minister of Aviation, performed the official opening ceremony, and the first aircraft to use the new airport was a British South American Airways (BSAA) Avro

Lancastrian named *Star Light*. The passenger terminal consisted of army tents and duck boarding next to the south side of the Bath Road, which were later replaced by prefabricated buildings. The initial control tower was a crude brick building roughly where the airport police station is now. I went to Heathrow Airport many times as a child starting about 1951. In 1925 Norman Macmillan, an RAF officer, made a forced landing and take-off at Heathrow and noted the flatness of the land and its suitability for an airfield. The land was at the time used for market gardening and wheat growing. Heathrow consists of the North and South runways running from east to west plus the one that runs from the south-west to north-east, which has recently been closed. However, when it was being used, particularly when landing towards the south-west, there was a gasometer at about 4 miles but there was also a very similar gasometer on finals for Northolt which had a similar runway direction. There were several occasions when aircraft landed at Northolt by mistake, resulting in the two gasometers subsequently being clearly marked – one with the NH for North Holt and the other one LH. When aircraft landed by accident at Northolt it was by an act of God that they didn't crash, because the runway was considerably shorter than London, and it usually resulted in all the passengers being taken off an aircraft to make it as light as possible so that it could just about get airborne and fly onto London itself. The northerly runway running west to east has a large groove in it going on for several hundred feet where an aircraft from the African continent landed with its brakes on and gouged the wheels down to the hubs.

4.   A Notice to Airmen (NOTAM) is a notice filed with an aviation authority to alert aircraft pilots of potential hazards along a flight route or at a location that could affect the safety of the flight. They are created and transmitted by government agencies and airport operators under guidelines specified by the Convention on International Civil Aviation (CICA). The term NOTAM came into common use rather than the more formal *Notice to Airmen* following the ratification of the CICA. A NOTAM is filed with an aviation authority to alert aircraft pilots of any hazards *en route* or at a specific location. They may be given for a number of reasons, such as hazards, important flights (by heads of state etc), closed runways, military exercises, passage of flocks of birds etc. Software is available to allow pilots to identify NOTAMs near their intended route or at the intended destination. Believe it or not, aircraft have landed at the wrong airport and even the wrong country.

5.   On 4 June 1967 a Canadair C-4 Argonaut passenger aircraft owned by British Midland Airways crashed near the centre of Stockport,

Cheshire, England. Of the 84 people on board, 72 were killed, the fourth-worst disaster in British aviation history. The aircraft overshot the runway on the first run and as the aircraft was making a second approach to the airport, the No. 3 and 4 engines suddenly cut out over the town of Stockport. The aircraft became uncontrollable and crashed at 10:09 am local time in a small open area at Hopes Carr, close to the town centre. Despite the crash occurring in a densely populated area, there were no fatalities on the ground. Investigators with the Accidents Investigation Branch (AIB) determined that the double engine failure had been caused by fuel starvation, due to a previously unrecognised flaw in the model's fuel system. Harry Marlow, the captain, survived but had amnesia and did not remember the accident sequence, and the first officer died.

6.   First flight 26 October 1931, introduced February 1932, retired from military service in 1959, although still in civil use.

7.   The photos include: (a) Steve Bohill-Smith (G-AOBX Yellow and Silver). Steve is a retired British Airways Captain, and G-AOBX is a group owned aircraft, owned by six ex-Concorde crew. The David Ross Flying group is named in honour of David Ross who bought G-AOBX as a basket case and restored it to airworthiness condition. The aircraft went on to win the Concourse Trophy for best Tiger Moth at Woburn. Sadly Dave passed away suddenly, and Steve set up the flying group in his memory. Steve has an unusual claim to fame, he held a Boeing 747 Display Authority and captained the Oasis 747 which flew in a number of UK air displays in the recent past. He flew commercially since 1972 including six years as a Concorde first officer, and has been flying Tiger Moths for 30 years which he considers to be 'real flying' – so different from the day job flying "by the seat of your pants". (b) Jerry Rendall (G-AOBX Yellow and Silver). Jerry is a retired British Airways Captain flying G-AOBX in the same group as Steve B-S. Joined the team in 2009.

8.   On 5 January 1941, while flying an Airspeed Oxford for the ATA from Prestwick via Blackpool to RAF Kidlington near Oxford, Johnson went off course in adverse weather conditions. Reportedly out of fuel, she bailed out as her aircraft crashed into the Thames Estuary near Herne Bay. HMS Haslemere spotted Johnson's parachute coming down and saw her alive in the water, but conditions were poor and despite a rescue attempt (which resulted in a fatality) Johnson's body was never recovered. A memorial service was held for Johnson in the church of St. Martin in the Fields on 14 January 1941 and the man who attempted to rescue her, Walter Fletcher, was awarded the Albert Medal posthumously. It has been more recently hinted that Johnson's death was due to friendly fire and that Tom Mitchell

claimed to have shot Johnson down when she twice failed to give the correct identification code during the flight. Mitchell explained that a request was made for the signal, but Johnson gave the wrong one twice. "Sixteen rounds of shells were fired and the plane dived into the Thames Estuary. We all thought it was an enemy plane until the next day when we read the papers and discovered it was Amy. The officers told us never to tell anyone what happened."

9.   The Oxford Aviation Academy Piper PA-34 Seneca at Oxford Airport. The primary focus for Oxford is the London region business aviation market as the sixth busiest for this sector in the UK. Within the private and business aviation sector, the airport handled over 8,000 private passengers in 2015. The main runway (Code 3C) is fully grooved and 1,552 m (5,092 ft). The airport can handle aircraft up to and including the Boeing BBJ and Airbus ACJ series. For the business aviation operator, the airport is an approximately 60 minute drive time from the West End area of central London but offers helicopter shuttles in 25 minutes to central London's Battersea Heliport which is co-owned with London Oxford Airport.

10.   On March 10, 1947 TWA Constellation 'Star of Hollywood' experienced sudden decompression during a transatlantic flight from New York City to Geneva, Switzerland. After stopping at Gander to refuel and take on passengers, it was 500 miles into the leg to Shannon, Ireland, when the astrodome (a clear plastic bubble on the top of the fuselage) shattered. Navigator George Hart was sucked out of the aircraft over the North Atlantic before the aircraft returned to Gander and passengers continued the flight on a replacement aircraft. TWA responded to the accident by equipping navigators on transatlantic flights with a safety harness.

11.   The Avro York is a high-wing cantilever monoplane using an all-metal construction, with many similarities to its predecessor, the Lancaster. The wings use a two-spar structure, which internally housed seven fuel tanks between the spars. Each engine drives a three-bladed propeller.

12.   I have since written a book on men molesting women, *Revenge of the Seven Magnificent Women* sold through Amazon.

13.   In 1983, the lake was searched for the body of Veronique Mireille Marre, a missing French student. As a result the remains of Margaret Hogg were found tied in the foetal position cable with a dry cleaning bag over her head and wrapped in a hessian cover. The diver initially thought them to be just a roll of old carpet. The police investigation was made easier by noting 'Margaret 11.11.63 Peter' engraved on the inside of the gold wedding ring recovered. Peter Hogg initially denied the murder before making a confession when he was sen-

tenced to four years imprisonment. He thought that he had been hard done by, as did many people in his home town of Cranleigh. As a lovely lady journalist explained in the documentary 'A Very British Murder', some people were quite pleased he as good as got away with it. Hogg recalled, "She came at me like a tiger, scratching, kicking and punching. After that I had to make a decision as to whether to bring in the authorities or try to cover the matter up. I was left in the position of being in a fairly strange town with no real friends around or very close relatives to help and with two very young children to bring up. I felt at the time, rightly or wrongly, that if I brought the police in, for instance, they might have been taken away and I'd be taken away and who knows when it ever would have been sorted out." Judge Thomas Pigot said he gave Hogg a minimum four-year term for the manslaughter of his wife because of his "exemplary character and his glowing testimonials to his qualities as a man and a father."

14. The accident on 14 April 1965 was fatal. It involved a British United Airways Douglas C-47, a scheduled international passenger flight from Paris Orly to Jersey. Despite the worsening weather conditions at Jersey, the crew continued with its approach but then abandoned it because visual range fell below minima. On its second approach, it first hit a tree before striking the outermost pole of the approach light system, causing the aircraft to crash into the approach lights and ignite, killing 26 of the 27 occupants. An article in the Jersey Evening Post commented, "The pilot should never have made an approach in those conditions. They were well below the minimum that should have applied to make an approach. He tried it and didn't get away with it." A weather report in Jersey eight minutes after the accident said that fog had reduced visibility to 70 metres.

15. *HMS Amethyst* (Lieutenant-Commander Skinner) sailed from Shanghai on 19th April to relieve *HMS Consort* at Nanking. She was fired at on 20th at around 0900, 60 miles from Nanking and grounded on Rose Island with heavy casualties, about 60 crew landed and many made their way to Shanghai with Chinese help. *Consort* was ordered from Nanking to assist *Amethyst*; *Black Swan* was ordered from Shanghai to Kiang Yin, 40 miles short of *Amethyst*. *Consort* arrived around 1500, but was heavily hit (20th) and unable to take *Amethyst* in tow, and so continued downstream. *HMS London* was then ordered to proceed up the Yangtse and meet *Black Swan* and *Consort* at Kiang Yin around 2000, but *Consort* was too damaged and ordered to Shanghai. On the 21st at c0200, *Amethyst* refloated and anchored two miles above Rose Island. Later in the morning, *London* and *Black Swan* tried to close *Amethyst* but came under heavy fire,

which was returned, and there were some casualties. Both ships returned to Kiang Yin where they were fired at again. Damaged and with more casualties, they proceeded to Shanghai. That evening, a naval officer and RAF doctor reached *Amethyst* by Sunderland flying boat. On the night of 21st/22nd April *Amethyst* evacuated more wounded and moved ten miles up river to evacuate more. She now had three naval officers, one RAF doctor, 52 ratings and 8 Chinese on onboard. On the 22nd, in the PM, Lt-Cdr Kerans, Asst Naval Attaché at Nankin arrived to assume command. Also on the 22nd, another attempt was made to land by a Sunderland but she was driven off by artillery fire. *Amethyst* moved a further four miles up river, where she remained for three months before escaping on the night of 30/31st July. *HMS Concord* was present at this time.

16. "Red Army soldiers don't believe in 'individual liaisons' with German women," wrote the playwright Zakhar Agranenko in his diary when serving as an officer of marine infantry in East Prussia. "Nine, ten, twelve men at a time - they rape them on a collective basis." The Soviet armies advancing into East Prussia in January 1945, in huge, long columns, were an extraordinary mixture of modern and medieval: tank troops in padded black helmets, Cossack cavalrymen on shaggy mounts with loot strapped to the saddle, lendlease Studebakers and Dodges towing light field guns, and then a second echelon in horse-drawn carts. The variety of character among the soldiers was almost as great as that of their military equipment. There were freebooters who drank and raped quite shamelessly, and there were idealistic, austere communists and members of the intelligentsia appalled by such behaviour. Beria and Stalin, back in Moscow, knew perfectly well what was going on from a number of detailed reports. One stated that, "many Germans declare that all German women in East Prussia who stayed behind were raped by Red Army soldiers." Numerous examples of gang rape were given, with "girls under 18 and old women included." Marshal Rokossovsky issued order No 006 in an attempt to direct "the feelings of hatred at fighting the enemy on the battlefield." It appears to have had little effect. There were also a few arbitrary attempts to exert authority. The commander of one rifle division is said to have "personally shot a lieutenant who was lining up a group of his men before a German woman spread-eagled on the ground." But either officers were involved themselves, or the lack of discipline made it too dangerous to restore order over drunken soldiers armed with submachine guns.

17. Scapa Flow (meaning 'bay of the long isthmus') is a body of water in the Orkney Islands, Scotland, sheltered by the islands of Mainland,

Graemsay, Burray, South Ronaldsay and Hoy. These sheltered waters have been used by ships for centuries and they have played an important role in travel, trade and conflict, especially during both World Wars. A consultation in ballast water management in 2013 measured the commonly used Harbour Authority definition of Scapa Flow at 324.5 square kilometres (125.3 sq mi) and just under 1 billion cubic metres of water.

Picture Credits

Air Speed Oxford at Duxford
Tony Hisgett from Birmingham, UK [CC BY 2.0 (https://creativecommons.org/licenses/by/2.0)], via Wikimedia Commons
Slingsby
Jelle Vandebeeck [CC BY 2.0 (https://creativecommons.org/licenses/by/2.0)], via Wikimedia Commons
Sedbergh
Kerry Taylor, Flickr
Miles Magister
Alan Wilson [CC BY-SA 2.0 (https://creativecommons.org/licenses/by-sa/2.0)]
Taylorcraft
Armchair Aviator's [CC BY 2.0 (https://creativecommons.org/licenses/by/2.0)], via Wikimedia Commons
Piper Colt
Ad Meskens [Attribution, CC BY-SA 3.0 (https://creativecommons.org/licenses/by-sa/3.0) or GFDL (http://www.gnu.org/copyleft/fdl.html)]
MG Y-Type
Sicnag [CC BY 2.0 (https://creativecommons.org/licenses/by/2.0)], via Wikimedia Commons
Nipper
RuthAS [CC BY 3.0 (https://creativecommons.org/licenses/by/3.0)], from Wikimedia Commons
BAC 111
Alan Wilson from Stilton, Peterborough, Cambs, UK [CC BY-SA 2.0 (https://creativecommons.org/licenses/by-sa/2.0)], via Wikimedia Commons
Husk Kit
Mattias Björklund [CC BY-SA 3.0 (https://creativecommons.org/licenses/by-sa/3.0)], from Wikimedia Commons

Trabant
User Asterion on en.wikipedia [CC BY 2.5
(https://creativecommons.org/licenses/by/2.5)], via Wikimedia
Commons
Heron
RuthAS [CC BY 3.0 (https://creativecommons.org/licenses/by/3.0)], from
Wikimedia Commons
Ambassador
Alan Wilson [CC BY-SA 2.0 (https://creativecommons.org/licenses/by-
sa/2.0)]
Airspeed ambassador cockpit
Lazlo Ferran, Pinterest, https://lazloferran.com/2014/10/06/1381/
Rapide
Mike Charlton www.ukairfieldguide.net
Dakota DC3
Towpilot [GFDL (http://www.gnu.org/copyleft/fdl.html) or CC-BY-SA-3.0
(http://creativecommons.org/licenses/by-sa/3.0/)], from Wikimedia
Commons
Jersey Airport
https://www.theislandwiki.org/index.php/File:1126Airport.jpg#filelinks
BAC 111
Guido Allieri - Italy [GFDL (http://www.gnu.org/copyleft/fdl.html) or
GFDL (http://www.gnu.org/copyleft/fdl.html)], via Wikimedia Commons
Berlin Tempelhof
Imanuel Marcus, https://publication79.com/2018/11/berlin-tempelhof-
an-airport-for-skaters-and-cyclists/
Viscount
MilborneOne [GFDL (http://www.gnu.org/copyleft/fdl.html) or CC BY-SA
3.0 (https://creativecommons.org/licenses/by-sa/3.0)], from Wikimedia
Commons
Viscount cockpit
http://vickersviscount.net/Pages_History/The_Turboprop_World-
Beater_VISCOUNT.aspx
Trident 3
Piergiuliano Chesi [CC BY-SA 3.0 (https://creativecommons.org/licens-
es/by-sa/3.0)]
Trident flight deck
Nimbus227 [Public domain], from Wikimedia Commons
Papa India Plaque
By Alan Hunt, CC BY-SA 2.0,
https://commons.wikimedia.org/w/index.php?curid=41045240
Boeing 737
Aero Icarus from Zürich, Switzerland [CC BY-SA 2.0 (https://creativecom-
mons.org/licenses/by-sa/2.0)], via Wikimedia Commons